International Science Between the World Wars

What is international science and how does it function? This book answers these questions through a detailed study of international congresses on genetics held from 1899 to 1939. It presents a portrait of international science as a product of continuous interactions that involved scientists and their patrons within specific political, ideological, and disciplinary contexts. Drawing on a variety of archival sources—ranging from Stalin's personal papers to the records of the Gestapo and from the correspondence among scientists in different countries to the minutes of the Soviet government's top-secret meetings—it depicts the operations of international science at a time of great political tensions.

Krementsov breaks with the view of science as either inherently national or quintessentially international, examining instead the intersection between national and international agendas in scientists' activities. Focusing on the dramatic history of the Seventh international genetics congress, he investigates contradictions inherent to scientists' dual loyalties to their country and their science. Through analysis of negotiations among three groups of actors involved with the organization of the congress, Krementsov examines the role of ideologies, patronage, and personal networks in the operations of international science.

Arguing that personal networks constitute a major structural component in the discipline's formation, Krementsov traces the emergence of international networks in genetics and explains their role in shaping the international community's reaction to national developments which threatened to undermine the very standing of genetics as an international discipline and which, in the end, profoundly affected the fate of the congress and the fate of the discipline.

Nikolai Krementsov is an Associate Professor at the Institute for the History and Philosophy of Science and Technology, University of Toronto. He lives in Toronto and St Petersburg with his wife and daughter. He is the author of *Stalinist Science* and *The Cure: A Story of Cancer and Politics from the Annals of the Cold War*.

Routledge Studies in the History of Science, Technology and Medicine
Edited by John Krige
Georgia Institute of Technology, Atlanta, USA

Routledge Studies in the History of Science, Technology and Medicine aims to stimulate research in the field, concentrating on the twentieth century. It seeks to contribute to our understanding of science, technology and medicine as they are embedded in society, exploring the links between the subjects on the one hand and the cultural, economic, political and institutional contexts of their genesis and development on the other. Within this framework, and while not favoring any particular methodological approach, the series welcomes studies which examine relations between science, technology, medicine and society in new ways, for example, the social construction of technologies, large technical systems etc.

International Science Between the World Wars

The case of genetics

Nikolai Krementsov

Routledge
Taylor & Francis Group

LONDON AND NEW YORK

First published 2005
by Routledge
2 Park Square, Milton Park, Abingdon, Oxon OX14 4RN

Simultaneously published in the USA and Canada
by Routledge
270 Madison Ave, New York, NY 10016

Routledge is an imprint of the Taylor & Francis Group

© 2005 Nikolai Krementsov

Typeset in Baskerville by
Newgen Imaging Systems (P) Ltd, Chennai, India
Printed and bound in Great Britain by
TJ International Ltd, Padstow, Cornwall

British Library Cataloguing in Publication Data
A catalogue record for this book is available from the British Library

Library of Congress Cataloging in Publication Data
A catalog record for this book has been requested

ISBN 0–415–35060–3

Men of science have two loyalties,
one to their country and one to their science.
Charles Davenport to the
US Secretary of State,
December 17, 1936[1]

As long as scientists themselves are
uncertain of their primary loyalty, their
position becomes tenuous and uncertain.
Robert K. Merton
December 1937[2]

Contents

Plates

Abbreviations

AAAS	American Association for the Advancement of Science
APRF	Archive of the President of the Russian Federation
APS	American Philosophical Society Library
ARAN	Archive of the Russian Academy of Sciences
AVPR	Archive of Russian Foreign Policy
GARF	State Archive of the Russian Federation
Glavlit	Censorship Administration
Gosplan	State Planning Administration
GSA	Genetics Society of America
IEB	International Education Board
IOC	International Organizing Committee for Genetics Congresses
IRC	International Research Council
JHB	*Journal of the History of Biology*
Narkompros	People's Commissariat of Enlightenment
Narkomzdrav	People's Commissariat of Public Health
Narkomzem	People's Commissariat of Agriculture
NKVD	People's Commissariat of Internal Affairs (secret police, successor of OGPU)
NYT	*New York Times*
OGPU	United State Political Directorate (secret police, predecessor of NKVD)
RAC	Rockefeller Archive Center
RGAE	Russian State Archive of Economics
RGASPI	Russian State Archive of Socio-political History
SNK	Council of People's Commissars
TASS	Telegraph Agency of the Soviet Union (Soviet news agency)
TsGANTD	Central State Archive of Scientific–Technical Documentation
TsIK	Central Executive Committee
USNA	US National Archives
VIET	*Voprosy Istorii Estezvoznaniia i Tekhniki* (a journal)
VASKhNIL	Lenin All-Union Academy of Agricultural Sciences
VIR	All-Union Institute of Plant Breeding
VOKS	All-Union Society for Cultural Relations with Foreign Countries
VSNKh	Supreme Council of the National Economy

Preface

I first came across the story of the Seventh international genetics congress more than a decade ago while collecting materials for a book on Soviet science during the Stalin era.[3] In the then just-opened archives of the Communist Party, I found decisions of the Politburo pertaining to the congress. In the Central State Archive of the October Revolution (now—the State Archive of the Russian Federation), I discovered numerous documents of various state agencies involved with preparations for the congress. In the archive of the then USSR Academy of Sciences, I dug out documents of the Institute of Genetics that was to have played host to the congress in Moscow, as well as personal papers of Soviet geneticists involved with its organization. Yet I felt that the documents I was unearthing were telling only one part of the story—a part that illuminated the negotiations between Soviet geneticists and their patrons over the issues of the congress. Another part, pertaining to the interaction between Soviet geneticists and their foreign colleagues, and particularly to those among foreign geneticists, was, understandably, missing in the records. I decided not to publish anything, but kept the materials for some future use.

A few years later, in the spring of 1992, I found myself in Philadelphia working through the correspondence between Soviet and US geneticists preserved among the manuscript collections in the Library of the American Philosophical Society. At that time I concentrated primarily on US geneticists' response to developments in Soviet genetics in the post-war period—the so-called Lysenko controversy and the resulting official banishment of genetics in the Soviet Union in August 1948. Plowing through various collections, I was struck by one strange feature: numerous copies of the same letter were sitting in the files of not only its addressee, but also in those of other geneticists. Many of these copies were marked "private" or "confidential" and bore notations: "for your information," "thought you'd be interested in this," and the like. When a couple of years later, I got an opportunity to explore the archives of British geneticists in London, Cambridge, Oxford, and Edinburgh, I encountered a similar picture: many personal collections had copies and duplicates of various pieces of correspondence related to Soviet genetics and Soviet geneticists. What is more, Western geneticists did not merely share information about what was happening in the Soviet Union, they coordinated their responses to Soviet events, planning and organizing a whole campaign in support of their colleagues there. At that time I decided to publish my observations in an article that appeared in the *Journal of the History of Biology* under the title "The 'second front' in Soviet genetics."[4]

While researching archives for that article, of course, I could not help but look through the pre-war files with materials related to the abandoned Moscow congress, taking notes and making copies of relevant documents, with the hope that one day I might be able to return to the story of the congress. Meanwhile, having learned that I was interested in that story, my colleagues began sending me copies of documents they had encountered in their own research in the papers of both Soviet and Western geneticists. The picture emerging from all these documents was quite intriguing: information regarding the congress had constantly been circulated through a close-knit *network* of geneticists from various countries, and their actions and reactions had been regularly debated and coordinated.

These archival findings, combined with interviews of several participants in the congress and my personal experiences of "international science," convinced me that the phenomenon I was observing was far from accidental. My suspicions were reinforced by numerous discussions with a member of my own personal network— a Professor of the University of Pennsylvania, Mark B. Adams—who at that very time was developing his ideas about the role of networks in the history of science in general, and the history of Soviet science in particular.[5] In the end, it is such a network of friends, classmates, colleagues, professors and their students, friends of friends, and family members that slowly emerged as a major protagonist in the intertwined stories of the Seventh international genetics congress, of genetics as an international discipline, and of international science between the world wars.

As is always the case with any historical work, I am indebted to numerous persons who facilitated my search for relevant documents. Guil Winchester generously shared with me a large collection of documents from Otto Mohr's archive she had found in Oslo, as well as her profound knowledge of the history of interwar genetics. Diane Paul gave me her extensive notes on J. B. S. Haldane's documents preserved in the Archive of the London University College, which greatly helped my own work in that archive. Tatiana Lassan provided access to and guidance in the enormous collection of N. I. Vavilov's materials at the All-Union Institute of Plant Breeding in St Petersburg (now housed in the Central State Archive of the Scientific Technical Documentation). Marina Sorokina helped locate a number of relevant documents in the Archive of the Russian Academy of Sciences in Moscow and allowed me access to her unpublished works on Soviet science in the 1920s. George H. Beale gave me invaluable material from his personal collection of documents related to the congress in Edinburgh and shared with me his personal recollections of the congress and its participants. Margaret Deacon granted me access to her unpublished history of the Edinburgh Institute of Animal Genetics and taped interviews with its members (held in the Library of the University of Edinburgh). Carola Sachse shared with me her collection of German documents related to the congress. Evgenii Gus'kov told me a number of stories about events at the Fourteenth international genetics congress in Moscow.

The staff of numerous libraries and archives were extremely helpful, including the Archive of the Russian Academy of Sciences, the Archive of Russian Foreign

Policy, the Central State Archive of Scientific–Technical Documentation, the Russian State Archive of Socio-political History, the Russian State Archive of Economics, the State Archive of the Russian Federation, the Library of the Russian Academy of Sciences, the US National Archives (Washington, DC), the Library of Congress (Washington, DC), the US National Library of Medicine (Bethesda, MD), the American Philosophical Society Library (Philadelphia, PA), the National Library of Scotland (Edinburgh), the Archives and Library of the University of Edinburgh, the Bodleian Library of Oxford University, the Lilly Library of the University of Indiana (Bloomington, IN), the Library of the University College (London), the Wellcome Library (London), and the Rockefeller Archive Center (Sleepy Hollow, NY).

I am indebted to the people and archives who have granted permission to repro-duce the illustrations. Every effort has been made to trace copyright holders, but in a few cases this has not been possible. Any omissions brought to the attention of the publishers will be remedied in future editions.

Several institutions provided financial support for this work for which I am very grateful. In 1992 the Mellon Fellowship of the American Philosophical Society gave me an opportunity to examine the society's incredible historical collections. In 1995, the Wellcome Trust and the Institute for the Advanced Studies in the Humanities at the University of Edinburgh enabled me for four months to explore various archives and libraries in Britain. In 1998, the Rockefeller Foundation's Special Interest Grant (with Susan G. Solomon) together with a travel grant by the Rockefeller Archive Center supported my explorations of relevant documents in the Center's enormous holdings. In 1999, an Everett Helm Fellowship at the University of Indiana (Bloomington, IN) made possible my work with H. J. Muller's materials at the Lilly Library. In 2000–2001, a senior fellowship at the Dibner Institute for the History of Sciences and Technology gave me a chance to draft the manuscript, while the Woodrow Wilson International Center for Scholars granted me a nine-month scholarship in 2002–2003, during which I was able to prepare it for publication. I would also like to thank the St Petersburg Branch of the Institute of the History of Science and Technology for supporting my research in Russia.

Earlier variants of this work were presented at several meetings, conferences, and seminars in Britain, Canada, Russia, and the United States, and I would like to thank their participants for useful critique and suggestions. I am indebted to many colleagues for their helpful comments and criticisms: Michael David-Fox, Vladimir Esakov, Mikhail Konashev, Marina Sorokina, who read or heard versions of various chapters. Ron Doel, John Krige, Susan G. Solomon, and Guil Winchester read the entire manuscript, made detailed comments, and helped me improve it in many significant ways. Mark B. Adams, Anne-Emanuelle Birn, and Daniel P. Todes read every version of the manuscript and offered numerous suggestions as to how make it better; their intellectual and moral sup-port was indispensable and invaluable. Naturally, I alone am responsible for any remaining mistakes and misinterpretations.

Prologue

A forty-year long road

On the evening of September 5, 1935, at the Onyx Restaurant of the American Hotel in Amsterdam, a lavish banquet marked the opening of an international botanical congress. The menu—printed on glossy red paper—featured the delights of European cuisine, with a distinct Dutch flavor:

Consommé Madrilène.
Sole bouillie
Sauce Persil.
Pommes nature

Poularde rôtie,
Petits Pois fins
Compote mêlée.
Pommes Chips

Fruits en Corbeille.

At one of the tables, fourteen people were enjoying their dinner and having a lively conversation. They came to Amsterdam from various countries—Austria, Britain, Germany, Japan, Sweden, and the United States—but what brought them all to that particular table was a shared interest in genetics. They talked about their research and reminisced about their meetings at the previous botanical congress held five years earlier in Britain, as well as at the Sixth international genetics congress held three years before in the United States.

They noted with disappointment the absence at the table of one of their colleagues, who had attended the earlier congresses and had enlivened them not only with his interesting reports, but also by the sheer force of his charming personality—the Soviet botanist and geneticist Nikolai Vavilov. So, they decided to send him a souvenir. A British geneticist, Cyril D. Darlington, who had only a year before visited Vavilov in Moscow and Leningrad, picked up a menu and wrote on the back: "To Nik[olai] Iv[anovich] Vavilov with red greetings to Red Russia from your friends." All those present at the table, including Irma Anderson-Kotto, George W. Beadle, Albert F. Blakeslee, David G. Catcheside, Cyril Darlington, Max Hartmann, Oche Keno, Ernst Lehmann, Otto Rosenberg, Georg F. L. Tischler, and Fritz von Wettstein, signed the improvised postcard.[1]

Although the geneticists missed Vavilov in Amsterdam, they certainly hoped to see him, as well as other Russian colleagues, in the not so distant future—at the forthcoming Seventh international genetics congress, which at that very time was being planned for August 1937 in Moscow. Indeed, over the course of the next year, geneticists all over the world were busily preparing for their sojourn to the Soviet Union, writing reports, selecting specimens for an exhibition that was to accompany the congress's sessions, and making travel arrangements. This extensive effort was coordinated by the congress's Soviet organizing committee, which regularly communicated with participants, informing them of the latest changes in the composition of program, available accommodations, and the means of transportation.

Alas, foreign geneticists' hopes of seeing Russian friends were never fulfilled. In mid-December 1936, with reference to "unofficial sources," the *New York Times* reported that the Soviet government had cancelled the congress and that its president—Vavilov—had been arrested. The news caused quite a commotion among Western geneticists, who immediately began bombarding Soviet officials with angry cables and letters. This active campaign apparently helped: within a week, much to their relief, geneticists learned that Vavilov had not been arrested and that the congress had been not cancelled, but "postponed." In the following months, Soviet geneticists indeed secured their government's permission to reinvite the congress to convene in Moscow a year later, in August 1938. But soon thereafter, the Permanent International Organizing Committee for Genetics Congresses presided over by the Norwegian geneticist Otto Mohr decided to withdraw the congress from the Soviet Union altogether and to hold it instead in Britain in 1939. Despite the relocation, Vavilov was elected as the congress's president, and nearly fifty of his compatriots submitted reports and exhibits for presentation at the congress. But not a single Soviet geneticist appeared in Edinburgh in August 1939.

How might we understand this peculiar chain of events? How did Moscow become the host of the international genetics congress in the first place? Why did the Soviet authorities first endorse, then cancel, and then reinvite the congress? Why did the international committee elect to relocate the congress, instead of holding it in Moscow a year later? How did Edinburgh come to host it? And why were Soviet geneticists absent from the congress in Scotland?

In searching for answers to these questions we will examine in close detail the content and context of interactions among three major groups of actors involved with the congress: Soviet geneticists, their domestic patrons, and their foreign peers. Analysis of these triangular relations, I believe, will illuminate not only the particular fate of the Seventh international genetics congress. It will help us understand the history of genetics as an international discipline during its first forty years of operations. It will shed light on the more general phenomena which we call "scientific internationalism," "international science," or simply "international scientific relations." And it will clarify the interplay between local and international scientific developments during the 1930s, in a world seized in the force field of political tensions among Stalin's Russia, Hitler's Germany, and Western democracies.

Genetics as an international discipline

Despite the fact that genetics is one of the most extensively studied disciplines in the history of science, its actual functioning as an international venture remains largely unexplored. Hundreds of works, ranging from short notes to monumental volumes, have documented the institutional growth of genetics in particular locales and traced the spread of ideas, techniques, and research tools among scientists in various countries.[2] Scholars have uncovered the emergence of "global" research agendas and "local" research styles.[3] But for the most part, the existing literature has focused on local developments in individual countries, particularly Britain, Germany, the Soviet Union, and the United States, while the role of international relations, and particularly international congresses, in the development of genetics has largely been neglected.[4]

This omission is particularly surprising, because from the start genetics was an international endeavor. Two events that came to symbolize the birth of this new sub-field of experimental biology convincingly illustrate this. In 1900 scientists from three different countries—Carl Correns in Germany, Hugo de Vries in Holland, and Erich von Tschermak in Austria—simultaneously "rediscovered" Gregor Mendel's laws of heredity.[5] Two years later, a German, Theodore Boveri, and an American, Walter S. Sutton, suggested that Mendelian "factors" (which the Danish geneticist Wilhelm Johannsen later named "genes") were located in the cell's chromosomes, thus laying a foundation for what would soon be called "the chromosome theory of heredity." Furthermore, the very name "genetics" for the budding discipline was suggested at and accepted by an international conference held in London in 1906.

During the four decades that followed these momentous events, genetics became an established discipline in various countries, including Austria, Belgium, Brazil, Britain, Canada, Denmark, France, Germany, Holland, India, Italy, Japan, Norway, Poland, Russia, Spain, Sweden, and the United States. Nearly a dozen specialized genetics periodicals that emerged during this period published works of scientists from their home countries, as well as those of researchers from abroad. International contacts in the burgeoning field became a way of exchanging and validating experimental data and theoretical concepts and thus maintaining a disciplinary consensus that embodied the "universality" of produced knowledge. Such contacts assumed additional importance as a way of propagating a specific production system that was taking shape in genetics during this time—the system built on and around a particular experimental organism, such as the fruit fly (*Drosophila*), the evening primrose (*Oenothera*), corn, mice, or wheat.[6] The exchange of new mutants, varieties, and stocks became an essential part of doing genetics, and international congresses became a major venue for such exchanges.

The seven international congresses held from 1899 to 1939 were milestones on the road traveled by genetics as an international discipline. From the first one—where just over one hundred scientists from six countries were present—to the seventh one, attended by more than six hundred participants from some forty countries, the international congresses testify to the rapid growth of genetics as an international enterprise. It would be mistaken, however, to take these figures as indicators of an unencumbered and uniform expansion of international activities in the field, for there were peculiar fluctuations in the participation of scientists from different countries in the congresses. After hosting the Fourth congress in Paris in 1911, French genetics all but disappeared from the international scene.[7] Similarly, after hosting the Fifth congress in Berlin in 1927, German geneticists' participation in the subsequent congresses steadily declined. In contrast, though only two scientists from Russia had attended the Paris congress as observers, at the next congress in Berlin, Russian geneticists formed the largest foreign delegation. At the Sixth congress held in 1932 in Ithaca, New York, however, only one geneticist from the Soviet Union was in attendance. Yet, despite such a meager representation, Moscow was selected as the locale for the Seventh congress scheduled to meet in 1937, and nearly six hundred Soviet geneticists were preparing to take part in its proceedings. After that congress was relocated to Britain and rescheduled for 1939, however, not even one of them came to Edinburgh.

These fluctuations in the attendance of international congresses by scientists from different countries suggest that the development of genetics as an international discipline was influenced not only by its practitioners' desire to expand and maintain mutual contacts and exchanges, but also by other factors and forces which at times facilitated and at times impeded their international activities. The interplay of these various factors and forces comes into sharp relief in the story of the Seventh international genetics congress.

Between "nationalism" and "internationalism": institutions, ideologies, and networks

Both practitioners of science and students of its history have spelt much ink debating whether science, in some Platonic sense, is a truly international or an inherently national phenomenon.[8] In my opinion, the real question is rather why and how national and international "dimensions" interact in scientists' activities at certain times and in certain places, what forces compel scientists to seek "internationalization," "nationalization," or "denationalization," and how scientists affect, mediate, exploit, or resist these processes.

The issues of internationalism have been a focus of attention by historians of science for a long time and have generated an extensive literature that falls into two uneven and almost unrelated parts. One deals with the issues in terms of institutions, studying international associations, research facilities, philanthropies, and societies. This literature ranges from histories of the International Research Council and CERN to studies of the Nobel and Rockefeller Foundations.[9] The second, considerably smaller part deals with the issues in terms of ideologies and cultures—both experimental and social practices. This literature examines assumptions, beliefs, ideas, standards, and techniques underpinning scientific internationalism, such as the "universality" of scientific knowledge, "academic freedom," the separation of science and politics, the pull and push of cooperation and competition among the national scientific communities, as well as nationalistic sentiments and local traditions embedded in the ideals and practices of international science.[10]

Although ostensibly dealing with the same issues, these two bodies of literature are separated by a wide gap. First of all, ideologies and cultures are not directly translatable into institutions, and they help little in understanding the institutional "incarnations" of internationalism, and vice versa. Second, the ideology of scientific internationalism has been examined mostly from the point of view of the scientific community, while the attitudes of its patrons (with a few notable exceptions such as the Nobel and Rockefeller Foundations) remain largely unexplored.[11] Finally, a number of events and phenomena, which are neither exactly institutions nor exactly ideologies/cultures, fall into this gap, including expeditions, occasional collaborations (such as, international polar and geophysical years), and, of course, congresses.

International congresses are, perhaps, the most explicit manifestation of the intersection between the national and international "dimensions" in scientists' activities, for their timing, location, program content, the representation of various countries, the composition of national delegations, and accompanying exhibitions and excursions are the results of negotiations among scientists from various countries. At the same time, congresses provide a vehicle for the advancement of local agendas, particularly for the scientists of the host country. National communities routinely use such congresses to enhance their disciplines' standing and visibility in the eyes of domestic patrons, which lead to sometimes quite fierce competition among national communities for the chance to host such a congress.

In dealing with the case of an international congress, neither the institutional nor ideological/cultural approach provides us with any clues as to what was going on and why things happened the way they did. It seems that we need to introduce an additional element in our analysis, which would bring together, and bridge the gap between, the different manifestations of what is commonly called "scientific internationalism."

Neither institutions, nor ideologies are Kantian "things in themselves": they do not exist in a vacuum or in the heads of historians who study them. They originate, come to being, and are effectuated by certain individuals and groups, which form particular *networks*. Following the ideas of Mark B. Adams about the critical importance of networks in the history of science in general and the history of Soviet science in particular, when I use the word "network" I am not referring:

> to anything arcane or technical—not the "networks" of the sociologist, dynamist, or social study theoretician, much less the computer specialist—but rather to the looser, more evocative meaning the word has come to have in everyday language, one familiar to every kind of historian: personal networks.[12]

It is the members of such personal networks who negotiate and determine the structures and agendas of the institutions they create.[13] It is the members of such networks who define and redefine the ideologies they adhere to and the cultures they practice.[14] And it is the multitude of such networks, which, intertwined together, form what we call the international community.[15]

A network, however, is more than a mere sum of individuals that form it—it is an entity with its own holistic characteristics and operating procedures. The major feature of a personal network is trust. Network members share and act upon certain information that may, but more often may not, be a part of public knowledge, which makes face-to-face contacts particularly important both for the formation of a network and for the preservation of its integrity, continuity, and efficiency. This particular feature suggests that periodic congresses serve (among other things) as a major vehicle for maintaining disciplinary networks, shaping their membership and defining their objectives. The story of the Seventh international genetics congress brings out with particular clarity a critical role that disciplinary networks play in the operations of international science.

International science between the world wars: politics, patronage, and disciplines

In their explorations of scientific internationalism, historians have concentrated primarily on the role of international politics in scientific activities. They have focused much of their attention on the period of the 1880s through the 1920s, examining the rapid "rise" of international science in the decades preceding World War I, its "disruption" during the war, and its slow "restoration" after the end of the hostilities.[16] They have also diligently documented the effects of the Cold War on relations among scientists within and between the great competing blocs—East and West.[17] On the other hand, in recent years, some scholars have described the "normalization" of international scientific relations brought about by the collapse of the Soviet Union in 1991 and the ensuing "end" of the Cold War.[18]

Much of this literature is based on the implicit assumption that international relations constitute an essential feature of "normal" science, which has an intrinsic value to its practitioners. It assumes that international science would go on and on, if not "interrupted" or "corrupted" by external political cataclysms, like world wars or the Cold War. It further postulates that, in the absence of wars, scientists always actively seek the "internationalization," while wars (whether "hot" or "cold") compel them to accept or even endorse the "nationalization" of their activities.

Although it has attracted insufficient attention from historians, the fate of international science during the interwar period challenges this simplistic idealization in two important ways.[19] First, it highlights the role of patronage in mediating the influence of "external" political factors on scientists' international activities. Second, it suggests that different disciplines vary in their "susceptibility" to external political influences.[20]

During the interwar period, the leading patrons of international scientific relations were private philanthropies—notably, the International Education Board (IEB) and the Rockefeller Foundation.[21] Setting their goal as "the promotion of science on an international scale," they fostered wide international exchanges through the program of postgraduate fellowships open to young talented researchers regardless of their country of origin. Working directly with leading scientists, Rockefeller philanthropies also supported the establishment of several large research institutions in Europe and the Americas. Genetics was a major focus of the Rockefeller international efforts, and during the 1920s and 1930s, Rockefeller philanthropies were to a large degree responsible for making genetics an international venture.[22]

Unlike private foundations and in stark contrast to the post-World War II period, the attitude of the majority of national governments to the international relations of their scientists during the 1930s could be characterized as encouragingly indifferent.[23] Unlike the case of international sanitary and public health conventions, governments' involvement with international scientific gatherings was minimal.[24] At best, some governments appointed symbolic "representatives" to scientific congresses. Governmental agents and agencies in most countries considered international relations in science to be scientists' private matters. As we will see, even when prodded by geneticists to intervene, government officials in the United States, Britain, and Scandinavia politely declined.

There were, however, two exceptions: Germany and the Soviet Union. By the mid-1930s, in both countries the patronage of science had become the prerogative of the party-state apparatus (though German scientists maintained links with other patrons, like the Rockefeller Foundation and private industry), and the goals of that apparatus defined the limits of scientists' international activities.[25] For instance, in 1933, the Soviet government prohibited its scientists from using Rockefeller fellowships and sharply curtailed their foreign travels. The influence of local patrons challenged scientists' adherence to the principles of international science.

In his letter to the US Secretary of State, written in December 1936 in relation to the announced cancellation of the genetics congress in Moscow, a prominent US geneticist, Charles Davenport, articulated scientists' dual position as citizens of both a particular country and an international "republic of letters": "men of science have two loyalties, one to their country and one to their science."[26] But, following the current ideal of scientific internationalism, he insisted that the latter takes precedence over the former: "it is by loyalty to their science that they are best able to make discoveries and advance knowledge which is of so much value to their country." Many scientists around the world shared Davenport's sentiments.

Both the Soviet and German governments, however, adhered to the opposite view—that scientists' loyalty to their science must be subordinate to the interests of their country. Both governments strove to employ their scientists' international relations to advance domestic and international policies—foremost, as a vehicle for propaganda. Scientists in both countries found themselves trapped between their allegiance to the ideals of international science and their obligations to domestic governmental patrons.

The influence of governmental patrons thoroughly undermined the "classic formula" of the ideology of scientific internationalism: "the participation of the nation in the scientist's fame spares the scientist any conflict between advancing his science and advancing the interests of his nation."[27] For many Soviet, as well as German scientists, advancing their science often meant entering into conflicts with either their domestic patrons or their foreign peers, or both.

The necessity of appealing to national governments for funding also encouraged the use of "nationalistic" rhetoric and the spread of "nationalistic" sentiments in the local scientific communities—rhetoric and sentiments, which in the mid-1930s contributed significantly to the emergence of "Aryan sciences" in Nazi Germany and "Marxist" or "proletarian sciences" in Soviet Russia. Historians have documented these "national" developments in considerable detail, empha-sizing the role of state policies and ideologies in fostering the "nationalization" of scientific activities in both Germany and the USSR.[28] Yet how various discipli-nary communities reacted at the time to such "national" developments within their own fields and how such reactions reflected on the larger issues of the ideology and practices of scientific internationalism requires further study.[29]

The history of genetics offers a unique opportunity to explore these questions, for genetics was one of the disciplines in which certain "national" variants gained particular currency during the 1930s.[30] In Germany, a number of researchers advanced a particular concept of "racial hygiene" based on the notion of the genetic superiority of "Nordic" or "Aryan" race,[31] while in the Soviet Union, the proponents of a peculiar "Michurinist" genetics led by Trofim Lysenko made a bid to replace what they termed "formal" or "Mendelian" genetics.[32] As we will see, the international community's reactions to these developments in both Germany and the USSR profoundly affected international relations in genetics and ultimately its fate as an international discipline.

Contrary to the ideal generalizations about "scientific internationalism" prevalent in the literature, the story of the genetics congress clearly reveals a certain "discipline-specificity" in the development of international scientific relations. Unlike many other disciplines (say, physiology or theoretical physics), the direct exchange of research material was an indispensable part of the very practice of genetics, making international contacts obligatory for successful research and maintaining the disciplinary consensus. A similar situation was characteristic of the earth sciences, such as geology, geophysics, oceanography, and meteorology. The very subject of these disciplines transcends national borders and, particularly before the advent of satellites, it required continuous cooperation and constant exchange of data among scientists from different countries.[33] However, the inter-national relations in the earth sciences during the 1930s appeared much less affected by "external" influences: in July 1937, exactly at the time when the Permanent Organizing Committee for Genetics Congress decided to withdraw the congress from the USSR, the Seventeenth international geological congress did meet in Moscow.[34]

What set genetics apart was that it became much more deeply enmeshed in certain public controversies of the day than any other discipline.[35] Like physics in the late 1940s and 1950s, during the interwar period, in the words of Otto Mohr, genetics was "brought to the very foreground of public attention."[36] Whether it was eugenic sterilization and immigration legislation in the United States and elsewhere, the rise of Aryan racism in Germany, or Lysenko's attempt to substitute his own "Michurinist" genetics for a "Mendelian" one as a basis for the Soviet Union's agricultural policies, all these "applications" of genetics became the matter of wide public debates. These debates threatened to undermine genetics' very standing as an international discipline by entangling it in politically charged "national" controversies. The international genetics community as a whole chose to dissociate itself from the local developments in various countries—first of all, Germany and the USSR—in order to fend off the real or perceived threats to the future progress of their discipline.

Of course, the genetics community was in no sense a monolith and individual differences in political sympathies, institutional agendas, career ambitions, and intellectual interests shaped personal actions and reactions. Yet continuous negotiations among the members of international networks helped define certain general trends, dominant frameworks, and common grounds that determined the community's reaction to the events in Hitler's Germany and Stalin's Russia, which in the end decided the fate of the Seventh international genetics congress and the fate of genetics as an international discipline.

"Dual loyalties"

Following my own "dual loyalties" to narrative and analytical histories, the book is divided into two parts. Part I narrates the forty-year history of international activities in genetics from the emergence of the discipline to the beginning of World War II, focusing on the seven international congresses held during this time. Chapter 1 documents the growth of genetics as an international discipline during the first third of the twentieth century, punctuated by four international congresses held in London in 1899, in New York in 1902, again in London in 1906, and in Paris in 1911. It describes the emergence of a new community—Soviet geneticists—and its late but spectacular entry to the international scene culminating in the Fifth congress held in 1927 in Berlin. Chapter 2 chronicles the extensive efforts of Soviet geneticists to arrange to host an international genetics congress, detailing their negotiations over the issue with their domestic patrons and foreign peers during the preparations for the Sixth congress convened in 1932 in Ithaca, New York. It follows Soviet geneticists' initial success in winning support of both their patrons and their peers for holding the Seventh congress in Moscow in August 1937, the congress's sudden cancellation by the Politburo of the Communist Party in November 1936, and Western geneticists' reaction to this unexpected turn of events. Chapter 3 traces Soviet geneticists' renewed negotiations with their patrons and their final success in persuading the Politburo to permit the congress's convocation in Moscow a year later, in August 1938. It describes the reaction of the international community to the events in Moscow and its ultimate decision to withdraw the congress from the Soviet Union and to hold it in Britain in 1939. It portrays the organizers' efforts and their eventual failure to secure the participation of their Soviet colleagues in the congress in Edinburgh.

Part II addresses several puzzles in the story of the Seventh international genetics congress: why did the Politburo first cancel and then postpone the congress, why did the international genetics community decide to relocate the congress to Britain instead of holding it a year later in Moscow, and why were Soviet geneticists absent at the congress in Edinburgh? It attempts to solve these puzzles through analysis of the triangular relations among three major groups of actors, which figure in the story of the congress: Soviet geneticists, their domestic patrons, and their foreign peers. Chapter 4 analyzes negotiations between Soviet geneticists and their domestic patrons within the context of Soviet internal and international politics, as well as within the institutional and intellectual context of Soviet genetics. It explores different goals pursued by Soviet geneticists and their patrons and the role of a particular science system that emerged in the Soviet Union in the 1930s in deciding the fate of the congress. Chapter 5 examines interactions between Soviet geneticists and their foreign peers, focusing on the sources and content of information available to Western geneticists and the role of the international context of the mid-1930s within which that information was assessed and used. It investigates various individual and collective agendas that shaped the actions of the international community. Chapter 6 examines the conflict between Soviet scientists' loyalties "to their state" and "to their science" embodied in relations to their domestic patrons and their foreign peers, analyzing the different understanding of what those loyalties actually meant to all the parties involved. It explores Soviet geneticists' role as interpreters and mediators in the ongoing "dialogue" between their patrons and their peers over the issues of science policy and ideology, examining the differences and contradictions between geneticists' agendas in "domestic" and "international" settings and the role of geneticists' personal networks in mediating these differences and shaping the fate of their congresses and their discipline.

The Epilogue tells a story of an international genetics congress that did meet in Moscow—albeit more than forty years after the ill-fated Seventh congress had been scheduled for the Soviet Union.

Part I

International genetics congresses, 1899–1939

Genetics as a discipline was born in the heyday of "scientific internationalism" in the first decade of the twentieth century. During this time science was considered to be international by its very nature—scientific facts and concepts were seen as universal. Science seemed to be an enterprise independent of locale, which could be studied in one place and practiced in another. Most scientists thought of themselves as citizens of the world, loyal not to the particular country they happened to reside in, but to an ideal "republic of letters" that united them all. The migration of scientists and exchange of ideas were treated as essential to the advancement of science. Standards of scientific excellence were seen as universal: not incidentally, exactly at this time, the Nobel Prize—the highest scientific award given to scientists irrespective of their country of origin—was instituted.

In 1914, World War I tore apart the rich tapestry of international scientific relations developed during the previous decades, driving scientists of different countries into "hostile political camps."[1] The aftermath of the war was marked by boycotts (and counterboycotts) of German and Austrian science.[2] But by the mid-1920s, scientists seemed to have overcome the war legacy and had returned to the practices of "international science," resuming exchanges of people and ideas and loudly proclaiming their adherence to the ideals of scientific internationalism. This situation continued until World War II, and then the Cold War that came in its wake, once again divided the world's scientists into opposing camps.

The history of genetics, however, does not fit easily into this neat picture of science as an international endeavor that would go on and on if it were not interrupted by major cataclysms such as world wars that demanded scientists' undivided loyalty to their countries to the detriment of loyalty to their imaginary "republic of letters." The story of the international genetics congresses indicates that even during the time of peace between the world wars, international relations in genetics were heavily imbued by the conflicts inherent to scientists' dual loyalties—to their science and to their country.

1 Genetics as an international science

Building an international discipline

Scientists engaged in studies of heredity maintained close contacts through correspondence and personal encounters at various international forums, most importantly conferences on plant breeding.[3] The first such conference, later hailed as the First international genetics congress, met in London in 1899. Initiated by William Bateson and held under the auspices of the Royal Horticultural Society, the conference was called the "international conference on hybridization (the cross-breeding of species) and on the cross-breeding of varieties."[4] During two days, on July 11 and 12, about one hundred thirty participants heard fourteen reports. Only six countries were represented at the meeting: France, Germany, Great Britain, Holland, Switzerland, and the United States.

The next meeting convened 3 years later across the Atlantic in New York City under the name "International Conference on Plant Breeding and Hybridization."[5] During three days, September 30–October 2, 1902, some seventy-five representatives from nearly a dozen countries met under the auspices of the Horticultural Society of New York. Although the number of participants at this conference was smaller than at the previous one, the number of presentations more than doubled: thirty addresses were presented and thirteen papers read by title. Furthermore, it was at this conference that William Bateson, his close friend and colleague Charles C. Hurst, and Hugo de Vries delivered reports on Mendel's "laws" of heredity.

Four years later, in 1906, this forum again assembled in London. About forty papers were listed in the program and forty-six published in the proceedings, along with descriptions of twenty-two special exhibits.[6] Almost three hundred delegates from thirteen countries had been invited to come to Britain. It was this meeting that for the first time assumed the name of the "international conference on genetics." In fact, the conference had been initially advertised and convened as an "international conference on hybridization and plant breeding."[7] But, in his inaugural address, its president William Bateson suggested that the emerging field of "the elucidation of the phenomena of heredity and variation" be named "genetics."[8] Apparently, this suggestion was welcomed and the conference proceedings were issued as the "Report on the third international conference on genetics." Furthermore, despite the remnants of the old name in the proceedings' subtitle—"hybridization (the cross-breeding of genera or species), the cross-breeding of varieties, and general plant-breeding"—the conference, for the first time, included several reports on animal genetics.

Bateson's suggestion of a new name for the studies of heredity and its eventual acceptance by the international community was far from accidental. For many years, heredity had been a subject of intensive studies by practitioners in a number of fields, including plant and animal breeding, cytology, eugenics, biometry, and embryology. The "rediscovery" of Mendel's laws offered a new approach to the phenomena of heredity based on the assumption that particular hereditary traits were transmitted from one generation to another by certain discrete "units" or "factors," which were inherited separately from each other and which the Danish geneticist Wilhelm Johannsen later named "genes." This approach, initially christened in honor of its originator "Mendelism," was enthusiastically embraced by a number of students of heredity, with Bateson as its most active "apostle."[9] However, Mendelism advocated by Bateson provoked sharp criticism from other students of heredity, notably a school of biometricians headed by W. F. R. Weldon and Karl Pearson. The main point of the controversy between Mendelians and biometricians was that Mendel's laws had been discovered and were subsequently demonstrated in the studies of *qualitative* (discontinuous) traits, such as the color of flowers or the shape of seeds. For biometricians, who were mostly preoccupied with *quantitative* (continuous) traits, such as the height of a plant or the weight of its fruits, any application of Mendel's laws to their subject seemed impossible.[10] The controversy raged with particular force in Britain, where it was exacerbated by the personal animosity and institutional rivalry between the leaders of two schools, while in other countries it was much less poignant.[11]

It seems likely that the controversy moved Bateson to invent a new name for the emerging discipline.[12] As social historians have convincingly argued, to succeed on the social scene, any group needs to resolve two distinct, but often interconnected problems: the internal problem of consensus and the external problem of legitimacy.[13] Applying this hypothesis to the process of discipline-building, one can suggest that Bateson's invention of a new name for the fledging discipline of genetics paved a way to the solution of both problems.[14] The new name was sufficiently neutral and allowed proponents of different approaches to hereditary phenomena to work together and hence to gradually develop necessary consensus over methods, tools, explanatory hypotheses, and research agendas of the new discipline. On the other hand, it seems probable that Bateson quite deliberately proposed the new name at an international conference in order to give the new discipline an international legitimacy and thus to distance genetics from domestic squabbles with the opponents of Mendelism.[15]

This strategy obviously paid off. Genetics began rapidly to acquire a disciplinary form. In 1908, in Berlin, Erwin Baur founded the first specialized journal in the field—*Zeitschrift für induktive Abstammungs- und Vererbungslehre* (*Journal for the Inductive Study of Evolution and Heredity*). The next year, a chair of genetics was created in Cambridge University, and Bateson's collaborator Reginald C. Punnett became the world's first professor of genetics. A year later, in 1910, the John Innes Horticultural Institution was founded in London with Bateson as its first director. The same year, Punnett established the *Journal of Genetics*. Although both British and German genetics journals focused on Mendelian genetics, they also published works by researchers who employed biometric or embryological approach and welcomed contributions by scientists from various countries.

When the next year, 1911, the Fourth international conference on genetics convened in Paris, it brought together nearly two hundred fifty delegates from seventeen countries. Fifty-eight reports were included in the proceedings.[16] It was at this conference that a further institutionalization of genetics as an international discipline took place. On September 23, at the end of the last session, the conference president Yves Delage announced that there was one more item on the conference agenda: the delegates should decide on the question of the place and date for the next, Fifth conference. Unlike at all the previous meetings, however, in Paris two countries appeared to be competing for the privilege to host the international gathering—both US and German geneticists extended an invitation. To deal with the problem, it was suggested to follow the example of international congresses in botany and zoology and to set up a "permanent committee for international genetics conferences."[17] The delegates felt that "the periodic international conferences should be tied to each other through a continuously active

Plate 1 The Fourth international genetics congress in Paris, 1911: (left to right) E. von Tschermark, W. Bateson, W. Johannsen, Y. Delage, and Ph. de Vilmorin. (From Ph. de Vilmorin (ed.) *IV Conférence Internationale de Génétique, Paris, 1911*, Paris: Masson et Co., 1913.)

entity and a homogeneous leadership possessing the authority necessary to make binding decisions." They unanimously elected representatives of nine countries—William Bateson from Great Britain as president, Erwin Baur from Germany, Erich von Tschermak from Austria, Wilhelm Johannsen from Denmark, Philip de Vilmorin from France, Jan P. Lotsy from Holland, N. H. Nilson-Elle from Sweden, Walter T. Swingle from the United States, and A. Lang from Switzerland—to the membership of the first international committee that was "charged with deciding on everything that concerns the general interests of the international genetics congresses." It was left to this committee to decide when and where—in the United States or Germany—the next congress would be held.

Of course, the practitioners of genetics did not neglect the opportunity to meet at other international gatherings both to promote their new field and to maintain links with established disciplines. International congresses in such traditional fields as zoology and botany provided a forum for those involved with the genetics of animals and plants, respectively. For instance, at the Second international botanical congress held in 1905 in Vienna, Erich von Tschermak delivered a long report on his Mendelian research.[18] Two years later, at the Seventh international zoological congress assembled in Boston in late August 1907, a large session was devoted solely to the issues of cytology and heredity with twenty-five reports. In Bateson's (perhaps biased and exaggerated) opinion, "Heredity, Cytology, and experimental zoology have kept the whole Congress. Nothing else has had any hearing worth the name."[19] It was at this congress that the first studies of heredity in the fruit fly—*Drosophila*, an organism that in just a few years would revolutionize genetics research—were presented.[20]

A similar forum for those interested in human genetics appeared at the First international eugenics congress. Eugenics—literally, "being well born"—had emerged in the mid-1880s as a field aimed at the biological improvement of the human kind, largely due to the efforts of Charles Darwin's cousin, Francis Galton.[21] Following his cousin's evolutionary concept, Galton believed that many human physical, mental, and moral traits were inherited, and hence, the survival of mankind as a species depended on improving the human stock. Galtonian eugenics involved two closely interrelated aspects: diminishing the reproduction of the physically, mentally, or morally "unfit," or *negative* eugenics; and increasing the reproduction of the hereditarily "fit," or *positive* eugenics. Eugenic ideas had attracted the attention of physicians, psychiatrists, anthropologists, animal breeders, demographers, biologists, sociologists, and public health officials, finding patrons among wealthy individuals and state bureaucracies.[22]

By 1910, various forms of eugenics movements had developed in Britain, France, Germany, and the United States, fueling international cooperation among various local eugenics societies, activists, and theorists, which culminated at the First international eugenics congress held in London in 1912.[23] During a week, more than one hundred participants listened to thirty-two reports on subjects ranging from practical eugenic measures to the interrelations between eugenics and historical research. Although eugenicists from Belgium, France, Germany, Italy, Great Britain, and the United States dominated the congress, delegates from Japan, Russia, Spain, and Switzerland also took part in the proceedings.

Eugenics had a strong appeal to many practitioners of genetics—both fields dealt with issues of heredity. But eugenics had much broader public exposure and support than the rather technical field of genetics and, aside from exciting intellectual issues, for many geneticists, forging an alliance with eugenics promised a very effective rhetorical cover for the "external" legitimization of their fledging discipline. As Paul Weindling has aptly observed, in Germany "eugenics nurtured an increasingly active and well-funded community of geneticists."[24]

The proceedings of the First international eugenics congress suggest that Weindling's observation is equally applicable to the relationship between eugenics and genetics in other countries.[25] At that congress a special section on "Biology and Eugenics" featured eight reports on various aspects of human heredity, two of them by geneticists. At the morning session, the US biologist Raymond Pearl presented a paper on "The Inheritance of Fecundity" in domestic fowl, "pointing out some possible eugenic bearings" of his studies. "These results on fecundity in fowls not only emphasize the importance of analytical studies to determine the precise mode of inheritance of human fecundity," he stated, "but they also furnish a guide and stimulus for the conduct of such studies."[26] Characteristically, the only comment on Pearl's paper came from the second geneticist present—Reginald C. Punnett. Noting that "workers on eugenic problems were sometimes criticized for experimenting with apparently useless things, such as sweet peas," Punnett emphasized, "Dr. Pearl had shown that such work might produce useful results."[27]

At the afternoon session, with the president of the Paris international genetics congress Yves Delage in the chair, Punnett himself gave "a lantern lecture" entitled "Genetics and Eugenics."[28] Starting with a declaration that "to the student of genetics, man, like any other animal, is material for working out the manner in which characters, whether physical or mental, are transmitted from one generation to the next," Punnett warned the audience that "our knowledge of heredity in men is at present far too slight and too uncertain to base legislation upon." He admitted that direct experimental studies of genetics in men were "hardly feasible," but insisted that collecting and analyzing pedigrees (a major method of eugenic studies at the time) could only be "carried out satisfactorily by those who have been trained in and are alive to the trend of genetic research." Characteristically, Punnett concluded his lecture by "expressing the hope that some imaginative millionaire would endow research on these [genetic] lines."[29]

International activities in genetics were quickly expanding when, in the summer of 1914, World War I erupted and put a stop to such international gatherings for almost a decade. The war also severely limited any further development of genetics in Europe that turned into one huge battlefield. Only American geneticists were able to actively pursue their studies during the war years, capitalizing on the momentum US genetics had developed on the eve of the war with the establishment of the American Genetics Association and its mouthpiece, the *Journal of Heredity*. The growth of US genetics was clearly reflected in founding a new journal, *Genetics*, in 1916.

One group of US geneticists in particular made a tremendous contribution to the advance of their discipline: Thomas Hunt Morgan and his students at Columbia University had begun to decipher the "mechanisms of Mendelian heredity."[30] Continuing their studies in Drosophila genetics started in 1908, Morgan and his pupils firmly established the chromosome theory of heredity, demonstrating the localization of genes on chromosomes, and began developing the concept of the gene as a material unit of heredity.[31] By the end of the war, they had published a number of articles and books summarizing their research.[32]

The war shredded the rich fabric of "international science," which had emerged during the preceding decades, dividing the international genetics community as it did many others. In the first postwar years, the feelings of embitterment and animosity between German and Austrian geneticists, on one hand, and their French and Belgian colleagues, on the other, were particularly strong.[33] Nevertheless, in the early 1920s, there were increasing calls for a return to the values and practices of internationalism.[34]

Eugenicists were one of the first disciplinary communities to answer these calls: by the spring of 1920, plans to hold the Second international eugenics congress in New York in September 1921 were well-advanced.[35] The forthcoming congress seemed like a good opportunity to resume international contacts in genetics as well, particularly because nearly one-third of the congress sessions were going to deal with genetic issues. The congress's organizers, including Charles Davenport (head of the US Eugenics Records Office) and Henry F. Osborn (the most prominent US paleontologist), approached Morgan with the suggestion that an international genetics congress "meet with them at the same time."[36]

Although he personally had certain reservations regarding such a joint congress, Morgan at once sought the counsel of William Bateson, the chairman of the permanent committee for genetics congresses. Bateson, however, adamantly refused the suggestion. He warned Morgan that by accepting the invitation for the joint congress with eugenicists "we might do ourselves great harm."[37] A few months later, on February 17, 1921, in the Galton lecture delivered to the Eugenics Education Society, Bateson clearly articulated his position vis-à-vis eugenics: "Genetics [*sic*!] are not primarily concerned with the betterment of the human race or other applications, but with a problem of pure physiology, and I am a little afraid that the distinctiveness of our aims may be obscured."[38] Morgan distributed Bateson's warning among leading US geneticists who apparently agreed that it was better to organize a separate genetics congress. However, finding a place for the genetics congress remained a problem.

As head of the international committee, Bateson felt particularly responsible for the resumption of the congresses.[39] As he declared in his letter to Morgan: "I am desirous of getting international relations back to normality as soon as possible." But he also felt that "a move made so soon would lead to bitterness and trouble." Some geneticists, including Erwin Baur, suggested that a congress could perhaps be arranged in 1921 on some neutral territory, for instance, in Copenhagen.[40] Baur thought that, "as Geneticists are vernunftige Leute [sensible people—N. K.], that French and Belgians might be induced to join even now."

But Bateson was certain that "this is of course out of the question and I doubt whether any member of those nations would join for several years." Indeed, it took almost five years for the international situation to stabilize and for French–German animosity to subside sufficiently to allow the international committee to accept the proposal of German geneticists to hold the congress in Berlin.[41]

When the congress finally met in September 1927, its participants were astonished to find that the largest foreign delegation had come from a country that had never before made an appearance at an international genetics meeting—Russia.

"Acclimatization" of genetics in Russia

Although a few Russian plant breeders did attend the 1911 Paris conference as observers, Russia was not represented at the prewar genetics congresses in any significant way and no Russian delegate joined the permanent international committee, because in that country genetics as a discipline came into being only after the revolutions of 1917. However, a mere decade after the turmoil of the revolutions and the ensuing civil war had ended in 1921, genetics had become a full-fledged discipline with dozens of laboratories, departments, and periodicals and hundreds of researchers all over the new Soviet Russia. In early 1929, when the first national conference on genetics convened in Leningrad, nearly 1,500 delegates took part in proceedings that featured more than 300 reports.

As elsewhere in the world, in Russia the initial impetus for this astonishingly rapid institutional growth came from three different fields: plant and animal breeding, experimental biology, and eugenics.[42] These fields supplied the "seed" personnel for the burgeoning discipline: the three "founding fathers" of Soviet genetics—Nikolai Vavilov, Nikolai Kol'tsov, and Iurii Filipchenko—and their numerous students and co-workers.

Russia was an agricultural country and, although somewhat later than in other countries, plant and animal breeding had been firmly instituted as a field of inquiry during the first decade of the twentieth century: by 1914 several hundred experimental agricultural stations engaged in breeding experiments were scattered across the vast expanses of the empire.[43] Although the news about the rediscovery of Mendel's laws had become known in Russia in early 1903, when a prominent botanist and member of the Russian Academy of Sciences, Ivan Borodin, published a series of articles on the subject,[44] "Mendelism" did not stir the enthusiastic response it had created in other countries among plant and animal breeders.[45] Furthermore, Russia's own "Darwin's bulldog"—influential plant physiologist Kliment Timiriazev—published several articles highly critical of "Mendelism" and its proponents, particularly Bateson.[46] Nevertheless, several professors at various agricultural schools began including outlines of "Mendelism" in their courses on plant and animal breeding.[47] Several of their students, including Vavilov, went abroad for postgraduate studies at leading genetics laboratories in Britain, France, and Germany. In 1913, the director of the Bureau of Applied Botany established under the aegis of the Scientific

Agricultural Committee of the Ministry of State Properties Robert Regel translated into Russian Erwin Baur's seminal work *Einführung in die experimentelle Vererbungslehre* under the title *Introduction to the study of heredity*.[48] Finally, in 1914, a professor at the Moscow Agricultural Institute, E. A. Bogdanov, published a voluminous tome of more than six hundred pages entitled *Mendelism, or the Theory of Hybridization*. This work, for the first time in the Russian language, provided a comprehensive survey of the advances of the new discipline in studying the heredity of plants and animals and answered its Russian critics.[49]

Also during the first decade of the twentieth century, as elsewhere in Europe and the United States, several university professors, notably Nikolai Kol'tsov in Moscow and Iurii Filipchenko in St Petersburg,[50] began developing a composite field that they called "experimental biology" or "experimental zoology." A major focus of this new field was the application of experimental methods to the study of the three main problems of evolution: variation, speciation, and individual development. Experimental biologists became quickly involved in genetic studies that promised "the elucidation of the phenomena of heredity and variation." They included elements of genetics in their courses on "experimental zoology," and in 1913 Filipchenko opened the first special course on "heredity and evolution." They translated major genetics texts, including works of Mendel, de Vries, Correns, and Baur, and published reviews and survey articles on "Mendelism" in various Russian periodicals. A new popular magazine, *Priroda* (*Nature*), created in 1912 with Kol'tsov's active involvement, became the mouthpiece of the new field.

Experimental biologists' attempts at institutionalizing this new field, however, met strong opposition from biologists of the older generation. They were engaged in studying evolutionary problems from the traditional—morphological and systematic—viewpoints and dominated existing zoology departments in the state universities. Nevertheless, the new biology found a niche within Russia's new private universities. In 1908, the prominent psychiatrist Vladimir Bekhterev and the zoopsychologist Vladimir Vagner created the Psycho-Neurological Institute in St Petersburg. This institute was engaged in both teaching and research, and it was at this institute that Filipchenko first delivered his course on "heredity and evolution." Also in 1908, Russia's first private university—the Shaniavskii Moscow City People's University (named after its sponsor, the rich industrialist Alfons Shaniavskii)—was established and soon became Kol'tsov's principal base. In 1913, Kol'tsov created a special laboratory of "experimental biology" at the university. Here Kol'tsov trained a group of bright young researchers, including Aleksandr Serebrovskii and Mikhail Zavadovskii—a group that would contribute substantially to the forthcoming institutionalization of genetics in Russia. In late 1916, Kol'tsov even managed to secure private funds for establishing the Institute of Experimental Biology, where he planned to organize a special genetics laboratory. But the implementation of this plan was disrupted by the Russian revolutions and the ensuing civil war.

As elsewhere in Europe and the Americas, in the late 1890s and early 1900s, eugenic ideas of "bettering the human race" also attracted interest among

Russian physicians, biologists, sociologists, anthropologists, psychiatrists, and social thinkers.[51] Treatises on eugenics, including works by its founder Francis Galton, were translated into Russian.[52] Prominent physicians and scientists, including Petr Kovalevskii and Vladimir Bekhterev, published articles on certain aspects of eugenics, particularly "degeneration."[53] The eminent philosopher Prince Petr Kropotkin even took part in the 1912 international eugenics congress in London. However, the institutionalization and development of eugenics as a research field in Russia occurred largely after the Bolshevik revolution and in close conjunction with genetics.

After the Bolshevik revolution these three fields—plant and animal breeding, experimental biology, and eugenics—provided launching pads for the institutionalization of genetics. The financial and institutional support for this active discipline-building came from the new Bolshevik state.[54] With the nationalization of all private enterprise in 1917, the state became the sole patron for science in Russia. The premium the state set on science and scientific education also made it an eager patron. The Bolsheviks' primary concern during their first years of power was the restoration and maintenance of the national economy, which they considered crucial for the building of what their political program called "the first socialist society": science was to play an important role in the building of socialism in Russia.

Although the Bolshevik revolution led to suffering, arrests, and deprivations for many Russian scientists, given the Bolsheviks' active support for science, it also created an unprecedented opportunity for institution- and discipline-building. Russian geneticists immediately seized that opportunity. During the civil war that ravaged the country for almost four years, accompanied by famine, epidemics, and terror, Russian geneticists managed to lay a foundation for their field. By the time the war ended in 1921, genetics had been firmly institutionalized in Soviet Russia.

Geneticists engaged various state agencies in support of their efforts. The People's Commissariat of Agriculture—Narkomzem—began funding genetics research at agricultural schools and experimental stations. The People's Commissariat of Enlightenment—Narkompros—supported work in universities and the Russian Academy of Sciences. The People's Commissariat of Public Health—Narkomzdrav—financed studies at medical schools and research institutes. Other agencies, such as the Supreme Council of the National Economy (VSNKh), the Council of the People's Commissars (SNK), and the Central Executive Committee (TsIK) also provided funds for genetic research at scientific institutions established under their auspices. The three enterprising men principally responsible for the flowering of genetics in Soviet Russia—Filipchenko, Kol'tsov, and Vavilov—tapped all available resources to organize genetics institutes and laboratories, convene conferences, create periodicals, and train a new professional generation.

In the autumn of 1918, Filipchenko organized Russia's first genetics department at Petrograd University. Two years later, he established a special genetics laboratory within the university's newly created Institute of Natural Sciences located on the former tsarist estate in Peterhoff, where he began work on quantitative genetics in wheat and other crops. In March 1921, under the auspices of the Russian Academy of Sciences, he also opened the Bureau of Eugenics, which immediately began publishing a bulletin.[55] Filipchenko used all three of his institutions as a training ground for a large group of students.

Although the Bolshevik revolution had destroyed the private philanthropies that had supported Kol'tsov's efforts to create the Institute of Experimental Biology, he managed to obtain alternative funding for his endeavors from the new Bolshevik state. Already in 1918, Kol'tsov managed to secure support from Narkomzem and Narkompros—through the Academy of Sciences—for creating two experimental stations outside of Moscow. Directed by his students Aleksandr Serebrovskii and Vladimir Lebedev, these stations became engaged in studying chicken genetics.[56] In January 1920, Kol'tsov also acquired Narkomzdrav's funding for his institute as a whole and for a number of periodicals published under its auspices. He procured for the institute a large building in the center of Moscow and funds for equipment and personnel. In the summer, Kol'tsov established a department of eugenics at his institute. Shortly thereafter this department became the basis for the Russian Eugenics Society. Kol'tsov served as both the president of the new society and the editor-in-chief of its mouthpiece—*Russian Eugenics Journal*—started a year later, in 1922.

In 1921, after the death of R. Regel', Vavilov became the head of the Bureau of Applied Botany in Petrograd, and within a year he transformed it into the State Institute of Experimental Agronomy. In 1923 he was appointed the director of this institute and also the director of another new institution he had helped to create: the Institute of Applied Botany and New (Plant) Cultures.[57] The *Proceedings* published by the new institutes regularly featured articles on genetics.

The discipline-building activities of Russian geneticists reflected their need both to find suitable patrons and to ensure the simple survival of genetics personnel. Given the Bolsheviks' pragmatic attitude toward science, a move to agricultural genetics was the most obvious. Not surprisingly, both Kol'tsov and Filipchenko became involved in studying genetics in agriculturally important subjects—wheat, poultry, and cattle. In addition to appealing to new patrons—notably, Narkomzem—this also provided a supplementary source of food for geneticists and their families. Kol'tsov's transfer of his studies and many of his staff during the civil war years to the experimental stations outside starving Moscow was in no small part motivated by the latter reason.

Eugenics offered another point of intersection between the interests of geneticists and their new patrons. Eugenic ideas of "bettering the human race" resonated very well with the Bolsheviks' early visions of creating a "new society" and a "new man." Both the commissar of enlightenment Anatolii Lunacharskii and the commissar of public health Nikolai Semashko became founding members of the Russian Eugenics Society. Although for some geneticists, notably Kol'tsov, eugenics provided a genuine source of inspiration and research possibilities, for others, it perhaps served mostly as a suitable rhetorical cover for legitimizing their genetic studies. In 1925, Filipchenko's Bureau of Eugenics (along with its bulletin) was renamed the Laboratory of Eugenics and Genetics, and in 1928 the word "eugenics" disappeared from its name completely.

The founders of Russian genetics maintained close ties with the heads of the state agencies that funded their endeavors, as well as prominent cultural figures that held the ear of the new rulers, such as the "great proletarian writer" Maxim Gorky.[58] Lenin's former secretary, the executive secretary of SNK, Nikolai Gorbunov headed the scientific council at Vavilov's Institute of Applied Botany and New (Plant) Cultures. During the civil war years, Filipchenko worked closely with Gorky in the Commission for Improving Conditions of Scientists in Petrograd. Kol'tsov cultivated contacts with Lunacharskii, Semashko, and Gorky.

During the 1920s, genetics laboratories appeared in various universities, medical and agricultural schools, and even zoos. An important center of genetic research—the Biology Institute (named after Kliment Timiriazev) directed by Russia's most prominent cytologist Sergei Navashin—emerged under the auspices of the Communist Academy, a Bolshevik counterpart to the Russian Academy of Sciences.[59] Genetics courses were introduced, and genetics textbooks were written and translated. A large number of students began to specialize in the new field.

The road to Berlin

The support of domestic patrons was, of course, imperative for the flowering of Soviet genetics, but no less important were international contacts. From its very birth, Soviet genetics developed in close contact with its foreign counterparts. Before the revolution, the three founders—Filipchenko, Kol'tsov, and Vavilov— had established close ties with their colleagues abroad. During his many visits to the Naples Marine Station and the Russian Marine Station at Villefranche in southern France, Kol'tsov had developed extensive contacts with German geneticists, notably Richard Goldschmidt and Max Hartmann.[60] Filipchenko had worked in Munich with Richard Hertwig in 1911–12. Vavilov had studied with William Bateson in Britain, Phillipe de Vilmorin in France, and Ernst Haeckel in Germany during 1913–14.[61] Although World War I, the revolutions, and the civil war had impeded contacts between Russian and foreign scientists for almost a decade, the moment the hostilities ended the old contacts were resumed and new ones were established.

In the autumn of 1921, Vavilov came to the United States. The stated purpose of his trip was to take part in an International Congress on Phytopathology. But he also visited agricultural stations and university departments all over the country and even established the Russian Agricultural Bureau in New York City to facilitate the exchange of materials and publications between Russian and American plant breeders. On his way back to Russia, he also toured centers of plant breeding in Britain (where he paid a visit to his teacher William Bateson), Germany, and Sweden.

But agricultural genetics was not Vavilov's only concern during his trip. On September 21, from San Francisco, he sent a long letter to the head of the US

Eugenics Records Office Charles Davenport.[62] Vavilov informed Davenport of the establishment of "the first Russian Eugenics Society" and the large amount of work done by Russian eugenicists, particularly Filipchenko and Kol'tsov. He expressed his regrets that he would not be able to attend the Second international eugenics congress held at the time in New York City and asked Davenport to collect recent eugenics literature for Russian colleagues.[63] At about the same time, Davenport received a letter from Russia, from the president of the Russian Eugenics Society Kol'tsov.[64] Sent through a Narkomzdrav representative in the United States, the letter informed Davenport of the creation of both the department of eugenics at the Institute of Experimental Biology and the Russian Eugenics Society. Kol'tsov noted that he would like to attend the international eugenics congress, but it seemed impossible at the moment. He also lamented the "intellectual famine" Russian scientists had been and were still experiencing, and asked Davenport for his assistance in getting recent genetic and eugenic literature. A few weeks later, Davenport received yet another letter from Russia, which had arrived via the Soviet Trade Delegation in Norway, this one from Filipchenko. Filipchenko notified his American colleague of the establishment of the Bureau of Eugenics in Petrograd and sent him its first bulletin. He also asked Davenport for help in acquiring eugenic literature.[65] Davenport immediately responded to the Russian requests and arranged for a large shipment of books and periodicals to both Moscow and Petrograd. This initial exchange soon grew into an extensive correspondence between American and Russian geneticists and eugenicists.

The efforts of Russian geneticists in establishing contacts with their American colleagues were reciprocated. The next year, Herman J. Muller, one of the original members of Morgan's "fly group" at Columbia University, came to Russia and visited genetics laboratories in Moscow and Petrograd.[66] He met the founders of Soviet genetics and their pupils, including Aleksandr Serebrovskii whose work on chicken genetics closely paralleled the research conducted by British and American geneticists.[67] Muller apprised his Russian colleagues of the remarkable progress the Morgan group had made during the last ten years and presented them a collection of *Drosophila* stocks he brought from the United States.[68] Muller's visit and his gift played a crucial role in the conversion of a large group of Russian geneticists to Drosophila genetics and in the adoption of the fruit fly as their primary research tool.

The institutional growth of Soviet genetics in the early 1920s was accompanied by the strengthening of formal relations to foreign genetics and geneticists. In 1923, the Russian Academy of Sciences elected both Bateson and Morgan its foreign members. The next year three more geneticists—Herbert S. Jennings, Wilhelm Johannsen, and Hugo de Vries—were elected to the academy.[69] During these years, Filipchenko, Kol'tsov, Vavilov, and several of their students went abroad to visit genetics laboratories or conduct research, reviving the old contacts and forging new ones.[70] They regularly corresponded with their colleagues in Britain, Germany, the United States, and other countries. In September 1924, Kol'tsov even managed to attend an International Conference on Eugenics in Milan.[71]

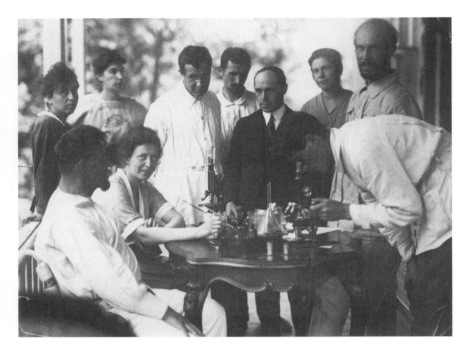

Plate 2 H. J. Muller's visit to Russia, 1922. S. S. Chetverikov (sitting first on the left), A. S. Serebrovskii (standing first on the right), H. J. Muller (standing third from the right). Courtesy of the APS.

The Bolshevik government eagerly supported scientists' efforts to rebuild their international relations for a number of reasons. First of all, the Bolsheviks hoped to use western advances in science and technology in their efforts to revive the country's economy devastated by almost a decade of continuous warfare. As Lenin once remarked: "To absorb everything valuable from European and American science is our first and foremost task."[72] In March 1921, the Soviet government set up the Bureau of Foreign Science and Technology in Berlin, with the specific mandate of "establishing vital and permanent relations with German (and other European) scientists."[73] At the same time Narkomzdrav sent its own official representatives to Germany, France, and the United States.

Economic reasons were closely tied to political ones. The new regime sought to employ international scientific relations to break down the diplomatic isolation and to dispel the image of Soviet Russia as the land of "barbarism" and a "threat to civilization" propagated by the Western press. In early 1925, a new agency—the All-Union Society for Cultural Relations with Foreign Countries (VOKS)—was created for the express purpose of enhancing the image of the Soviet Union abroad.[74] Science was a major focus of VOKS's activity: scientific advances were trumpeted in the VOKS bulletin published in French, German, and English.

Russian scientists used all the available channels to expand their international contacts.

The convergence of the interests of scientists and their state patrons in fostering international relations was particularly apparent at the first international scientific gathering held in the Soviet Union—the bicentennial jubilee of the Russian Academy of Sciences.[75] On February 18, 1925, the academy's vice-president, mathematician Vladimir Steklov, and its permanent secretary, orientalist Sergei Ol'denburg sent a long letter regarding the forthcoming anniversary to Lenin's successor as the head of SNK Aleksei Rykov.[76] The academicians asked for the state's permission to invite a large number of foreign scientists to the jubilee and for the establishment of a special governmental commission, with Rykov as its chairman, "to assign the celebration a state character." They noted that many foreign scientists were eager to come to Leningrad for the jubilee and emphasized that: "This jubilee will have a particular importance in international politics. Foreign scientists will see for themselves that all the stories about the destruction of cultural treasures, about the reign of barbarism in the USSR, are nothing but groundless fictions."

Rykov enthusiastically responded to the call. He immediately wrote a memorandum for the Politburo—the highest ruling body of the Central Committee of the Communist Party presided over by Joseph Stalin[77]—with a proposal to "give the jubilee an imposing character." He explained his reasons: "There would be an exceptional interest in this celebration abroad, the foreign press would have to publish detailed reports. Speeches and reports of our academicians will be coordinated with us [that is the Politburo—N. K.]. The whole plan of the celebration will be approved by us. Under such conditions, I think, we can use this occasion with great benefits for ourselves." The very next day the Politburo decided "to consider it desirable that foreign scientists attend the 200-anniversary of the Academy of Sciences" and instructed SNK to fund the jubilee and appoint a special jubilee commission under Rykov's chairmanship. Although scientists in a number of countries ignored the celebration and only ninety-eight (instead of the invited three hundred) foreign guests came to Leningrad for the festivities, the jubilee was a success and it certainly served the goals of both Soviet scientists and their patrons.

Soviet geneticists did not miss the opportunity the jubilee afforded to strengthen their own international contacts. The academy sent invitations to attend the jubilee to all its foreign members, including the "godfather" of genetics, chairman of the permanent committee for international genetics congresses, William Bateson. Bateson had planned for a long time to visit Russia on his own. In the spring of 1925, he had even asked his former student Vavilov for help in expediting a Russian visa for his trip during the summer.[78] But family matters forced him to cancel the trip. The invitation to come to Leningrad for the jubilee in early September, therefore, came at an opportune moment, and Bateson gladly accepted it. Bateson was not the only geneticist among the guests. A prominent cytologist from Finland, Harry Federley, and an eminent German neurologist with a keen interest in genetics, Oscar Vogt, joined Bateson to form a sort of unofficial genetics delegation. The trio was taken on a tour of Vavilov's institutes in

Plate 3 The "genetics delegation" during the jubilee of the Russian Academy of Sciences, Peterhoff, 1925. Front row: (left to right) I. I. Sokolov, V. A. Dogel', Iu. A. Filipchenko, N. I. Vavilov. Back row: H. Federley, O. Vogt, W. Bateson. (From *Nikolai Ivanovich Vavilov. Nauchnoe Nasledie v Pis'makh*, Moscow: Nauka, 1994, vol. 1.)

Leningrad and his experimental station at a former tsarist estate south of the city. They also visited Filipchenko's department of genetics at Leningrad University and his laboratory in Peterhoff. When the celebration moved from Leningrad to Moscow, they visited Kol'tsov's Institute of Experimental Biology, as well as Navashin's laboratory at the Timiriazev Biology Institute. They met the leaders of Soviet genetics and their students and were much impressed by the facilities and personnel.[79]

International contacts of Soviet geneticists began to expand quickly. The same year, one of Kol'tsov's students, Nikolai Timofeeff-Ressovsky, went to Germany to help Vogt establish a genetics department at the Kaiser Wilhelm Institute for Brain Research. At the beginning of the next year, Georgii Karpechenko, a talented young cytologist, whom Vavilov was grooming to head genetics at his institute, embarked on a six-month tour through the discipline's European centers. He started with the Kaiser Wilhelm Institute for Plant Genetics directed by Erwin Baur and then, via Holland, he proceeded to Britain to visit Bateson's John Innes

Institution.[80] In turn, Karpechenko's stay in Britain spurred several British geneticists, including C. Leonard Huskins and R. Ruggles Gates, to visit Russian genetics institutions in the summer and fall of 1926.[81] Also in 1926, Vavilov undertook a long expedition to collect wild varieties of cultivated plants in the Mediterranean, visiting France, Spain, Abyssinia, Italy, Greece, and other countries and making acquaintance with leading geneticists there.[82]

Of course, the ultimate opportunity for Russian geneticists to expand and solidify their international contacts would be attendance at an international genetics congress, yet their participation in such a congress was far from assured. Although Russia had fought in World War I on the side of the Allies, in its aftermath, Russian scientists were isolated de facto, if not de jure, from many scientific activities spearheaded by the allied countries, particularly by the International Research Council and various international disciplinary unions it controlled.[83] This situation naturally drove scientists of the two "pariahs of Versailles"—Soviet Russia and Weimar Germany—into each other's embrace.

Before the war, ties between Russian and German science had been very strong; Germany had always been the favorite place for Russian scientists' postgraduate studies in a variety of disciplines. Although during the war the scientific communities of both countries had been swept by the wave of nationalism and had loudly proclaimed each other sworn enemies,[84] almost immediately after the war the old relations were reactivated. In the situation where scientists in both countries found themselves cut off from the rest of world science (albeit for different reasons), their bilateral contacts acquired special importance.[85]

For Soviet geneticists, then, the decision of the permanent international committee for genetics congresses to hold the first postwar congress in Germany proved to be a very fortunate one. Given the policy of non-recognition of the Soviet Union upheld by the United States, combined with the worsening of Soviet Russia's relationship with France and particularly Britain in 1927, Germany was probably the only country in the world to which a delegation of Soviet geneticists would have been allowed to come for the congress. And given the particularly close bilateral relations between the Soviet Union and Germany, it seemed that there would be no problem in securing the government's permission and support for such a visit.

The Soviet government's encouragement of international (and particularly Soviet–German) scientific contacts did not mean, however, that scientists were allowed to go abroad as they pleased. They first had to obtain permission of the state agency under whose auspices they worked. Then they had to submit a request to a Narkompros "inter-agency" commission established specifically to vet scientific trips.[86] After sifting the requests, Narkompros in turn funneled the documents to a special "Departure Commission" created in April 1924 within the Central Committee of the Communist Party to approve and monitor all foreign travel.[87] Without the blessings of the Departure Commission no one could leave the country.

Soviet geneticists managed to work their way through the bureaucratic hurdles. First of all, only sixteen of them applied specifically for the trip to Berlin to take part in the congress.[88] Others, instead, gave "research in laboratories and libraries" as the purpose of their trip abroad and listed a number of scientific institutions in countries other than Germany, such as Holland, France, or Czechoslovakia, as their primary sites of visits, but mentioned Berlin as a transit stop in their travels. Second, a number of Soviet geneticists undertook the trip at their own expense, without asking for subsidies from state agencies, which greatly improved their chances of getting approval. Furthermore, even when the Departure Commission had initially denied permissions to some applicants, geneticists managed to reverse the decision. For instance, in early June 1927, the commission refused the application of Sergei Chetverikov, head of the genetics laboratory at Kol'tsov's Institute of Experimental Biology, to attend the congress, which had been presented through Narkompros.[89] Kol'tsov immediately wrote a letter to his fellow-member of the Russian Eugenic Society, Nikolai Semashko, asking for help.[90] The commissar of public health intervened. At the end of July, the Departure Commission approved Chetverikov's trip "to Germany with scientific purposes" under Narkomzdrav's auspices.[91]

The Fifth international genetics congress held in Berlin in September 1927 demonstrated a tremendous growth of genetics as an international discipline: more than nine hundred scientists from thirty-five countries took part in its proceedings with almost one hundred fifty papers presented. Soviet geneticists formed the largest foreign delegation (second only to the hosts—the Germans) to the Berlin congress and made quite an impression.[92] As one observer remarked: "Russia was represented by a surprisingly large number of men."[93] Their reports covered practically all areas of genetics studies, demonstrating to the international community that a new, large, and gifted group of researchers had entered the genetics world. Two reports in particular caught the eye of the congress members. Vavilov presented his theory of the centers of origins of cultivated plants formulated on the basis of the enormous collection he had gathered during his travels. Georgii Karpechenko, a young cytologist at Vavilov's Institute of Applied Botany, demonstrated the first ever successful inter-generic hybrid between cabbage and radish—*Raphanobrassica*. An observer noted: " . . . the greatest drive in genetics research . . . was that concerned with cyto-genetics—with explaining the cellular mechanisms of heredity and evolution. The cytological paper of Karpechenko (Leningrad) was outstanding in this field."[94] Although it failed to attract much notice from the congress participants at the time, a report by Sergei Chetverikov laid the foundation for population genetics. Not surprisingly, it was at the Berlin congress that Russia officially joined the international genetics community: a Soviet representative—Nikolai Kol'tsov—was elected to the permanent international committee for the genetics congresses.

The Berlin meeting also stimulated the first attempt at bringing an international genetics congress to Russia. On September 3, 1927, the head of Narkompros Anatolii Lunacharskii sent a letter to the Central Committee Department of Agitation and Propaganda (Agitprop).[95] Noting that the Fifth international genetics congress was about to open in Berlin, the commissar suggested inviting the next congress to Moscow in 1930. He remarked that this proposal had been initiated by the president of the Berlin congress Erwin Baur, and stressed that the convocation of the congress in the USSR "will improve our cultural relations with foreign countries and promote strengthening of our science." It is almost certain that Lunacharskii's letter was instigated by Kol'tsov, who had long-standing relations with the commissar through the Russian Eugenics Society. Furthermore, just a few months earlier, in mid-June, both Kol'tsov and Lunacharskii had traveled to Berlin to take part in the "Week of Russian Science." During this trip Kol'tsov actively discussed various issues of the forthcoming congress with his German colleagues, particularly Baur and Goldschmidt. Agitprop officials forwarded Lunacharskii's letter for decision to one of the governing bodies of the Central Committee—its Secretariat.

In a few days, the Secretariat received a similar request from another quarter— the Council of the People's Commissars (SNK). The SNK appeal was prompted by a letter written by a member of the Soviet highest legislative body, TsIK, director of the Institute of Applied Botany Nikolai Vavilov. It was co-signed by the head of the institute's Scientific Council, Nikolai Gorbunov, formerly the SNK executive secretary.[96] Vavilov and Gorbunov asked for permission for the Soviet delegation to the Berlin congress to officially invite the next congress to the USSR. They noted: "the convocation of this congress in the USSR will have great importance in raising the prestige of Soviet science as well as in establishing more normal relations among separate countries." A deputy-head of SNK, Ian Rudzutak, endorsed the proposal and, sent it along with an SNK resolution: "to consider it expedient to convene the next genetics congress in the USSR," to the Secretariat for final approval.[97]

While all these papers were traveling from one bureaucrat's desk to another, on September 11, 1927, the congress opened in Berlin. It seems likely that Soviet geneticists kept sending inquiries to the Central Committee apparatus, for some-time in mid-September one of Agitprop officials sent his own memorandum to the Secretariat.[98] Noting that the Berlin congress had already started and its Soviet members had already left Russia, he asked for a decision immediately. On September 16, the Secretariat permitted Soviet geneticists to officially invite the next congress to convene in Moscow.[99] But despite all the efforts of both German and Russian geneticists to schedule the next congress for Moscow, it was decided to hold the next congress in 1932 not in the Soviet Union, but in the recognized center of the discipline—the United States.

US and Soviet genetics

Despite this setback, between the congresses Soviet geneticists greatly expanded their international contacts, particularly with US colleagues. A special role in this process was played by the Rockefeller philanthropies, which, despite the absence of formal diplomatic relations between the two countries, awarded five Soviet geneticists fellowships for postgraduate studies in the United States between 1927 and 1932.[100]

The story of Rockefeller fellowships for genetics began at the end of 1922, when Wickliffe Rose, then director of the International Health Board of the

Rockefeller Foundation, proposed setting up a new board with the goal of "promotion of education throughout the world."[101] The new "International Education Board" (IEB) aimed to advance postgraduate education in agriculture and natural sciences, particularly physics, chemistry, and biology.[102] With Rose as its first director, the IEB was to locate "inspiring productive men in each of these fields; ascertain of each of these whether he will be willing to train students from other countries." The major directions of the IEB efforts were fellowships for the "international migration of select students to the centers of inspiration and training" and support for institutions where the fellows would be trained. On April 30, 1923, the board of trustees approved the design for "the promotion of science on an international scale."[103]

In November 1923, Rose went to Europe to locate "inspiring and productive men." Over a five-month period he visited nineteen countries, establishing contacts with more than two hundred leading scientists.[104] When he returned to the United States in April 1924, Rose brought with him a list of scientists and institutions eager to participate in the IEB programs, as well as a list of candidates for the fellowships. He also scouted US institutions in search of suitable places for European fellows. Morgan's laboratory at Columbia University became one of these institutions and during the first year of IEB operations it played host to three European fellows, two from Germany and one from Russia.

Indeed, the first Russian Rockefeller fellow, Evgenii Gabrichevskii, came to Morgan's lab in January 1925.[105] A graduate of Moscow University and a student of Russia's most prominent evolutionary morphologist Aleksei Severtsov, Gabrichevskii had become involved in genetic studies of mimicry in insects in the early 1920s. He entered into correspondence with Morgan and Punnett, both of whom were quite impressed with his research. In the summer of 1924, Morgan recommended Gabrichevskii to Wickliffe Rose, which resulted in the award of an IEB fellowship. Gabrichevskii spent more than two years with Morgan.[106] He finished his fellowship in the spring of 1927, just as Morgan was reviewing another application from Russia.

In March 1927, a student of Filipchenko, Theodosius Dobzhansky, applied for an IEB fellowship to spend a year at Morgan's lab.[107] His application was endorsed by his teacher and seconded by the prominent Russian ichthyologist and evolutionist Lev Berg. At the end of August the Board approved the award, and on Christmas day Dobzhansky arrived in New York City. The next autumn he followed Morgan to Caltech, extending his fellowship for another year.[108] In California, Dobzhansky regularly met with his compatriot Mikhail Navashin who had also received an IEB fellowship in 1927. The son of Russia's most prominent cytologist, Sergei Navashin, Mikhail had chosen to study with Ernest Babcock at the University of California, Berkeley. Navashin's coming to Berkeley, however, was delayed for almost a year, for he had troubles obtaining the US entry visa.[109] In the end, combined efforts of the officers of the Rockefeller Foundation and the University of California prevailed: Navashin was able to enter the United States and spent a year in Babcock's lab. When his fellowship ended, the same laboratory made home to yet another Soviet fellow—Vavilov's co-worker

Georgii Karpechenko—who arrived in Berkeley in November 1929. The next year two more Soviet geneticists—Isaak Agol and Solomon Levit—received Rockefeller stipends. Students of Serebrovskii, they traveled to Austin to take their fellowships with H. J. Muller at the University of Texas. During the subsequent summer, they spent two months at the Genetics Department of the Carnegie Institution on Long Island headed by Charles Davenport.[110] On his way back to the USSR, Agol also stopped for three months at Goldschmidt's laboratory at the Kaiser Wilhelm Institute for Biology in Berlin-Dahlem.

Soviet fellows made quite an impression in the United States. As associate director of the Rockefeller Foundation European Office, Daniel O'Brien informed Serebrovskii in early 1931: "Your assistant, Dr. Agol, is evidently doing excellent work on his fellowship."[111] Quoting a letter from Muller, O'Brien stated that Agol's report was "the biggest hit in the Genetics Section [at the AAAS meeting in Cleveland] with the work done here this fall" and that "Professor T. H. Morgan tried to persuade him to leave Texas and come to the California Institute of Technology, but he refused."

The Rockefeller fellowships were not the only channel for Soviet geneticists' visits to the United States. In the late 1920s, in order to prepare cadres for industrialization, the Soviet government began sending abroad at its own expense a number of young party members for postgraduate training. One of these young trainees was Anton Zhebrak, a recent graduate of the Timiriazev Agricultural Academy in Moscow. In 1930, on Kol'tsov's recommendation, Zhebrak was

Plate 4 The First All-Russian conference on genetics, Leningrad, 1929. E. Baur is delivering report, behind him G. A. Levitskii (sitting). At the table: Iu. A. Filipchenko, N. I. Vavilov, Richard Goldschmidt, G. D. Karpechenko, unidentified, unidentified, V. E. Pisarev. (From *Nikolai Ivanovich Vavilov. Nauchnoe Nasledie v Pis'makh*, Moscow: Nauka, 1997, vol. 2.)

accepted as a graduate student in the genetics department of Columbia University chaired by Morgan's successor Leslie C. Dunn.[112]

Foreign travels of Soviet geneticists were reciprocated by visits of foreign geneticists to the Soviet Union. After the Berlin congress, Leslie C. Dunn toured centers of genetics research in Moscow.[113] Several foreign geneticists, including Erwin Baur, Richard Goldschmidt, and Harry Federley, attended the First All-Russia conference on genetics and breeding held in Leningrad in January 1929. The same year a British geneticist, Cyril Darlington, came to the Soviet Union. In the summer of 1931, a prominent British biologist, Julian Huxley, visited the USSR as a guest of the newly established Soviet travel agency Intourist. In the winter of 1931–32, another member of the Morgan group, Calvin Bridges, spent six months working in Vavilov's genetics laboratory at the USSR Academy of Sciences in Leningrad.

By the time the next, Sixth international genetics congress was scheduled to meet in the United States in 1932, many Soviet geneticists had become respected members of an international network of scholars engaged in genetics studies, having developed close personal contacts with leading specialists in various countries. They hoped that the forthcoming congress would further strengthen their position within the world community and allow them to invite the next congress to meet in Russia.

2   The road to Moscow

The Great Break

While Soviet geneticists were busily developing their international contacts, their homeland was going through a new revolution—a "revolution from above."[1] Joseph Stalin began to consolidate his own power over the Communist Party and that of the party apparatus over the nation. The year 1929 marked a dramatic change—a "Great Break" (*Velikii Perelom*), as Stalin named it—in all aspects of the country's life. The Bolsheviks launched a grandiose plan of rapid industrialization in order to build the "material-economic basis of socialism." Crash industrialization demanded enormous financial, material, and human resources: the peasantry was collectivized and the state established a total monopoly over resources and production.

Science was profoundly affected by the radical reorganizations of the Great Break. The system of higher education was reformed to supply personnel for new industrial centers. As in all other spheres of Soviet life, in science the Bolsheviks created a huge, centralized, hierarchical complex of institutions and a bureaucratic apparatus to supervise and control it. They exerted tight control over the personnel of scientific institutions: the scientific community was "Bolshevized" and its "commanding heights" were seized by party members and "nonparty Bolsheviks."[2]

For genetics and geneticists, the turmoil of the Great Break appeared a mixed blessing. In the situation of "sharpening class struggle" and attacks on "bourgeois specialists" manifested in the infamous "Shakhty trial" of several engineers accused of "wrecking," a number of geneticists fell victims to the new terror.[3] Sergei Chetverikov, a founder of Soviet population genetics and head of the genetics department in Kol'tsov's institute, was arrested and exiled from Moscow in 1929 for his alleged "counterrevolutionary activity."[4] As a result, the department was dissolved and a number of Chetverikov's students had to move to the provinces.[5]

Several powerful patrons of genetics, including Gorbunov, Lunacharskii, and Semashko, lost their governmental positions as part of Stalin's move to consolidate his personal power. Having lost their ministerial offices, the old patrons "migrated" into the new scientific establishment, becoming members of academies and directors of academic institutions. Lunacharskii became head of the TsIK Scientific Committee (1929–32) and member of the Academy of Sciences (1930). Gorbunov became a vice-president of the newly established Lenin All-Union Academy of Agricultural Sciences (VASKhNIL) in 1929.

With the demise of the old party patrons came the death of the early "revolutionary dreams" of creating a "new society" and a "new man" through advances in biomedical sciences. A number of new fields that had pursued those dreams (or had used them as a convenient rhetorical umbrella to protect their own research agendas) and that had been flourishing during the first post-revolutionary decade came under fierce ideological attacks for the "biologization" of social issues. Research in experimental endocrinology, animal and human behavior, and hematology that had claimed to study such subjects as rejuvenation, the prolongation of life, and manipulation of behavior began to shift their focus to less controversial and ideologically dangerous subjects. As might be expected, one such field was eugenics: in 1930 both the Russian Eugenics Society and its journal ceased to exist.[6] The next year, the *Great Soviet Encyclopedia* labeled eugenics a "bourgeois science."[7] But research in human genetics continued. Russian eugenicists moved on to study what they now termed "anthropogenetics" and "medical genetics."[8]

Notwithstanding the turmoil, the Great Break also greatly accelerated the institutional expansion of Soviet genetics as a discipline. Despite the removal of Semashko and Lunacharskii from their posts and the dissolution of the Russian Eugenics Society, genetics institutions under both Narkomzdrav and Narkompros continued to grow. In 1929 a small laboratory of human genetics in Narkomzdrav's Medical-Biological Institute was established, directed by party member Solomon Levit.[9] After Levit's return from his Rockefeller fellowship in the United States, the laboratory was transformed into the Institute of Medical Genetics named after Maxim Gorky. During the early 1930s genetics departments and laboratories were established at Moscow University (under Aleksandr Serebrovskii) and reestablished at Leningrad University (under Georgii Karpechenko and Aleksandr Vladimirskii). Genetics also prospered within the Academy of Sciences. After Filipchenko's sudden death from meningitis in 1930, Vavilov inherited his genetics laboratory. Three years later it was converted into a large Institute of Genetics where many of Filipchenko's students continued to work.

The policy of "mobilizing" science for the socialist construction announced in the late 1920s especially stimulated the growth of agricultural institutions. The severe agricultural crisis prompted by the collectivization led in late 1929 to the creation of VASKhNIL under Vavilov's presidency. Vavilov considered genetics a key discipline in the development of Soviet agriculture, and he actively supported its institutionalization and development. On the basis of his Institute of Applied Botany, he created the gigantic All-Union Institute of Plant Breeding (Vsesoiuznyi Institut Rastenievodstva—VIR), where seeds of various cultivated and wild plants collected throughout the world were used to breed new varieties for Soviet agriculture. He promoted the creation in 1931 of the All-Union Institute of Animal

Breeding, where Serebrovskii became head of the genetics department. He also lobbied for introducing genetics courses in agricultural schools. Because of his considerable efforts in the early 1930s, agricultural institutions became a bastion of Soviet genetics.

In June 1932, in compliance with the government's drive for introducing planning in science, Soviet geneticists organized a huge, well-publicized conference "On the Planning of Breeding and Genetics Work." At this conference, under the pretext of "better planning and organization" of research, they elaborated a plan aimed at the further institutional expansion of their discipline.[10] Simultaneously, they prepared the ground for the further development of their international contacts, particularly participation in the Sixth international genetics congress.

The road to Ithaca

While Soviet geneticists struggled with the turmoil of the Great Break, the organization of the Sixth international genetics congress scheduled to meet in 1932 in the United States run into unexpected difficulties: the world economic crisis—the Great Depression—threatened to make it impossible. The organizing committee set up in early 1930 was composed of renowned US geneticists: T. H. Morgan (president), Edward M. East (program chairman), Robert Cook (treasurer), Clarence C. Little (secretary), Charles B. Davenport (finances), Rollins A. Emerson (local committee), Leslie C. Dunn (transportation), Milislav Demerec (exhibits), and Donald F. Jones (publications). The committee debated whether they should postpone the congress, given the lack of funding even for US participants, not to mention their guests from all over the world. In the end, the committee decided to stick to the plan. Cornell University, home of the largest agricultural school in the United States, agreed to host the congress and defray part of the costs for accommodations. A number of US institutions involved with genetics research paid for their employees' attendance. The organizing committee was also able to tap into private funding from various foundations and individuals, most importantly the Carnegie philanthropies. Nevertheless, it was clear that the general attendance would not be very large.

The organizing committee sent personal invitations to about twenty Soviet geneticists, including Vavilov, Kol'tsov, Serebrovskii, and all Rockefeller fellows who had worked in the United States during the previous years. US geneticists planned to use the congress to bring a number of Soviet colleagues to various laboratories around the country. For instance, Charles Davenport hoped that a leading cytologist of Vavilov's institute—Grigorii Levitskii—would be able to spend several months at his lab either prior to or after the congress.[11] But for Soviet geneticists just coming to the congress would prove to be a very difficult task.

Soviet geneticists had begun lobbying state agencies for permission to attend the congress well in advance. In July 1930, Serebrovskii sent a letter to the TsIK Scientific Committee—a new government body, which had been set up a few years earlier and had gained much power during the Great Break, serving as an intermediary between scientists and the party apparatus, particularly in the issues

Plate 5 The organizing committee for the Sixth international genetics congress. Front row (left to right): R. Cook, E. East, T. H. Morgan, C. B. Davenport, R. A. Emerson. Back row: C. C. Little, L. C. Dunn, D. F. Jones, M. Demerec. (From *Journal of Heredity*, 1932, vol. 23.)

related to foreign travel.[12] Serebrovskii notified the Scientific Committee that he had received a letter from the chairman of the congress's commission on transportation, Leslie C. Dunn, and that he had been appointed a member of that commission in charge of travel of Soviet delegates.[13] Serebrovskii urged the committee's officials: "1) to raise the question on [our] general attitude toward the USSR's participation in the congress; 2) to decide in principle on the number of Soviet delegates; 3) to include necessary funds in the budget for 1932."

Following the established bureaucratic procedure, the Scientific Committee sent inquiries regarding "the desirability of Soviet Union representatives' participation in the congress" to the Commissariat of Foreign Affairs, Narkompros, the Academy of Sciences, and the Communist Academy.[14] All of them but the Commissariat of Foreign Affairs eagerly supported the idea. In his response the deputy-commissar of foreign affairs, Lev Karakhan noted that he could neither recommend nor oppose the issue "from the point of view of science." From "the issue's political side," he continued, "it is difficult to give any definite answer now, two years before the congress."[15] As a result, in late September the Scientific Committee informed Serebrovskii that, "this issue will be discussed in 1932."[16]

On January 2, 1932, the Scientific Committee officials indeed returned to the issue of the genetics congress. They sent a letter to the Communist Academy inquiring as to whether the academy considered the congress's attendance by

Soviet representatives necessary.[17] The academy's governing body—its presidium—apparently forwarded the inquiry to the Timiriazev Biology Institute, for in mid-February the Scientific Committee received a long letter from the institute's new director, chairman of the Society of Marxist-Biologists, Boris Tokin. "It is absolutely necessary to take part in the congress," Tokin stated, and proposed a detailed plan of action for the Soviet delegation. First of all, Tokin insisted, it was necessary "to present a comprehensive critique of bourgeois eugenics" and "to make our voice heard in broad proletarian masses, among Negroes, and such." Second, he suggested that the Soviet delegation deliver a report on "the crisis of modern genetics" in which "positions of materialist dialectics" would be advanced. And finally, Tokin recommended that the delegation present a report "demonstrating our achievements in the field of genetics and breeding under the conditions of socialist construction."[18] In response, the Scientific Committee asked Tokin to present the congress's program "at once."[19]

At this point, however, much heavier artillery entered the battle. In March, the Scientific Committee received a package from Nikolai Vavilov, who by that time had become the president of VASKhNIL and director of the Academy of Sciences' genetics laboratory.[20] Enclosed were an official letter from the congress's general secretary C. C. Little addressed directly to the Scientific Committee and two issues of *Genetics Congress Quarterly*—a newsletter distributed by the US organizers—as well as a letter by Milislav Demerec regarding an exhibition that was to accompany the congress. Informing the Scientific Committee that he had been appointed a vice-president of the forthcoming congress, Vavilov noted that he had already appealed to Narkomzem to "send a large Soviet delegation" and requested that the Scientific Committee also raise "independently" the issue of the Soviet delegation and its funding.[21] Five days later, the committee approved "the plan of Soviet participation in international congresses in 1932." Under number 10, the committee officials resolved:

> to consider it expedient that representatives of Soviet scientific institutions take part in the international genetics congress convening in the USA (Ithaca) on August 24–31, of this year. To send to the congress Comrade Serebrovskii (from the Communist Academy) and Comrade Vavilov (from the Academy of Sciences).[22]

As required by the rules, the committee forwarded its resolution to the Central Committee of the Communist Party.

About a month later, Vavilov sent the Scientific Committee another long letter.[23] His main point was that "there are all necessary foundations for the convocation of the next international genetics congress in the USSR, and we hope that the congress's members will enthusiastically support this idea." He insisted that it was necessary to send a large representative delegation to the congress. A few weeks later Vavilov again appealed to the committee.[24] He reiterated his point on the need of sending a large Soviet delegation, emphasizing that it would "allow us to seek the agreement [of the congress's members] for the convocation

of the next Seventh international genetics congress in the USSR." "The participation of a large competent delegation," he continued, "will give much greater
weight to the Soviet proposal." He asked the Scientific Committee to raise this
issue in the Council of People's Commissars (SNK).

Meanwhile, during May and June, a number of other agencies, including
Narkompros, the Ukrainian Academy of Sciences, and the USSR Academy of
Sciences, bombarded the Scientific Committee with requests for the inclusion
of various individual scientists working under their auspices in the Soviet delegation
to the genetics congress. The committee invariably answered that it was too late to
include anyone, for the list had already been sent off to the Central Committee.[25]
Even former Rockefeller fellow and now head of the Narkompros Science
Department, Isaak Agol, was denied attendance, despite the letters on his behalf he
had been able to solicit from certain members of the Scientific Committee itself.[26]

At the end of July, Vavilov again wrote to the Scientific Committee: "the General
Assembly of the USSR Academy of Sciences petitioned [the government] for permission to convene the Seventh international genetics congress in the USSR.
VASKhNIL also considers it expedient to raise the question of the congress's convocation here."[27] Vavilov gave his reasons: "The convocation of the congress in this
country will have first of all great political importance and will provide the opportunity to raise even higher the level of Soviet science." He yet again emphasized the
need of sending a large delegation to Ithaca. The Scientific Committee concurred
and sent its recommendations to the party apparatus: "To consider expedient the
convocation of the next genetics congress in the USSR; to petition the responsible
organs [the bureaucratic euphemism that meant the Central Committee—N. K.]
for permitting the Soviet delegation to raise this issue, if conditions are favorable."[28]

But all these paper battles turned out to be irrelevant, for the ultimate decision
rested with the highest agency—the Politburo. None of the Scientific
Committee's commendations even reached this level, for a very simple reason—
already in December 1931, the Politburo's Departure Commission headed by
a Central Committee Secretary, Nikolai Ezhov, had suggested that all foreign
travels of Soviet scientists be cut back in order to save hard currency for industrialization. Ezhov further recommended that the number of scientists sent abroad
through the Scientific Committee should not exceed five a year.[29]

However, as always, Soviet scientists sought to circumvent the bureaucratic
barriers. Vavilov took a very clever, but risky gambit to secure at least his own
attendance. During the previous years, he and his co-workers had embarked on
numerous expeditions to various continents to collect plants and seeds for the
Institute of Plant Breeding. They had visited Argentina, Iran, Japan, Peru,
Ethiopia, Italy, Canada, and many other countries, gathering an extraordinarily
rich collection of wild and cultivated forms of various plants, which were to be
used for breeding new varieties of cultivated plants. In late 1931, Vavilov began
planning another expedition to North and South America with the aim of gathering information on cultivating plants in arid and artificially irrigated regions.
This aim had a particular appeal for his patrons in Narkomzem, because the current agricultural plans emphasized the need to expend production in the eastern

regions where the problem of irrigation was particularly acute. The idea of an American expedition thus received the backing of Narkomzem officials and Vavilov decided to tie it together with his visit to Ithaca.

So, at the end of June 1932, with Vavilov's prompting, the head of Narkomzem, Iakov Iakovlev appealed to another Central Committee Secretary, Pavel Postyshev. Iakovlev asked for permission to send Vavilov and a vice-president of VASKhNIL, Mechislav Burskii, to the Americas to collect seeds of various plants (particularly potato and cotton) and, while in the United States, to take part in the congress.[30] Postyshev forwarded the letter to his subordinates for evaluation. Although Postyshev's staff favorably assessed the proposal, on July 15, Ezhov's Departure Commission vetoed the proposed trip. As it happened, objections came from another quarter—the secret police (the United State Political Directorate—OGPU).[31] On July 4, the OGPU Economic Division had sent Ezhov a long memorandum. Marked "top-secret, extremely urgent, for your eyes only," the memorandum stated:

> For a number of years since 1924 the All-Union Institute of Plant Breeding, headed by Vavilov, has sent numerous expeditions to different parts of the world, including America. It has gathered an international collection of seeds and plants. The collected material has still not been studied, and almost no practical conclusions and achievements have been introduced into the national economy—this work never went beyond the institute's walls.[32]

Although OGPU did not object to sending a Soviet delegation to the congress, it considered "the organization of any botanical expedition to America inexpedient," and the Departure Commission followed this recommendation.

Yet Vavilov would not give up. Two weeks later a deputy-head of Narkomzem sent another petition, this time to a higher authority—member of the Politburo, Lazar Kaganovich.[33] Emphasizing that it would be "absolutely unacceptable, if representatives of the USSR were not present at the International Genetics Congress," the Narkomzem official urged Kaganovich to reverse the Departure Commission's decision on Vavilov and Burskii's trip to the United States. Kaganovich inscribed on the appeal: "I think Narkomzem's proposal can be accepted." On August 3, just two weeks before the congress opening, the Secretariat permitted Vavilov to go to the United States.[34]

As a result of all these negotiations, only one Soviet geneticist—Nikolai Vavilov—appeared in Ithaca.[35] At the session on "genetics and evolution" organized by East, Vavilov shared the podium with three founders of evolutionary genetics—Ronald Fisher, J. B. S. Haldane, and Sewall Wright. In his report Vavilov elaborated his theory of the centers of origin of cultivated plants, summarizing the result of his numerous expeditions and an enormous amount of work done by his co-workers at the Institute of Plant Breeding. He also announced a discovery made by one of his younger colleagues from Odessa, Trofim Lysenko: a technique that its author named "yarovization" or "vernalization," which allowed changing the vegetation period of various plants and, therefore, in Vavilov's opinion, opened a new possibility for hybridization of varieties with different vegetation periods.

Vavilov's announcement of Lysenko's discovery made quite a splash in the United States. The media was excited by the possibilities of "growing of subtropical wheat in cold climate" and using vernalization as a "weapon against drought."[36] Several US geneticists decided to repeat Lysenko's experiments.[37]

It was very important for Vavilov as the only Soviet representative at the congress to apprise his foreign colleagues of the progress of Soviet genetics: he even managed to bring to Ithaca several exhibits prepared by his co-workers, most notably, new polyploid hybrids created by Karpechenko. But of course, equally important was the opportunity to renew his personal acquaintance with the world's leading geneticists who had come to Ithaca. Vavilov spent much time in private meetings with Morgan, East, Darlington, Muller, and Haldane. He also frequently met with his former compatriots: Theodosius Dobzhansky, who had become a leading figure in Morgan's lab at Caltech, and Nikolai Timofeeff-Ressovsky, who had become Germany's leading Drosophila geneticist.

As a vice-president of the congress, Vavilov also took part in various business meetings, including, most importantly, the one dealing with the organization of

Plate 6 During the Sixth international genetics congress in Ithaca, 1932. Left to right: N. I. Vavilov, T. H. Morgan, and N. A. Timofeeff-Ressovsky. (From *N. I. Vavilov. Dokumenty i Fotografii*, St Petersburg: Nauka, 1995.)

the next congress. At that meeting Vavilov was elected the Soviet representative of the International Organizing Committee for Genetics Congresses (IOC), replacing Kol'tsov who had held this position since the Berlin congress. The IOC elected in Ithaca included geneticists from fifteen countries: Erich von Tschermak (Austria); Rene Vandendries (Belgium); Oivind Winge (Denmark); Harry Federley (Finland); Roger de Vilmorin (France); Richard Goldschmidt (Germany); J. B. S. Haldane (Great Britain); Alessandro Ghigi (Italy); Saitiiro Ikeno (Japan); Tine Tammes (Netherlands); Otto Mohr (Norway); Nils Hermann Nilsson-Elle (Sweden); Otto Schlaginhaufen (Switzerland); Nikolai Vavilov (USSR); Rollins A. Emerson (USA). Otto Mohr—the first foreign postdoctoral fellow in the Morgan group at Columbia University in 1918—was elected president. The committee was to choose a place and a date for the next congress and to administer its affairs until a local organizing committee was appointed and took over. Vavilov came to Ithaca with the permission of the Soviet government to invite the next congress to meet in Moscow.[38] He presented the invitation to the IOC, which, at a formal session, decided that the next congress would meet in summer 1937, but left open the issue of its location for further consideration.

Setting up the Moscow congress

The inability to attend the congress in Ithaca dealt a heavy blow to Soviet geneticists' efforts to strengthen their international relations. Yet they used all means at their disposal to further that goal. In spring 1932, following Vavilov's nomination, the USSR Academy of Sciences elected the geneticists T. H. Morgan, N. H. Nilsson-Elle, E. von Tschermak, and H. de Vries as honorary members. In February 1933, the prominent American geneticist H. J. Muller was elected a corresponding member.[39] In September of that year, on Vavilov's invitation, Muller moved to the Soviet Union and began working in Vavilov's laboratory of genetics at the Academy of Sciences. A few months later the laboratory was moved to Moscow and transformed into the Institute of Genetics. Muller's students, Daniel Raffel and Carlos Offerman joined him in Moscow shortly thereafter. The same year, the Bulgarian geneticist Doncho Kostov joined the institute. In 1934, Cyril Darlington visited the institute and delivered a series of lectures. Soviet geneticists also made a special effort to translate and publish in Russian all new monographs and textbooks in their discipline.

However, in furthering their international contacts, Soviet geneticists had to work against new restrictions on foreign travel and foreign communications in general, which were being put in place by the party apparatus. In May 1933, the Politburo suddenly forbade Soviet scientists from accepting Rockefeller Foundation fellowships.[40] This put a stop to the plans of two geneticists, Nikolai Dubinin, a new head of genetics in Kol'tsov's Institute of Experimental Biology, and Mikhail Gershenzon, another talented student of Kol'tsov, to take their fellowships in the United States. A year later, the apparatus established new rules for foreign correspondence and the publication of scientific works abroad. The exchange of reprints with foreign scholars became officially possible only through

VOKS, and all papers officially submitted for publication abroad had to be approved by the Censorship Administration (Glavlit).[41] Even the exchange of books became difficult. As Vavilov mentioned in his letter to the British geneticist Sidney C. Harland (who at that time worked in Brazil): "I just got back my book on the scientific foundations of wheat breeding, which I had sent you. The censorship has returned it to me. This is stupid, for it has nothing on politics."[42] During 1932–35, Soviet scientists' visits to foreign countries, which had not exceeded ten a year at best, were steadily curtailed and finally came to a complete stop.[43]

Under such conditions, the possibility of having international congress in Moscow held a special appeal for Soviet geneticists, and they did their best to ensure that such a possibility became a reality. In early May 1935, when Vavilov received a letter from Mohr inquiring about the status of the Soviet invitation to hold the Seventh international genetics congress in the USSR, he immediately went to work.[44] Vavilov at once informed the IOC chairman that he would discuss the matter with the government.

According to Soviet rules, hosting an international congress required approval of the Orgburo and the Politburo of the Central Committee of the Communist Party. To prepare the ground for such approval, Vavilov raised the issue at a sitting of the governing body of the USSR Academy of Sciences—its presidium. In a letter to the presidium Vavilov noted that he had conferred with the commissar of agriculture, Mikhail Chernov and the head of the Central Committee's Science Department, Karl Bauman and that both had endorsed the idea.[45] Not surprisingly, on June 2, without much discussion, the presidium decided that "it is desirable to have the congress convene in the Soviet Union in August 1937" and that the presidium should petition the government for permission.[46] On July 3, Vavilov wrote to Mohr that he had secured the support of Narkomzem and Narkompros, as well as that of the Academy of Sciences, for holding the congress in Moscow. "As soon as I know more definitely about the decision of our Government, I shall immediately inform you," he assured.[47]

Securing governmental permission took time. On July 13, the presidium sent an official petition to Bauman, who in turn sent his own recommendation to the Secretaries of the Central Committee—the general secretary Joseph Stalin, Andrei Andreev (who oversaw agriculture), and Nikolai Ezhov (who oversaw personnel and security issues). The question was put on the agenda of the Orgburo, which on July 31 authorized the Academy of Sciences to host the congress and instructed the Science Department to prepare its suggestions regarding the organization and membership of the congress.[48] Two days later the Politburo rubber-stamped this decision.[49]

At the end of August, Vavilov informed Mohr that he had secured the government's permission, and that now it was the turn of the IOC to confirm its acceptance of the official invitation sent by the Academy of Sciences.[50] A month later, Mohr sent Vavilov a personal letter telling him that the IOC members had unanimously voted in favor of the USSR as the best place for the congress. In mid-November, Mohr sent a letter of official acceptance to the Academy of Sciences presidium.[51]

As soon as the IOC's official answer had arrived, the presidium proceeded to discuss a preliminary program and membership of the Soviet organizing committee. On December 5, the presidium approved the membership and program prepared by Vavilov.[52] Surprisingly, or so it may seem at first sight, the chairman of the organizing committee was not Vavilov, but a person with no relation to either genetics or the Academy of Sciences whatsoever—Aleksandr Muralov. A long-time party member and a deputy-commissar of agriculture, Muralov had by a party decree replaced Vavilov as VASKhNIL president in early 1935. It seems almost certain that Vavilov quite deliberately put Muralov at the head of the organizing committee: given Muralov's connections to various party and state officials, he seemed an ideal spokesman for the congress. Vavilov and a vice-president of the Academy of Sciences, Vladimir Komarov, became vice-chairmen of the organizing committee; former Rockefeller fellow and now director of the Institute of Medical Genetics, Solomon Levit—general secretary; senior geneticist at the Institute of Genetics, H. J. Muller—head of the program committee; former Rockefeller fellow, Mikhail Navashin—chair of the exhibition committee. The organizing committee also included such well-known geneticists as Nikolai Kol'tsov, Aleksandr Serebrovskii, and yet another former Rockefeller fellow Georgii Karpechenko. Also included were a number of officials from the Academy of Sciences and VASKhNIL: former VASKhNIL vice-president and now the permanent secretary of the Academy of Sciences, Nikolai Gorbunov; VASKhNIL academician and head of the Odessa Institute of Genetics and Breeding, Trofim Lysenko; VASKhNIL vice-president Georgii Meister; and director of the Academy of Sciences Institute of Botany, Boris Keller.

On the next day, Vavilov wrote to Mohr: "We nominated the members of the Organization Committee.... These nominations . . . must now be ratified by the Government. As soon as this is done, the Committee will immediately start to work."[53] Again, it took a while to secure the necessary ratification. At the end of December, Bauman presented the proposed membership to the Orgburo, but only a month later, on January 29, 1936, did the Orgburo approve it.[54] Two days later the Politburo rubber-stamped the decision and commanded Muralov to present the organizing committee's suggestions regarding the congress's work in three months.[55] On February 5, the Politburo decision was finally issued in the form of an SNK decree and forwarded to the Academy of Sciences.[56]

The organizing committee began its work as soon as all the formalities had been observed, and, on February 17, held its first formal meeting, which was largely devoted to the program.[57] The committee decided that the congress should focus on three main subjects: genetic aspects of evolution, the breeding of domestic animals and cultivated plants, and human genetics. About a month later, on March 13, Muralov presented SNK a preliminary budget for 1936, requesting 333,300 rubles.[58] Three days later, the committee met again, this time to discuss the exact date and place for the congress's sessions. Initially, following the model of the Fifteenth international physiological congress held in the summer of 1935, it had been planned to officially open the genetics congress in Leningrad (at Vavilov's Institute of Plant Breeding) and then hold sessions in Moscow (at the Institute of Genetics also headed by Vavilov). But citing various logistic difficulties encountered by their colleagues who had organized the physiology congress, the committee rejected this plan and decided to hold the genetics congress during the week of August 23–30 in Moscow only.[59] Vavilov regularly informed Mohr of these discussions and decisions.

On April 23, the committee held another meeting, appointing Vavilov the congress's president and Morgan its honorary president. It also amended the preliminary program. The amendment was made at the request of more than thirty American geneticists, including C. B. Bridges, R. C. Cook, L. C. Dunn, H. S. Jennings, and C. C. Little who had asked the organizing committee to add to the program a "discussion of questions relating to racial and eugenic problems."[60]

In fact, the request had probably been initiated by Julius Schaxel, a German émigré biologist who at that time headed a laboratory at the Academy of Sciences in Moscow.[61] In late November 1935, after the decision to hold the congress in Moscow had been approved by all interested parties, Schaxel sent a letter to his former compatriot Walter Landauer (who at that time worked at the Storrs Agricultural Station in Connecticut) suggesting to "put to discussion [at the congress] the national-socialist race theory."[62] Landauer eagerly responded to this suggestion that resonated so well with his own disposition toward the issue and prepared a draft letter that he circulated among practically all American geneticists involved with human genetics, many of whom enthusiastically supported the proposal.[63] On April 2, he sent the letter along with his explanatory note to the congress's secretary Levit. In his note, Landauer also suggested, that "Russian ethnologists working with racial minorities may well take a prominent place in the discussions."[64]

This request by American geneticists presented a certain problem for the organizing committee, for, as we have seen, in the Soviet Union, eugenics had been banned during the Great Break. So, putting "eugenic problems" on the congress's agenda was obviously politically unwise. Not surprisingly, the organizers decided that "reports on the disciplines related to genetics" should not be included in the program. They agreed, however, that the last session of the congress should be devoted to the discussion of "human genetics and race theory," omitting any mention of eugenics and "eugenic problems" altogether.[65]

At the end of April, the government approved the staff of the organizing committee's technical apparatus that included eleven workers—several secretaries and interpreters, an accountant, a messenger, a stenographer, and a typist.[66] A month later, following the Politburo's order to present the organizing committee's suggestions regarding the congress's work, Muralov submitted a lengthy report to the Politburo head Joseph Stalin and the SNK head Viacheslav Molotov.[67] Enclosed was a draft of SNK decree that assigned numerous tasks to various governmental agencies to ensure the congress's timely and successful preparation. A large portion of the decree dealt with the renovation and remodeling of genetics institutions that were to be visited by the congress participants. In total, Muralov requested "4–5 million rubles" to fund the congress.

On June 13, the organizing committee sent out Information Letter No. 1 and began sending personal invitations to various geneticists to deliver reports at the plenary sessions.[68] Over the course of the summer the committee communicated with foreign and Soviet geneticists who planned to attend the congress and regularly met with various government officials regarding the congress's funding and the organization of an exhibition that was to accompany the congress. Intourist was put in charge of accommodations and transportation for foreign participants. The committee also kept its patrons apprised of the latest developments: in mid-August, Muralov submitted a progress report to SNK.

At the beginning of September, the Academy of Sciences presidium listened to Muralov's report on the organizing committee's activities to date and approved its plan of preparations and a preliminary scientific program.[69] At the end of the month, Muralov and Levit sent a lengthy memorandum on the congress's scientific program to the Central Committee's Science Department.[70] The memorandum listed six major subjects to be discussed at the congress: (1) evolution in light of genetic research; (2) plant genetics and breeding; (3) animal genetics and breeding; (4) genes, mutations, and structural bases of heredity; (5) distant hybridization and polyploidy; (6) human genetics and racial theories. It also named the Soviet and foreign geneticists invited to deliver keynote reports on these subjects.

In mid-October, SNK approved the organizing committee's operational budget for the rest of the year to the sum of 160,000 rubles.[71] By that time the organizing committee had received responses from nearly nine hundred geneticists from all over the world. The largest number of letters arrived from the United States (369), next was Britain (83), then Germany (82), Canada (32), Japan (25), Sweden (22), Holland (20), China (16), France (15), Switzerland (15), Poland (14), and India (13).[72] At the beginning of November, the organizing committee prepared its Bulletin No. 1 and sent it to the printers.[73] Everything seemed to be going smoothly.

Suddenly, on November 14, 1936, the Politburo decided: "to cancel the convocation of the Seventh international genetics congress in the USSR in 1937."[74]

Cancellation turned postponement

The Politburo decision came as a shock. Even members of the organizing committee, who were informed about this decision in the form of an SNK top-secret decree three days later, did not know the reasons behind it or the details of how it had been reached. Yet, despite the warning on the SNK decree—"not for circulation"—they had to provide some explanation to foreign and Soviet geneticists invited to attend the congress.

On November 25, the head of the program commission, Muller, sent a long letter to his fellow-member on the organizing committee, Gorbunov, asking for instructions—what to tell his correspondents, particularly foreigners who had been asked to present texts of their plenary reports by January 1937. He noted:

> In my letters reasons and details need not be given.... It could be stated simply that "it has been found impracticable to hold the congress this coming summer". Or if this information would in itself be objectionable, I might merely state that I was no longer connected with the Program Committee, and that further inquiries should be directed to you.[75]

Apparently, Muller received some kind of encouragement, for at the beginning of December he sent letters to several Western geneticists, including Mohr, Emerson, Dunn, and Darlington, saying that "it has been found impracticable to hold the Congress here next summer."[76] Almost simultaneously, Vavilov sent a similar letter to Mohr informing him that "by the decision of the Government it was found that during the next year and very possibly during 1938 it would be impossible to have the Congress in the USSR." Noting that he did not know "definitely the reasons for this decision," Vavilov concluded:

> Your rights as President of the International Committee are now again in full power and now it depends on you and the Committee to decide in which country to have the Congress. The official letter from the Academy of Sciences will be sent [to] you in a few days.[77]

At the same time, following the SNK decree, the Academy of Sciences presidium decided to dismantle the local organizing committee and to send an official letter to Mohr informing the IOC chairman, that "due to a number of unforeseen circumstances . . . it is impossible to convene the Seventh International Genetics Congress in the USSR in 1937." However, as always, such decisions required approval of the powers that be. So, in early December, Komarov and Gorbunov sent a memorandum to Molotov asking him to approve the course of action and the draft letter to Mohr.[78] In fact, the academy officials prepared two drafts. One stated that the decision to cancel the congress was made by "the Soviet government," the other omitted any mention of the government's part in the whole affair.

Molotov forwarded the memorandum and the enclosures to his subordinates, who in turn asked the Commissariat of Foreign Affairs for an opinion regarding the wording of the official information. The commissar Maxim Litvinov preferred the variant that did not mention "the government's decision."[79] He expressed his regret "regarding such, apparently inevitable, outcome," and concluded: "this case shows the need for an extremely careful approach to the matters of convocation in the USSR of international congresses, and, in cases of the Government's approval of such congresses, the necessity of strengthening the work of respective organizing committees."

Soviet geneticists could not so easily abandon the hope of having the congress in Moscow and, while the bureaucrats prepared papers to dispose off the whole issue of the congress, geneticists began a concerted effort to save it. The wording of the Politburo decision—"to cancel the convocation of the Seventh international genetics congress in the USSR in 1937"—was open to different interpretations. It could be read as meaning that the very idea of having the congress in Moscow had been abandoned. But it could also be read as implying that, while the congress had been canceled for 1937, it might be held at a later date. This was an opening certainly worth exploring. So, sometime in late November–early December, prompted by Vavilov, Gorbunov sent a letter to Molotov.[80] Co-signed by a trusted party appointee to the academy presidium, vice-president Gleb

Krzhizhanovskii, the letter warned the head of the Soviet government that "a complete abandonment of the congress could provoke undesirable speculations and declarations undermining the prestige of Soviet science," and asked for permission to convene the congress in Moscow a year later—in August 1938. The officials even suggested a way to present such a postponement:

> The Academy of Sciences presidium considers the change in the dates of the congress the most convenient form [of dealing with the problem] that could be explained by the preparations for the 20th anniversary of the October Revolution, [and] by the meeting of the International Geological Congress in 1937.

Molotov was perhaps too busy to listen to the academicians' advice—among his many preoccupations at the moment was the All-Union Congress of Soviets that at the beginning of December was to adopt a new, "Stalin" Constitution of the Soviet Union—and the academicians' forewarning was quickly confirmed. The news about the troubles with the congress leaked out.

On December 9, Edward M. East sent Milislav Demerec a note asking for any information Demerec might have about the congress. The reason for East's inquiry was a letter he had received from Kol'tsov. In a short postscript, Kol'tsov noted: "It seems that the Seventh International Genetics Congress is going to be postponed."[81] Alarmed, Demerec immediately called up the New York office of Intourist. As he reported to East:

> Last week they received a cable from Moscow giving the date of the Geologists' Congress and stating that the date of our congress would be sent in the near future. They doubt very much that it will be postponed. However, they are cabling today to Moscow for information and shall let me know as soon as it is received. I shall keep you informed on future developments.[82]

Two days later, on December 12, Intourist did let Demerec know what they had learned: "We are very sorry to have to inform you that we have this morning received from our Moscow office a cable informing us that the VII International Congress on Genetics will not be held in Moscow during 1937."[83] But Demerec was away from his office and received the Intourist letter only on December 16, when it was, in a way, too late.

For, on December 14, the *New York Times* published a "wireless" dispatch from its Moscow correspondent: "The Seventh International Congress of Genetics which was to have been held here next August . . . has been canceled by order of the Soviet Government, it is learned unofficially."[84] But the dispatch covered more than just the cancellation of the congress. It also announced that Vavilov, the president of the forthcoming congress, together with Agol, former Rockefeller fellow, had been arrested, and the congress's general secretary Levit had come under heavy fire from party officials. It provided what seemed to be the reasons for canceling the congress:

> An interesting story of a schism among Soviet geneticists, some of the most prominent among whom are accused by Communist party authorities of holding German Fascist views on genetics and even being shielders of "Trotskyists," lies behind the cancellation. The fact that so many of the Soviet Union's most distinguished geneticists are under fire is believed to be [the] motive for the government action.

The "schism" the article referred to was an ongoing controversy on the "issues in modern genetics" between two groups of Soviet agriculturists, each headed by a member of the congress's organizing committee—Vavilov and Lysenko.[85] The controversy had been going on for almost a year and was coming to a head exactly at the time of the *New York Times* publication—on December 19, an open discussion between the two groups was to begin at a session of VASKhNIL.

The news spurred Western, particularly American and British, geneticists into immediate action. A number of prominent scientists sent cables and letters to the Soviet Ambassador to the United States Aleksandr Troyanovskii, asking for detailed information on the fate of Vavilov and Agol, as well as that of the

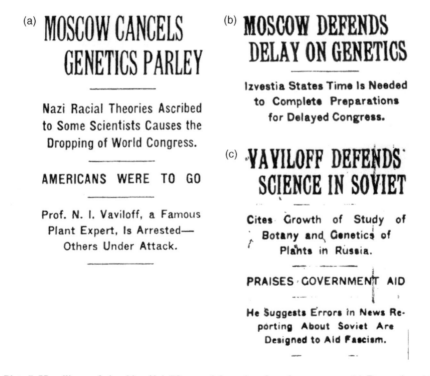

(a) **MOSCOW CANCELS GENETICS PARLEY**

Nazi Racial Theories Ascribed to Some Scientists Causes the Dropping of World Congress.

AMERICANS WERE TO GO

Prof. N. I. Vaviloff, a Famous Plant Expert, Is Arrested— Others Under Attack.

(b) **MOSCOW DEFENDS DELAY ON GENETICS**

Izvestia States Time Is Needed to Complete Preparations for Delayed Congress.

(c) **VAVILOFF DEFENDS SCIENCE IN SOVIET**

Cites Growth of Study of Botany and Genetics of Plants in Russia.

PRAISES GOVERNMENT AID

He Suggests Errors in News Reporting About Soviet Are Designed to Aid Fascism.

Plate 7 Headlines of the *New York Times* articles related to the congress, (a) December 14, (b) December 21, and (c) December 22, 1936.

congress. Among Troyanovskii's correspondents were the Nobelist T. H. Morgan, the prominent anthropologist from Columbia University Franz Boas, the editor of the *Journal of Heredity* Robert Cook, the president of the American Association for the Advancement of Science Edwin G. Conklin, and the secretary-treasurer of the American Genetics Society Milislav Demerec. The Soviet consul in San Francisco also received a number of letters from West-coast scientists. The Soviet Ambassador in London received similar requests from British geneticists, while Swedish geneticists appealed to the Soviet Ambassador in Stockholm.[86]

Geneticists not only pestered Soviet diplomats with requests for information, they also tried to secure assistance from their own government officials. On the day of the *New York Times* publication, Dunn sent a cable to Emerson, asking him "to get [the Secretary of Agriculture] Henry Wallace to see somebody in the Soviet Embassy."[87] Emerson immediately sent his own cable to Wallace.[88] Two days later, Charles B. Davenport even urged the Secretary of State to "transmit in proper diplomatic fashion to the government of [the] USSR" his protest against the maltreatments of his colleagues.[89] Cyril D. Darlington sent a similar request to the Foreign Office and tried to enlist the British Association for the Advancement of Science into a parallel action.[90] American and British officials, however, decided to stay clear of the issue. As the Foreign Office put it in its answer to Darlington: "the matter does not appear to be one in which His Majesty's Government could properly or usefully intervene."[91] The State Department sent a similarly worded response to Davenport.[92] There is also no indication that Henry Wallace paid a visit to the Soviet Ambassador or even responded to Emerson's cable.[93]

But Soviet diplomats obviously felt differently. Troyanovskii immediately forwarded all the letters he had received from American scientists to Moscow to the Commissariat of Foreign Affairs, as did the Soviet Consul in San Francisco.[94] To add fuel to the fire, on December 17, the *New York Times* published a sarcastic editorial on the cancellation of the genetics congress under the telling title "Science and Dictators."[95] The next day, *Science* reprinted without comment the first *New York Times* information under the title "Abandonment of the Moscow Meeting of the International Congress of Genetics."[96]

In addition to alerting Soviet and local political establishments, geneticists immediately mobilized their scientific contacts. They put the issue of the congress on the agenda of the annual meetings of the American Genetics Society and the American Association for the Advancement of Science, which were scheduled to begin on December 30 in Atlantic City, "with a hope," as Demerec put it, "that the opinion of American scientists may help to open the eyes of responsible factors in Russia."[97]

The active campaign in the West obviously did "open the eyes" of the Soviet authorities. For on December 21, one of the Soviet central newspapers, *Izvestiia*, published an unsigned editorial article under the title "A response to the slanderers from 'Science Service' and 'New York Times'," which was reported in the *New York Times* the very next day.[98]

The editorial was initially provoked by a story, entitled "Science, Innocent Bystander," distributed on December 14 by an American news agency—Science

ОТВЕТ КЛЕВЕТНИКАМ
ИЗ „САЙЕНС СЕРВИС" И „НЬЮ-ЙОРК ТАЙМС"

По поводу отсрочки созыва международного генетического конгресса, американское агентство «Сайенс Сервис» выступает с заявлением о том, что в СССР «интеллектуальная свобода не существует», а газета «Нью-Йорк Таймс»—с сообщением об «аресте в СССР Агола и Вавилова».

Мы имеем по этому поводу сообщить следующее:

1) В СССР действительно не существует той «свободы» генетической науки, под которой в некоторых государствах понимают свободу убийства людей или свободу уничтожения целых народов из-за их будто бы «неполноценности»

2) Действительная свобода исследовательских работ, действительная интеллектуальная свобода существует только в СССР, где наука работает не в пользу и не по найму кучки капиталистов, а на благо и в интересах всего народа, всего человечества. Одним из свидетельств этому является, в частности, происходящая ныне в Сельскохозяйственной Академии имени Ленина публичная (в присутствии более чем 500 научных работников) дискуссия по вопросам генетики. На заседании Академии, якобы «арестованный», Вавилов выступает, как уже известно из советской печати, 22 декабря с докладом, критикующим научные воззрения молодого ученого Лысенко, а последний — выступает с докладом, критикующим антидарвинистский характер некоторых теоретических положений Вавилова. Насчет ареста Вавилова «Нью-Йорк Таймс» просто наврал.

3) Господин Агол, ничего общего не имеющий с наукой, действительно арестован следственными органами за прямую связь с троцкистскими убийцами. С такими господами СССР неизменно будет так же поступать и впредь, каким бы якобы научным защитным флагом они ни пытались прикрыть свою преступную деятельность против государства. В СССР действительно не существует «свободы» для убийц и «свободы» для пропаганды террора.

4) Генетический конгресс, ранее назначенный на 1937 год, действительно отложен на некоторое время по просьбе ряда ученых, пожелавших удлинить сроки своей подготовки к конгрессу. Единственной целью этой отсрочки является поэтому — стремление обеспечить наилучшую его подготовку и наибольшее участие ученых различных стран в его работе.

Plate 8 The editorial in *Izvestiia* edited by Stalin, December 21, 1936.

Service. "Editorializing on the basis of the *New York Times* report," the story lamented the absence of "intellectual freedom" in the USSR manifested in the cancellation of the genetics congress.[99] Although, as far as I was able to determine, no one among the American scientists, who had appealed to Soviet diplomats for information, had been at the time aware of its existence, the story found its way to the Soviet Union, through the Soviet news agency—TASS—with which Science Service had an arrangement for the exchange of scientific news.

TASS routinely prepared summaries of important news from the Western media for the top-level officials in the party apparatus. So, on December 19, the "Bulletin of Foreign Information," which carried the summary of Science Service and *New York Times* reports related to the congress, landed on Stalin's desk. Obviously, the Soviet leader was annoyed by what he read. Apparently under his orders, someone among his subordinates had prepared a draft of "the response," a document, which Stalin heavily edited.[100]

The editorial fiercely refuted all the accusations of limiting academic freedom: "Real freedom for research work, real intellectual freedom exists only in the USSR where science works not for the benefit and not under the hire of a narrow group of capitalists, but for the good and in the interest of the peoples of all mankind."[101] As an illustration, it referred to the discussion on "issues in genetics" which had opened two days earlier at the VASKhNIL session. It then stated that Vavilov had not been arrested and would in fact tomorrow deliver a plenary report at the discussion. Stalin added: "The *New York Times* simply lied about Vavilov's arrest." The editorial then noted that Agol had indeed been arrested, but his arrest had nothing to do with genetics or the congress—he had been arrested for "terrorist Trotskyist activities" (Stalin changed this to "his direct connection to Trotskyist murderers"). Ominously, the article did not even mention the name of the third geneticist referred to in the *New York Times* dispatch—Solomon Levit. At the very end, the editorial announced that the genetics congress had not been canceled but merely postponed, because many Soviet scientists involved had "requested more time for preparation."

As if the editorial was not enough, the next day *Izvestiia* carried a lengthy "Telegram to the *New York Times*" by Vavilov himself, which reiterated the main points of the editorial, with one notable exception—it did not even mention Agol.[102] The following day, December 23, the *New York Times* published a transla- tion of Vavilov's "telegram," which Vavilov himself had delivered to the New York Times Moscow office.[103] The newspaper also admitted that earlier informa- tion about Vavilov's arrest was an "inadvertent error in transmission."[104] The same day, Troyanovskii sent cables to all the American scientists who had appealed for clarifications a few days earlier: "Your information is incorrect. Professor Vavilov not arrested. Genetics congress not canceled, merely postponed on account of desire of many scientists to have more time for preparation."[105]

The ambassador's cables, together with the *New York Times* publications, calmed the worries of American geneticists about the fate of Vavilov, but explained very little regarding the reasons for the congress's cancellation or the prospects of the future congress in Russia. As Dobzhansky put it in a letter to Dunn: "An excellent piece of diplomacy. Vavilov not arrested—but it does not mean he was not arrested. Who are the many scientists? Postponed until when?"[106]

Quite soon Western geneticists would learn the answers to these questions.

3 The road to Edinburgh

Oslo

With the announcement of the Soviet cancellation Western geneticists immediately began a concerted effort to move the congress elsewhere. Even when they learned that the congress had been not cancelled, but "postponed," they felt that "the local group apparently has no right to make a postponement. If it is unable to fulfill its obligation, the whole matter should be reported back to the International Committee for a decision."[1]

This in effect meant that the responsibility for the congress fell again on the shoulders of the IOC chairman Otto Mohr. But from December 19, 1936, when he first learned about the cancellation, until the beginning of March 1937, when he received the first official letter from Moscow informing him that the congress had been postponed till August 1938, Mohr was caught in a web of contradictory signals: Moscow's official silence, Soviet geneticists' private messages, and their Western colleagues' heated debate on what to do about the congress.

Mohr first became aware of the problem on December 19, when the American representative on the IOC Emerson sent him the following telegram: "Moscow congress cancelled. Urge prompt effort to place the congress elsewhere 1938. Not wise to hold next congress United States. Can Scandinavian countries sponsor it."[2] Mohr found the cable "entirely incomprehensible."[3] Just a few weeks earlier, in mid-November, he had spent several days with Muller in Copenhagen (at a conference organized by Niels Bohr), and at that time Muller had given him no indication of either postponement or—far less—cancellation of the congress. On the contrary, Mohr had the impression that "the arrangements were progressing well according to scheme."[4] A couple of days before Emerson's cable, Mohr had received a private note from Muller announcing that "it has been found impracticable to hold the congress here next summer." "No doubt," Muller continued, "an official communication regarding the matter will be issued soon." But no official statement followed, and Mohr found it difficult to believe Emerson's information. He did send a cable to Moscow organizers, though: "Emerson cables congress cancelled. Send information."

Mohr was in for a long wait. Only on December 26 (i.e. after the *Izvestiia* editorial had appeared) did he receive a reply from Muralov: "Congress is not cancelled

Plate 9 Otto Mohr during the Sixth international genetics congress in Ithaca, 1932. Courtesy of the APS.

but in compliance with request of a number of geneticists time will be changed. Exact time will be determined in near future."[5] Two days later (the day after the VASKhNIL session had ended), Mohr received a telegram from Vavilov: "Congress postponed. Soon mailing information."[6] On January 5, Mohr also received letters from Emerson and Demerec, which included clippings from the *New York Times* and made the whole picture even muddier. The same day, Mohr wrote detailed responses to his American colleagues, noting that he would "if necessary go to Moscow in order to get full information."[7] Two days later, Mohr sent a long letter to Muralov begging for immediate and exact information on what had happened in Moscow.[8]

By that time Mohr almost certainly had received "unofficial" information from Vavilov's letter of December 9: "By the decision of the Government it was found that during the next year and very possible during 1938 it would be impossible to have the Congress in the USSR." Vavilov concluded:

> Your rights as President of the International Committee are now again in full power and now it depends on you and the Committee to decide in which country to have the Congress. The official letter from the Academy of Sciences will be sent you in a few days.[9]

But Moscow officials kept silent, which added considerably to Mohr's anxiety.

If Moscow kept silent, Western geneticists spoke out at the top of their voices. The issue spurred a heated debate among American geneticists. During the December meeting of the American Genetics Society it was, of course, the talk of the day. One of the first sessions was devoted to a report by a special commission (chaired by Jennings, with Dunn and Emerson as members) on the situation with the forthcoming congress. The report summarized all the information available to date, noting disparities between the official version of events (as presented in the press and cables from the Soviet ambassador) and private messages from both geneticists in the USSR (first of all Muller) and the IOC chairman Mohr. The commission suggested that the meeting adopt a special resolution on the issue, musing "whether recent developments do not indicate that Russia is not ready to be a host to a Genetics Congress and that it would be advisable to hold it at some other place." The resolution urged the IOC to "arrange for holding the Seventh International Congress at the earliest practicable time."[10] Two weeks later, on January 15, Demerec prepared and circulated among all the members of the society a long summary with all the information available on the congress, including the resolution adopted by the December meeting.

But, of course, most actions took place not at the meeting's official sessions, but in private discussions behind the scenes. During these discussions Dunn, Demerec, and Emerson decided that Mohr should go immediately to Moscow. The aim of the suggested trip was two-fold. On one hand, US geneticists were anxious to find out what the actual situation in Moscow was in regard to the cancellation of the congress and whether the Soviet organizers proposed to reinvite the congress. On the other hand, they wanted to know what Soviet geneticists—first of all, Muller and Vavilov—thought regarding a place for the congress in case it was not held in Russia. The Americans also hoped that Mohr would be able to get "an interview with someone in the government to discover what the official attitude toward genetics actually is."[11] They were even ready to pay for Mohr's trip.

Not all American geneticists, however, were of the same mind about this proposal. Cook, for one, thought that the Soviet government had acted "high-handedly" in the whole affair. He did not believe that "anything is to be gained by further negotiations with the Soviet authorities" and insisted that if American geneticists were to go to the postponed congress in Russia they would be "nothing but suckers." Cook wanted to convey to Mohr "that American geneticists resent the action of the Soviets."[12] Indeed, in the 1937 February issue of *Journal of Heredity*, he published his own barbed editorial on the subject.[13]

Many Western geneticists shared Cook's resentment, but did not agree with the course of action he proposed. As Demerec put it to him:

> The question before us now seems to be not how to get even for the slap we got but how to repair the damage done. After USA, Russia has the largest group of active geneticists and any move, which would antagonize Russian government, may isolate that large group and prevent their attendance of international congresses. It seems to me that a great deal of caution should be used by the International Committee in handling this matter. There is no question that this committee has the right to change the place of the congress but it is questionable if this right should be exercised in opposition to Russian government.[14]

Cook reluctantly agreed with the arguments of his colleague. American geneticists urged Mohr to take a trip to Moscow and even provided him with funds "to ease and expedite plans for rescuing the Congress."[15]

But Mohr was hesitant. He first consulted with the Norwegian foreign minister and the Norwegian ambassador to the USSR, who happened to be his personal friend. At the urging of his American colleagues, he sent another cable to Moscow at the beginning of February: "Please answer my letter. Imperative to know whether my coming to Moscow will be of help."[16] Ten days later, on February 13, he received a cable signed by Gorbunov and Vavilov:

> The false information and direct inventions of *New York Times* are completely disproved by the telegram of academician Vavilov addressed to *New York Times*. Date of congress is fixed [for] 1938 exclusively in order that it can be prepared for better. We are sending you detailed information.[17]

The cable did not even mention Mohr's suggestion of coming to Moscow and no "detailed information" arrived for almost a month.

Although official Moscow kept its silence, by that time Mohr had received another letter from Vavilov, dated January 4.[18] This one was much more optimistic. Noting that the letter "is private, for your personal information," Vavilov elaborated on the official explanation regarding the congress's postponement:

> The fact that the International Geological Congress, which was announced prior to the Genetics Congress, is also to be held in Moscow this year has entailed some difficulties as regards hotel accommodations. The latter problem is further complicated by the large influx of people from provincial cities and villages expected in connection with the big agricultural exhibition, which is being arranged in Moscow for this summer. On this account alone some of our Soviet geneticists and plant-breeders thought it might be desirable, if possible, to postpone the Congress.

Vavilov further stated that "taking into consideration all those circumstances the Soviet Government decided to postpone the Congress." He concluded, however, on an optimistic note:

> The question of the Congress depends in our case on the decision of the
> Government and on its financial help. There is immense interest in the Congress
> on the part of geneticists and plant- and animal-breeders, and I believe it will be
> possible to arrange the Congress here, if not in 1937, then in 1938.

Notwithstanding Vavilov's belief, Mohr was disturbed by the official silence and
plagued by numerous letters from geneticists from all over the world regarding the
future congress. He entered into correspondence with Swedish, Dutch, and British
geneticists asking whether any of the national groups "may arrange the congress in
1938, or eventually in 1939." He was not very hopeful in regard to Scandinavian
countries. When the location for the forthcoming congress had been discussed in
early 1935, Swedish geneticists had initially invited it to convene in Lund-Malmo,
"but dropped their promise owing to practical difficulties." Mohr's pessimism
proved justified. Swedish geneticists again declined to became involved with the
congress: they were preparing for the international botanical congress scheduled
for Stockholm in 1940 and felt that they would not be able to arrange for two major
congresses in a row. Mohr thought that perhaps British geneticists "may be willing
to help us out of these difficulties."[19] He even asked the British representative on the
IOC, J. B. S. Haldane, to accompany him on his trip to Moscow. Although "entirely
in favor" of Mohr's going to Moscow, Haldane himself could not join him, for as
he put it: "my proper place is in Spain."[20] At the time Haldane was planning his
second trip to join the Republican forces in the Spanish civil war.[21]

In late February, Mohr's hopes came true. He received a quite unexpected
letter from Francis A. Crew, director of the Edinburgh Institute of Animal
Genetics, which seemed to offer a way out of the trouble. Noting that "it is years
since we either met or corresponded," Crew stated, "a sufficient stimulus has now
presented itself to make me take up my pen." Declaring that after the reported
cancellation of the congress, he himself certainly had "no intention of going
to Russia" and that "the Congress ought to be withdrawn there from," Crew
suggested Edinburgh as the best place for the congress and asked Mohr to support
his suggestion.[22]

Moscow

While Mohr was trying to find a place for the congress elsewhere, Soviet geneticists
used every means at their disposal to lobby the party apparatus to hold the congress in Moscow. They were encouraged by the December 21 *Izvestiia* editorial
announcing that the "congress was not cancelled, but merely postponed."
Although Soviet scientists did not suspect that Stalin had personally edited the
article, they certainly knew that such a statement could not have appeared in
Izvestiia without approval at the highest level. As Muller remarked in his letter to
Huxley written on the New Year's eve, "it should not be assumed that the
Congress will not be held here at all."[23]

Plate 10 The USSR Academy of Sciences officials. Left to right: N. Gorbunov, V. Komarov, and G. Krzhizhanovskii at the December 1936 General Assembly of the USSR Academy of Sciences. Courtesy of ARAN.

The *Izvestiia* announcement made all the December negotiations regarding the dissolution of the congress's organizing committee and the draft letter to Mohr obsolete. So on January 15, in reversal of its own December decision on the dissolution of the organizing committee, the Academy of Sciences presidium chaired by the newly appointed president Vladimir Komarov resolved: "to appeal to the head of SNK V. M. Molotov regarding the changes in the structure and timing of the International Genetics Congress."[24] In a few days, Komarov and Gorbunov, in close consultation with Muralov and Vavilov, began drafting a long memorandum for Molotov. Exactly two weeks later, on January 29, the presidium again returned to the issue of the congress—this time to discuss the new membership of the organizing committee. It was proposed to appoint Komarov the chairman, with Vavilov and Muralov as his deputies. VASKhNIL vice-president Meister was nominated as general secretary, while Keller, Lysenko, Karpechenko, Muller, Navashin, Mikhail Zavadovskii, Schaxel, and Vavilov's deputy in VIR Andrei Sapegin were nominated as members.[25]

The academy officials, however, were not the only ones concerned with the congress. On January 30, Stalin and Molotov received a memorandum from Iakov Iakovlev, the recently appointed head of the Central Committee's Agricultural Department, formerly the commissar of agriculture, and a staunch supporter of

Lysenko's agricultural nostrums, particularly vernalization. Apparently sometime in late December–early January, perhaps as a result of Stalin's involvement with the *Izvestiia* editorial, Iakovlev was entrusted with examining the work of the congress's organizing committee. He conducted a thorough investigation of its activities, as well as the congress's scientific program, and found them unsatisfactory. In his opinion, the program "had been prepared in such a way that it would have given upper-hand to the supporters of fascist genetics."[26] Among the subjects that would be particularly open to this undesirable situation, Iakovlev listed "human genetics" and "evolution in light of genetics research."

"In order to ensure the state's interests at the congress," Iakovlev suggested a plan of action: to change the membership of the organizing committee and the congress's scientific program; to ensure the presence of an overwhelming majority of scientists "from democratic countries and opponents of Fascist genetics"; to appoint a special commission (with himself as chair) from the Central Committee and SNK to oversee the preparations; to hold the congress in August 1938.

The changes in the membership of the organizing committee proposed by Iakovlev amounted to a complete removal of all geneticists but Muller and Vavilov. Komarov was nominated the chairman, with Muralov, Vavilov, and Lysenko as deputies, while Meister, Keller, and Gorbunov remained members. The changes in the scientific program were no less drastic. Iakovlev suggested that the congress take as its major themes the following three topics: (a) distant hybridization; (b) vernalization; and (c) the material basis of heredity. In all three topics, main speakers were to be Soviet geneticists: Meister, Lysenko, and Muller respectively. Iakovlev also thought it wise that the Central Committee's commission he proposed to create approve the abstracts of plenary reports in advance.

A few days later, Stalin and Molotov received another piece of information regarding the congress from Bauman, the head of the Science Department: "As you know, the question of genetics congress and the discussion on issues in genetics, which had been held at the session of VASKhNIL in December 1936, aroused great interest among foreign scientists, particularly in the USA."[27] As an illustration, Bauman enclosed copies of the letter by Landauer to Schaxel of December 26, 1936, and of Schaxel's response. Bauman noted that "all the information coming from us says that the genetics congress is not cancelled, but postponed" and that there had been many inquiries from abroad regarding the exact date of the congress. He concluded: "I consider it expedient to permit the convocation of the congress in the USSR in 1938."[28]

The correspondence Bauman enclosed definitely piqued the interest of the addressees, particularly the last two paragraphs of Landauer's letter, which Molotov marked on the margin with red pencil:

> In light of contradictory information [available in the United States], naturally, everyone feels that they know only part of the truth. Those who are instinctively anti-Russian, of course, are saying that this is merely the newest demonstration of the absence of freedom in Russia and of the weakness of the government. Although these conclusions are perhaps stupid, one should

not underestimate their effects. Those who sympathize with Russia are unable to provide a rational explanation.

We knew that Vavilov had published a note to the effect that the whole affair had nothing to do with intellectual freedom. As far as I understand, this note is aimed at the foreign bourgeoisie. At least, if I understand the situation correctly, in Russia there could be discussed or published anything that is not treason. A question that comes to mind of true friends of Russia is whether certain generalizations of Mendelian genetics are considered to be treason? Is it considered impermissible to apply to humans [the principles of] genetic diversity in the same form that had been established for other animals? These are the main questions that need elucidation.[29]

Molotov also marked two last paragraphs in Schaxel's letter, which purported to answer Landauer's questions:

The freedom of the Soviet citizen is not only written in in the new Constitution, but is firmly embedded in the conscience of the masses, and here it is not utopia anymore. Because of this, if some scientists, like Serebrovskii, talk about artificial insemination of women to improve the race or, [like] Kol'tsov, talk about selective advantage of mass mortality from infectious diseases, our public reacts very sharply, for they see in this a return to barbarity that in our country is completely eliminated. Our people feel offended by suggestions that look like the Nuremberg laws of German Fascism on sterilization, castration and special barracks for breeding humans.

For such scientific nonsense our scientists are never being persecuted [*presleduiutsia*], least of all, arrested. But their thoughts are publicly exposed as mistaken in general and special publications. They have every opportunity to continue their scientific work.[30]

The same day Molotov forwarded Bauman's package to his deputy Valerii Mezhlauk for action. Mezhlauk notified the boss that "the issue is under control. Comrades from the Academy of Sciences promise to give their proposals in two days."[31]

Indeed, keeping to their promise, two days later, on February 7, Komarov and Gorbunov sent their memorandum to Molotov, who at once forwarded it to Mezhlauk.[32] The memorandum briefly recounted the work done by the local organizing committee, noting that "in many respects, preparations for the congress had not been finished in time and there emerged absolutely correct doubts regarding a possibility of the sufficiently proper organization of the congress in 1937." "Therefore," the authors stated, "transferring the congress to another date was absolutely necessary." They proceeded to illustrate the "comparative weight of Soviet genetics and breeding," emphasizing that "the very fact of the unanimous response to the Academy of Sciences invitation to hold the congress in the USSR is a sign of great interest in Soviet genetic and breeding work" on the part of the world community. The authors described "what the congress would bring to Soviet genetics and breeding," stressing that it "would have great significance in informing foreigners about the conditions and importance of science in the USSR."

A special section of the memorandum addressed the issue of the congress's program. Stating that the most important, central problems were "evolutionary theory in light of the newest genetic advances" and "questions of practical genetics and the breeding of agricultural plants and animals," Komarov and Gorbunov suggested that "the discussion of racial problems in light of genetics initiated by American scientists" should be removed from the program, because "there are special eugenics congresses to address questions of eugenics." The academy officials also noted that the majority of invited speakers would be scientists from the United States, Britain, France, and Scandinavian countries and that "a large number of leading German geneticists (Goldschmidt, Stern, and others) emigrated from Germany during Fascism."

The memorandum also included a section detailing Western reaction to the congress's "postponement." Stressing that "false information" in the Western media and its "refutation by *Izvestiia*" provoked "numerous letters from leading scientists with questions about the fate of the congress," the authors quoted extensively, though very selectively, from Mohr's letter of January 7:

> I sincerely hope that the alleged rumors are without foundation. But as chairman of the International Committee I need, as you will readily understand, any information, which enables me to answer the questions, which have already started to come from the committee members.

And further:

> When I recommended the acceptance of the USSR government's liberal invitation, I, for one, did it out of sincere respect and admiration for the splendid scientific achievements of the Soviet geneticists, an opinion that is shared by all competent scientific authorities.[33]

The memorandum concluded with the suggestion that the congress be convened in August of 1938. As enclosures, it contained the proposed membership for the new organizing committee, "which could ensure better effectiveness of work for preparing the congress" and a draft of the new program.

Furthermore, four days later, on February 11, Gorbunov sent Mezhlauk one more example of Western reaction to the congress's "postponement"—the Russian translation of Demerec's information letter of January 15—noting that it "deserves attention."[34] Mezhlauk underlined the quoted phrase in red pencil and forwarded the translation to Molotov's secretary with inscription: "If V. M. [Molotov] does not have this memo, please apprise him." Molotov carefully read Demerec's summary, marking in the margin passages that attracted his attention. He particularly noted Demerec's statement that "private reports from Russia revealed that the organizing committees of the Congress had been disbanded" and underlined the phrase that "Russia is not ready to be a host to a Genetics

Congress." After reading the document Molotov sent it back to Mezhlauk with his own notation: "To Comrades Mezhlauk and Gorbunov. The letter shows that Comrades from the Academy of Sciences who were supposed to handle the post-ponement of the congress in a sensible way [*po-chelovecheski*], did it like idiots [*po-golovotiapski*]. This indeed deserves 'attention' V. Molotov." Nevertheless, despite Molotov's displeasure, the negotiations between Soviet geneticists and their party patrons regarding the congress continued.

On February 25, Mezhlauk received from the Commissariat of Foreign Affairs a memo compiled by the Soviet Embassy in Washington.[35] The memorandum listed all the American scientists who had corresponded with Troyanovskii and summarized their inquiries: "All letters express the deep respect of American scientists for Professor Vavilov." It also quoted extensively from Demerec's letter to the Ambassador:

> The work of Professor Lysenko is also known here. Professor Vavilov was the one who with great enthusiasm introduced his work during the last interna-tional congress of genetics held at Cornell University in 1932. However, exper-iments made in this country since then failed to support the extravagant claims of Lysenko. A feeling is prevalent here that his success is due more to the spec-tacular advertising rather than to the intrinsic value of his work. Among all European nations the USSR today holds leading positions in both theoretical and applied genetics. It is, therefore, with great concern that all scientists view an apparently successful attempt of scientific demagogues to wreck what the world considers as one of the most important scientific developments.[36]

Mezhlauk filed the memo with all other materials regarding the congress.

Between worlds

At the beginning of March 1937 Mohr finally received a fat package from Moscow, which contained the first official letter, dated February 17 and signed by Muralov and Vavilov. The Soviet organizers apologized for the delay: "The situation in regard to this matter was such a complicated one that, in spite of desire to give you full information immediately about it, we were unfortunately not able to do so until now." The letter began by refuting the publications in the American press (enclosed was the text of Vavilov's telegram to the *New York Times*). It proceeded with recount-ing the discussion on "issues in genetics" at the December VASKhNIL session, noting that, "as a result of this session, the Academy of Agricultural Sciences has estab-lished a special fund of one million rubles for the full financing of experimental work on the most fundamental problems of genetics and breeding, which were raised at the session." (As enclosures, the package contained the daily bulletins pub-lished during the session with summaries and texts of almost all reports and com-ments.) Only then, the authors turned to the issue of the congress, repeating the official explanation for its postponement. The most important, however, was a statement that the organizers "have now obtained permission from the Government to hold the Congress in Moscow in 1938." Muralov and Vavilov proposed that the IOC approve the new date for the congress and expressed their hope that Mohr would put his authority behind "the desired solution of the problem."[37] Mohr's offer to come to Moscow again received no reply.

On March 13, Mohr acknowledged the receipt of the Moscow letter and coldly informed its authors that "conforming to the mandate given to the International Committee I regard it necessary to put the entire question before this committee." He warned his Soviet correspondents that "the unexpected postponement of the congress has caused some uncertainty also among those very people who were most eager to attend a congress in the USSR," and promised to keep them posted.[38]

This time, Mohr did not mention his desire to visit Moscow. As he explained in a letter to Cook three days later, "one reason why I have postponed a personal visit to Moscow is also a visit I had by an American who came straight from Moscow with direct greetings from my personal friend there, with whom he had been in direct touch."[39] The "personal friend" was of course H. J. Muller and the "American" was a journalist, Roald Lund, who had indeed met with Muller several times and who, upon coming to Norway, shared with Mohr his first-hand impressions of Moscow, Muller, and the situation in Soviet genetics.[40] Although, by his own admission, genetics was not "his line" and he did not know "just what the argument is about," Lund's impressions were not very encouraging.[41] He was quite certain that "they will not under any circumstances hold the congress, and are postponing as a first step toward forgetting." He also told Mohr that Muller was soon leaving Russia for Spain to join the Republicans as a member of an international medical team.

This information, brought directly from Moscow, apparently contributed to Mohr's hesitancy in wording his suggestions to the IOC. He took a while preparing "the question" for the attention of the IOC members. And now it was the turn of Soviet organizers to get anxious.

As we have seen, in early February the Academy of Sciences officials had provided the party apparatus with all the justifications for holding the congress in Moscow in August 1938. Molotov delegated the preparation of the decision on the congress to his deputy Mezhlauk, who collected the papers sent in by all the interested parties. Over the course of a month, however, Mezhlauk did nothing, and at the beginning of March, the Academy of Sciences officials again sent the Komarov–Grobunov memorandum to Molotov. This time the head of SNK himself read the memo and presented the issue to the Politburo. The negotiations between Soviet geneticists and their party patrons finally came to an end. On March 19, 1937, the Politburo decided: "To approve the Academy of Sciences suggestion on the transfer to August 1938 of the meetings of the Seventh International Genetics Congress in the USSR. To delegate decisions on the membership of the organizing committee and scientific program to SNK."[42] Two days later this decision was issued as the SNK top-secret decree No. 469 and forwarded to the Academy of Sciences.[43] Vavilov and his colleagues could celebrate a major victory in their fight to save the congress. But the very next day came Mohr's letter of March 13, which greatly alarmed Soviet scientists involved with the congress.

On March 23, Gorbunov forwarded a translation of Mohr's letter to Molotov, Iakovlev, and Bauman.[44] In an enclosed note, Gorbunov suggested that "taking into account feelings of certain foreign scientists," the organizing committee should provide Mohr with additional information and invite him to come to Moscow, so that the IOC chairman "could counter possible attacks against holding the congress in the USSR." Gorbunov asked for instructions. Molotov attentively read the translation and twice underlined Mohr's statement:

> Conforming to the mandate given to the International Committee I regard it necessary to put the entire question before this committee. And I will not deny that the unexpected postponement of the congress has caused some uncertainty also among those very people who were most eager to attend a congress in the USSR.
>
> The very nature of our science explains why quite a few members of our committee have already asked whether it would not, under the present conditions, perhaps be better to have the next congress in a country that is not in the foreground of political attention. Whether this can be arranged is another question, but under all circumstances I feel it my duty to put also this eventuality before the International Committee.

Perhaps, as on previous occasions, Gorbunov received Molotov's instructions by phone. Whatever the case, four days later, on March 27, together with Komarov, Gorbunov called a meeting to discuss the course of action. The group that gathered at the Academy of Sciences presidium included all the members of the old organizing committee (except Muller, who had already left for Spain) together with a few new members proposed by the academy presidium, as well as key personnel of the organizing committee's technical apparatus. They decided to send Mohr the following telegram:

> Confirm the receipt of your letter of March 13. With the approval of the Soviet government, the organizing committee suggests that the date for the congress be set for August 1938. To discuss the issues of better preparations for the congress consider desirable your coming to Moscow at our expense.

The meeting also decided that it was necessary to send to all foreign participants an announcement that the congress was being moved to August 1938. They also confirmed the proposal of the Komarov–Gorbunov memorandum that "the issue of race theory be excluded from the congress's program."[45]

The same day, Gorbunov sent Molotov the draft of the cable to Mohr, marked "Urgent," stressing that it should be sent "as soon as possible."[46] Gorbunov provided Molotov with a list of the IOC members and noted that "[representatives of] Italy, Switzerland, and Germany will be definitely voting for holding the congress in another country," while "[representatives of] France, Britain, Norway, Sweden, Austria, Denmark, Finland, and, of course, the USSR will be voting for us."[47] He stressed that "the remaining FIVE [*sic!*] countries are oscillating; we have organized a number of friendly letters from our scientists, which probably will convince them to support us, for all of them had been earlier definitely for holding the congress here." Molotov authorized the cable, but crossed out the clause "with the approval of the Soviet government." The next day, Molotov's secretary called up Gorbunov and informed him about Molotov's decision. The cable, with Molotov's correction, was fired off at once.

Mohr, however, did not hurry to pack his suitcase and go to Moscow. Instead, on April 8, he sent all the IOC members a lengthy memorandum, "for information" only. The memorandum recounted Mohr's official correspondence with the Soviet organizers (enclosed were copies of the letters and cables exchanged to date). Mohr proceeded to note that, judging by the bulletins of the VASKhNIL session he had received from Russia, "deep disagreements regarding basic genetic principles had arisen among the leading Soviet geneticists" and, in his opinion, these disagreements could affect the congress's work. He further stated that before putting the new Soviet invitation to a vote by the IOC, he considered it necessary to ask whether there are "other variants." He had sent out such inquiries and was now awaiting answers, Mohr noted, and meanwhile would like to gather from the IOC members a "general opinion" regarding the issue, which is necessary "to make my trip to Moscow useful."[48]

Soviet geneticists obviously realized that now the fate of the congress was in the hands of their foreign colleagues, and they did their best to convince Western geneticists to support the congress's convocation in Moscow. On April 5, Vavilov sent letters to the IOC members whom he knew personally—Federley, Tschermak, and Haldane—as well as to Demerec, assuring his friends that "we will do all we can to ensure the congress's success."[49] On the very day Mohr sent out his memorandum to the IOC members, Vavilov wrote him a long letter.[50] After apologizing profusely for the delay in writing, Vavilov declared: "We have the assurances of the Government that it will do everything possible in the way of arranging accommodations for the delegates and aiding financially in the organization of the Congress." He repeated twice the invitation to Mohr to come to the USSR "any time this year that is convenient to you." "Here we can discuss all questions of the program and other details of the Congress," he stated. Knowing about Mohr's close friendship with Muller, Vavilov noted that Muller was in Spain at the moment, but should return to Moscow in about four months. He also briefly recounted the disagreements with Lysenko and his followers, which had been the subject of discussion at the December VASKhNIL session, and repeated again: "All questions we shall be able to discuss when you come here."

The next day, Vavilov also sent a long letter to Muller, informing him about the developments in Moscow since Muller had left for Spain in early March:

> The Government and the Central Committee are now definitely in favor of the Congress. Molotov himself spoke by telephone with Komarov about the Congress, about the program, about the Organization Committee. For half an hour they spoke frankly about all questions. It was quite an unusual event, as you will understand. Molotov and Litvinov are themselves now engaged in arranging that the Congress be held in the USSR, and they promised to do the best for its successful organization.[51]

Noting that "now we have started a campaign for the Congress, and we ask you to help us in this matter," Vavilov emphasized: "Of course, you understand that it is very important for the benefit of genetics to have it in the USSR."

Other Soviet geneticists sent similar letters to their friends abroad. Serebrovskii, for example, wrote to Dunn:

> I hope that the International Committee will accept our proposal to organize the Genetical Congress in August in Moscow and that our friends in U.S.A. will support this invitation since postponing. The delay of the Congress was erroneously enlightened [*sic!*] in the American Press. Since Your visit to this country in 1927 great progress have [*sic!*] occurred and we shall be able to show to our foreign guests much interesting.[52]

Mikhail Navashin wrote a long letter in the same vein to Babcock:

> The Genetics congress as you know has been postponed until 1938. It was a good measure since many of our colleagues desired to have more time for preparations .... Now we are awaiting [*sic!*] for the decision of the International committee and hope the congress will be held later in the summer of 1938. Wish you could attend it so that we see each other. It will be first time since 1930.[53]

The answers to Mohr's memorandum from various countries began to arrive at the beginning of May, and the majority of them supported the idea of Mohr's going to Moscow to get first-hand impressions of what was going on there. Furthermore, in mid-May, Muller came from Spain to Britain on his way to the United States. He actively and quite successfully lobbied British geneticists to support the congress's convocation in Moscow. As Darlington wrote to Mohr on May 14:

> A fortnight ago I persuaded Haldane, somewhat against his will, to tell you that many of us here were in favor of holding the Genetics Congress in England. This week Muller has been staying with me, and we have discussed the whole situation thoroughly. Eventually we both came to the contrary view—with which Huxley also agrees—namely that the congress should be held in Moscow, and for this reason, that sound genetics in Russia may suffer a serious reverse if we withdraw.[54]

It seems that Mohr had finally made up his mind and decided to undertake his trip. But, on May 20, he received another letter from Darlington: "I have just heard ... that Kol'tsov and Serebrovskii have been arrested .... Huxley suggests to me that we ought to organize a protest signed by all leading geneticists in this country."[55] By a strange coincidence, on this very day, American geneticists received and circulated "reliable" information (relayed through a Rockefeller fellow from Poland) that "seventeen professors of several of Moscow's universities and institutions are imprisoned" as a result of the December discussion.[56] Mohr immediately fired off an indignant letter to the Soviet organizers: "If it is true, every thought of an International Genetics Congress in [the] USSR next year will in my opinion have to be abandoned."[57]

As it happens, the news of new arrests in Russia was untrue—it was "constructed" from reports published in Russian émigré newspapers by Peo Koller, a Hungarian émigré working at that time in Crew's institute in Edinburgh.[58] On May 28, Mohr received a cable from Vavilov: "Information you received about Kol'tsov and Serebrovskii completely wrong letter follows."[59] But this wrong information proved decisive in shaping all the following discussions and decisions in the West.

Mohr's letter regarding the putative arrests of Kol'tsov and Serebrovskii prodded the Soviet organizers into action. On June 10, Serebrovskii himself sent Mohr a letter:

> Dr. Vavilov showed me your letter in which you write about mine and Prof. Kol'tsov's arrests. I am not surprised at all that the enemies of the USSR again and again distribute false accusations against my country. But I am sorry that even our friends take seriously this gossip and admit the possibility that in the USSR an intellectual can be arrested for his scientific opinions. I will be very happy to know that in your country these false rumors distributed by the enemies of Communism will find a deserved valuation. I hope to see you in Moscow.[60]

On June 16, Komarov again called up a meeting to discuss the situation.[61] After a prolonged debate, it was decided that "there are all necessary conditions for successful convocation of the congress in the USSR in August 1938." The committee came to a decision to send letters to that effect to the IOC members and leading Western geneticists, noting specifically "that slanderous exploits against Soviet science, which had recently appeared in foreign publications and had aimed at terminating the convocation of the congress in the USSR, are absolutely false and bear the character of provocation." The next day, the organizing committee sent Mohr yet another letter urging him to come to Moscow:

> We are anxious to get without delay positive answer from the International Organization Committee, which is especially necessary in order to get in touch in time with foreign members of the Congress. Your visit will do very much for the efficiency of the preparation for the Congress. Kindly let us know beforehand the day of your arrival.[62]

But Mohr had obviously made up his mind. He answered: "I think I had better not go to Moscow now, since my visit might easily give you a misleading impression as to my hope of the possibility of an international congress in Moscow in 1938." He explained that the IOC members were quite unsure of "whether Moscow will be right place for an International Congress next year." He further declared that "this question will now be put before the International Committee for decision."[63] It seems likely that while writing his response to the Soviet organizers Mohr already knew that the British Genetical Society had decided that it would accept the IOC invitation to host the congress in Britain, if, "in the opinion of the International Committee, it will be impossible to hold the congress in Russia in 1938."[64] And obviously, in Mohr's opinion, it was indeed impossible.

Meanwhile, during June and July, in the United States, Muller actively communicated to his colleagues that it was imperative to hold the congress in Russia. He explained that if the congress were pulled out from Russia it "might cause grave injury to the developing science of genetics in the USSR."[65] But Muller's lobbying, though successful in swinging the opinion of some American geneticists in favor of Moscow, proved too late to change the situation decisively.[66]

On July 21, Mohr sent out another lengthy memorandum to the IOC members. He again recounted his correspondence with the Soviet organizers and expressed his regret that "unfounded rumors" had found their way into the press. But, he warned his readers again, the "disagreements" among Soviet geneticists "are of such nature that they cannot be disregarded, even though I feel convinced that both the foreign attendants and the USSR geneticists would have freedom to express their opinions at a congress in Moscow." He put before the IOC members two alternatives: first, to accept the new Soviet invitation and hold the congress in 1938 in Moscow; second, to accept the invitation to hold the congress in 1939 in Britain.[67]

By mid-September, contrary to Gorbunov's predictions, the majority of the IOC members had chosen the second alternative. Only the representatives of France, Britain, and the USSR had voted for having the congress in Moscow, while representatives of Japan and Belgium had not answered Mohr's memorandum in time. At about the same time, Muller had accepted Crew's invitation to come to work at the Edinburgh Institute of Animal Genetics and shortly thereafter left Russia for good. On November 18, the British Genetical Society decided to hold the congress in Edinburgh in August 1939. Four days later, Muller wrote Mohr a long letter from Edinburgh, commenting: "It was not a mistake, the way the international committee finally decided" not to hold the congress in Russia.[68]

Edinburgh

Considering the congress's relocation from Moscow, many Western geneticists feared that it might bar their Soviet colleagues from coming to the congress in another country. As Emerson warned Mohr in the spring of 1937, "the feeling in Russia may be so strong that their geneticists may not be allowed to attend the Congress."[69] Yet for a while it seemed that this fear was unfounded.

In February 1938, the general secretary of the British organizing committee Francis Crew sent Vavilov an official letter inviting him and a large number of his colleagues to take part in the congress in Edinburgh. Crew also informed Vavilov that the committee had unanimously elected him the president of the forthcoming congress.[70] This unprecedented gesture of appointing a foreign delegate as the congress's president was meant to soften the blow of the congress's withdrawal from Moscow and to ease possible difficulties in arranging Soviet geneticists' attendance of the congress in Scotland.

Vavilov gladly accepted the honor of presidency and used it extensively to lobby the Soviet authorities for permission for a large delegation to go to Edinburgh. As he stressed in his application to the Academy of Sciences presidium: "the president of the congress would be given every opportunity to speak about achievements of Soviet science; British biologists are paying particular attention to the participation of Soviet geneticists in the congress."[71] Vavilov immediately wrote a long letter to Molotov, telling the head of SNK that he had been elected the president of the forth-coming congress and that a number of Soviet geneticists had been asked to deliver plenary reports at its various sections.[72] Vavilov emphasized that "there are all rea-sons to believe that Fascist Germany would not allow its geneticists to take part in the congress, because . . . a Swedish geneticist, stringent antifascist, [Gunnar] Dalhberg, had been appointed the chair of the section on human heredity."

During the year, Muller, who had as a matter of course become a member of the program committee in Edinburgh, discussed with Vavilov the membership of the Soviet delegation.[73] About fifty Soviet geneticists were preparing reports and exhibits for the congress, with a number of them delivering keynote reports and invited lectures. In October, Vavilov sent Crew a request to expand representation at the congress sessions of "plant and animal breeding in light of genetics," stat-ing that "if it were possible to pay more attention to this line, it would be very desirable."[74] He stressed that "many breeders and even geneticists feel that there is a real gap between the most interesting genetical work on the chromosome theory, etc. and the needs of practical breeding work."

Plate 11 Members of the Institute of Animal Breeding in Edinburgh, spring 1939. H. J. Muller (second row, third on the left), F. A. Crew (second row, seventh from the left), P. C. Koller (second row, third from the right), Guido Pontecorvo (third row, third from the left). Author's collection.

Preparations for the congress proceeded on schedule, and it seemed that geneticists from all over the world would come to Edinburgh. As Crew boasted in September 1938: "Russia is well represented, also Germany and Italy. Disregarding the possibilities of war, I see no reason why we should not have a really fine Congress."[75] Nevertheless, British geneticists took additional steps to ensure the participations of their Soviet colleagues. In the spring of 1939, the British Embassy in Moscow presented the Commissariat of Foreign Affairs with a request to appoint official Soviet representatives to the congress and provided a list of Soviet geneticists invited by the organizers.[76] Furthermore, in early July, in response to Vavilov's appeal for help in securing the participation of Soviet geneticists in the Edinburgh congress, Muller drafted a letter to the Soviet ambassador Ivan Maiskii and asked a number of colleagues to support his plea.[77] Stressing "the prominence of Soviet participants in the Congress," the letter requested the ambassador's assistance in expediting their arrival in Edinburgh. As it happened, Maiskii was going to visit Edinburgh on July 15, and Muller planned to present his letter (signed among others by Crew, Haldane, Darlington, and Huxley) to the ambassador in person. Apparently the plan worked, for on July 19, the ambassador wrote to Crew promising to send inquiries to Moscow.[78]

British geneticists also tried to enlist the help of their own diplomats. Apparently under Darlington's instigation, a prominent British botanist, Sir Daniel Hall (a good friend of Vavilov, whom he had even recommended for the membership in the Royal Society in 1935), sent a letter to Lord Halifax. Hall informed the Secretary of Foreign Affairs that he had learned "on good authority that the Soviet Government is being pressed to withdraw permission to Vavilov and his colleagues to attend the congress," and asked Lord Halifax to "make representation to the Soviet Government that the British Government would view with dismay the withdrawal of Dr. Vavilov from the Presidential Chair, and that such action would have a bad effect upon enlightened public opinion all over the world."[79] The next day, Lord Halifax's private secretary informed Hall: "the Secretary of State is having the matter looked into."[80]

By the end of July, the preparations for the congress had been completed. The organizing committee printed the program of the forthcoming congress. It was planned to have pre-congress excursions and informal meetings in London, Cambridge, and Oxford, and then to open the congress sessions in Edinburgh. Nearly seven hundred geneticists from some fifty countries were expected to attend and to present almost four hundred reports. Soviet genetics and geneticists featured prominently on the program's numerous sessions and sections with forty-two papers.

On the eve of the congress, the early fears of Western geneticists proved justified. On August 4, Crew received a letter from Vavilov dated July 26: "Soviet geneticists consider it impossible to take part in the congress held in Scotland instead of its originally planned location—the Soviet Union."[81] The letter came as a complete surprise and occasioned a great deal of trouble for the organizers.[82] They had to redo the entire agenda, rearrange all the time-tables, print out a new program, decide what to do with the forty-two papers they had received from the Soviet participants, and somehow cope with the absence of the elected president.

The organizers did the best they could. A new program was printed, bearing the notation: "after this program had been printed and only ten days before the actual opening of the congress, no fewer than fifty names and titles had to be removed and the whole program hurriedly recast." Papers of the Soviet geneticists were removed from the proceedings. And it was left to the congress's participants to decide what to do about the presidency.

On August 15, the congress office opened in London to receive the first guests, and the program of pre-congress activities began with a reception by the host and originator of international genetics conferences—the Royal Horticultural Society. For a week, congress participants toured centers of genetics research in Britain, arriving in Edinburgh on the evening of Thursday, August 22.

The next morning at 10:30, in McEwan Hall of the University of Edinburgh, Otto Mohr opened the first plenary session with a formal address. He briefly recounted the story of the congress's withdrawal from Moscow and its relocation to Edinburgh and thanked the organizers for "the splendid way in which they have been able to overcome all difficulties."[83] He suggested that the general

Plate 12 F. A. Crew during the congress in Edinburgh, August 1939. Author's collection.

secretary of the organizing committee Francis Crew "be invited to be the President of the Congress" and "the volume and spontaneity of applause" led him to conclude that his suggestion met with unanimous approval. Crew took the chair and delivered a thank-you speech, noting:

> You invite me to play a part that Vavilov would have so adorned. Around my unwilling shoulders you drape his robes, and if in them I seem to walk ungainly, you will not forget that this mantle was tailored for a bigger man....In one respect at least I can claim to be Vavilov's equal, for I, as he would have done, will serve this congress to the utmost of my ability.[84]

It seemed that the congress would go on as planned. But on that very day, August 23, 1939, in Moscow, Germany and the Soviet Union signed a non-aggression treaty that became known as the Molotov–Ribbentrop pact. The war that had been looming over Europe for over three years was quickly becoming a reality. The next evening, British citizens in Germany were advised to leave the country, while similar advice was issued for German subjects in Britain. The rapid deterioration of the international situation caused much anxiety to the congress's participants. In the words of one observer: "That night and the following day there was an exodus."[85] The German delegation had to heed official advice and leave for home. Many European geneticists started thinking in the same direction, anticipating difficulties with transportation. Hungarian, Scandinavian, and Swiss delegates left. A number of British geneticists also left Edinburgh and hurried back home to their families. It seemed that the congress would disintegrate. Yet, it continued. The transportation for the largest foreign delegation—nearly two hundred US geneticists—along with a number of delegates from Canada, Australia, India, and other distant lands could not be arranged on the spot, and it was decided to continue the congress's sessions but to shorten the proceedings by one day. On Tuesday evening, August 29, the farewell party continued long into the night with toasts to "absent friends" and those "who were in danger and distress." The morning broke off the festive mode: a number of sailings out of Britain had been cancelled, and the congress's members found themselves stranded. The next day Germany invaded Poland.

World War II had begun.

Part II

Between patrons
and peers

The story of the Seventh international genetics congress is in many respects a puzzling one. The actions and reactions of both the patrons of Soviet genetics and its foreign peers in the whole affair seem quite unusual. Why did the Politburo cancel and then "postpone" the congress? And why were Soviet scientists not allowed to attend the congress in Edinburgh? Whatever reasons the Politburo had for canceling the genetics congress, they certainly did not affect the holding of either the 1935 international physiology congress, or the 1937 international geology congress in Moscow. Nor did they stop a joint Soviet–American expedition to the Urals mounted by astronomers in the early summer of 1936 to observe a total eclipse of the sun.[1] Nor did they prevent the participation of a number of foreign mathematicians in a conference in Moscow in 1938. Why was genetics singled out?

Similarly, why did the international genetics community appear so sensitive to the "postponement" of the congress and decide to withdraw it from Moscow? During the 1930s, other disciplinary communities were faced with similar "postponements," but did not react in the same way. Short of an actual war that occasioned, for instance, the postponement and subsequent withdrawal of an international congress of psychology and another one on malaria from Madrid in 1936, or the Anschluss of Austria in 1938 which led to an attempt to withdraw an international psychological congress from Vienna (an attempt made obsolete by the outbreak of the world war), other disciplinary communities were quite unwilling to change locations of their international congresses. The postponement for a year of the Second international congress for studies on population originally scheduled for 1934 did not occasion its withdrawal from Berlin.[2] Nor did the postponement in 1936 of the First international conference on fever therapy, "because of numerous requests to permit more time for the preparation of material," lead to its relocation from New York City.[3] On the other hand, representatives of the international geological community eagerly went to Moscow for their congress in 1937. A proposal to boycott the 1932 international physiology congress in Rome, as a way of protesting "against fascist attacks on academic freedom within Italy," found no support in the US physiological community.[4] And neither did French nor American mathematicians invited to attend a conference in Moscow in 1938 choose to boycott it in protest against the Soviet violations of "academic freedom." Why was the fate of the genetics congress so different?

To answer all these questions we need to examine in close detail the continuous interactions among three major groups of actors involved with the congress: Soviet geneticists, their domestic patrons, and their foreign peers. The following chapters analyze each side of these "triangular" relations within the context of local and international developments in genetics, as well as within the Soviet and international political context of the time. Chapter 4 scrutinizes negotiations between Soviet geneticists and their domestic patrons. Chapter 5 investigates interactions between Soviet geneticists and their foreign peers. Chapter 6 explores Soviet geneticists' role as interpreters and mediators of the "dialogue" between their patrons and their peers over the issues of "scientific internationalism."

4 Soviet geneticists and their patrons

The Seventh international genetics congress was the subject of continuous negotiations between Soviet geneticists and their party patrons. Yet the content, dynamics, and context of these negotiations before and after the Politburo decision to cancel the congress differed dramatically. Why did the Politburo endorse hosting the congress in Moscow in the first place? Why did they cancel it in November 1936? Why did they reverse their own decision some four months later? And why did they prohibit Soviet geneticists' attendance at the congress in Edinburgh? Answers to these questions will help us understand the Soviet authorities' changing attitudes towards "scientific internationalism" and illuminate the complex relationships among ideologies, patronage, and disciplinary development, which profoundly affected the negotiations.

Party patrons and international science

As we have seen, Soviet geneticists had been trying to organize an international congress in Moscow since 1927. They understood very well the advantages of holding the congress in their country. On one hand, they certainly hoped that the congress would bring increased visibility, prestige, and consequently funding for their discipline. For instance, geneticists used the projected congress as a pretext for applying to their patrons for permission to launch a new periodical—the *Soviet Journal of Genetics*.[5] At the same time, given the mounting difficulties of foreign travel in the 1930s, the congress would provide Soviet geneticists an opportunity to expand and strengthen their international contacts.

As for the Soviet authorities, they had initially been very eager to have an international genetics congress convene in Moscow and had repeatedly endorsed Soviet geneticists' attempts to host the congress. Yet, their attitude towards "international science" underwent a visible transformation over time. In the 1920s, the Politburo endorsed Soviet scientists' international contacts in order to tap Western expertise in science and technology and to break down the diplomatic isolation of the new regime. Accordingly, the authorities encouraged and often funded visits by Soviet scientists to foreign countries, whether to attend conferences, to collect plants, to undertake postgraduate studies, or to stage a propaganda show, such as the "Week of Russian Science" in Berlin in the summer of 1927. In the 1930s, however, the authorities sharply curtailed foreign trips by Soviet scientists. Partially this curtailment was related to the need to save hard currency for industrialization. Yet there was more to this policy than purely financial concerns, for in 1933, the Politburo prohibited Soviet scientists to accept Rockefeller fellowships that cost nothing to the state purse. During the 1930s, instead of sending their scientists abroad, the Soviet leadership gave much more weight to foreign scientists' visits to the Soviet Union.

Starting in 1930, the USSR played host to a number of international scientific gatherings, including the Second international congress of soil scientists (1930), the Fourth international conference on hydrology (1933), the Fourth international congress on rheumatism (1934), the Fifteenth international physiological congress (1935), and the Seventeenth international geological congress (1937). The Soviet government lavishly funded each of the meetings. For instance, it allocated three and a half million rubles for the physiology congress, with the actual expenses reaching nearly four million.[6] The government's major goal in such spending was certainly not science per se, but propaganda.

The international scientific meetings were used to showcase the advances of the first socialist country in education, science, technology, and medicine. Soviet scientists were well aware of this goal and used it extensively in their negotiations with their patrons over the issues of international congresses. For instance, in a report to SNK on "the political significance" of the congress of soil scientists, officials of the Academy of Sciences pointed specifically to numerous publications by the congress's participants in their home countries, which "had given a very precise and accurate picture of everything they had seen in the USSR, in counterpoint to all those slanders against the USSR, which are so characteristic of the Western press."[7] Soviet scientists used such justifications in setting up two congresses scheduled for 1937 in Moscow—the Seventh international genetics congress and the Seventeenth international geological congress. For example, while trying to secure the government's permission for hosting the genetics congress, Vavilov emphasized that "first of all, the convocation of the congress in our country will have great political significance."[8] Vavilov's rhetoric was echoed in every letter to the party patrons on the issues of international scientific congresses.

The 1935 physiology congress illustrates how the Soviet authorities used the international gathering to achieve their political goals. "To assist the convocation of the XV international physiological congress in the USSR," the Politburo appointed a special commission of high-ranking party and state officials, including the chairman of the Central Executive Committee (TsIK), the commissar of public health, a deputy-commissar of foreign affairs, heads of the Central Committee's Agitprop and Science Department, and chairmen of the Moscow and Leningrad city councils.[9] Furthermore, shortly before the congress's opening, Stalin suggested that the Politburo appoint an additional commission, headed by the Secretary of the Leningrad Party Committee Andrei Zhdanov, "to manage the physiological congress."[10] The TsIK chairman Ivan Akulov opened the congress with greetings from the Soviet government, which had been edited and approved by Stalin himself and which trumpeted the achievements of Soviet science.

The congress's president, Nobelist Ivan Pavlov responded with a passionate speech glorifying the government's efforts in supporting and promoting science.[11]

The Politburo closely monitored and tried to influence what was happening at the congress itself. For instance, on August 14, at its evening session, the congress had to decide where and when to hold the next meeting. Early that morning, Zhdanov had sent a coded cable to Stalin, asking for his "directives" regarding the issue. The reason for Zhdanov's inquiry was that some delegates had suggested Germany as a possible place for the next congress. Stalin promptly responded: "[We] consider it necessary not to allow the next congress to convene in Germany. Do give appropriate instructions to the Soviet delegation."[12]

Propaganda around the "achievements of Soviet science" was carried out at the highest level. When the congress moved from Leningrad to Moscow, Molotov gave a special hour-and-a-half long audience to the members of the International Organizing Committee for Physiology Congresses. On August 17, Molotov hosted a lavish banquet for the congress's participants in the Kremlin, which was attended by many top-level party and state officials. The head of the Soviet government delivered a fifteen-minute long toast, in which he boasted of the tremendous growth of Soviet science and emphasized the importance of science to the Soviet Union.[13] When the congress's scientific program had been finished the foreign delegates were taken on tours throughout the Soviet Union.

The Soviet press covered the congress extensively, publishing daily numerous photographs and speeches by participants, the journal of events at the congress, and accounts of banquets and parties arranged by various Soviet agencies. So did the Western media.[14] The congress clearly achieved the propagandistic goals the Soviet government had set for it and proved a very effective tool in shaping

Plate 13 International physiological congress in Moscow, August 1935. Left to right: O. Frank, W. Cannon, V. Molotov, I. Akulov, I. Pavlov, A. Hill, L. Lapicque, G. Kaminskii, L. Fedorov. (From B. I. Zbarskii and V. M. Kaganov, *XV Mezhdunarodnyi Fiziologicheskii Kongress*, Moscow: Biomedgiz, 1936.)

foreign participants' impressions of Soviet science, Soviet life, and Soviet people.[15]
A page from the diary of one American delegate illustrates just how effective the
"physiology show" was:

> The entertainment of the delegates had been such as one reads in the
> "Arabian Nites." We had been received & banquetted in palaces, enormous,
> costly, wonderful structures, undamaged by the Revolution & the civil wars.
> Gorgeous halls, parks, illuminations, hundreds of fountains, tables groan-
> ing under the wate of choice food & native wines, skies fild with the latest
> splendors in fireworks or with countless descending parachutes! Profusion,
> magnificence, at times barbaric!
>
> After the congress we had gone with 120 other delegates on a tour, which
> had been a royal progress & nothing less!
>
> But perhaps the most thrilling experience was that in the Central Park of
> Culture & Rest in Moscow. To this park some 250 delegates went one evening
> in autobuses. The news of our coming had preceded us. At & inside the gate
> was an enormous crowd (many thousands). Thru this we past in single file
> along a narrow lane between oceans of radiant faces, mostly yung. Clapping,
> clapping, clapping—a greeting to the foren scientists. I hav as a teacher some
> times felt the ecstasy of knowing that peple really cared for me. But as a
> scientist in America I hav never been made to feel more important than
> a 1st class butler. Here it had been different.[16]

One can suggest that the success of the physiology congress contributed to the
changing attitude of the Soviet authorities towards Western science. In the 1920s,
the Bolsheviks had viewed Russia as a backward country with underdeveloped
science and technology, which, in Lenin's words, needed "to absorb everything
valuable from European and American science." Yet at the same time, as the first
country that had carried out a proletarian revolution, they had regarded the
Soviet Union as the leader of the world community in social and political
developments. During the 1920s, the Bolsheviks actively supported the rapid
expansion of national science and technology in an effort to catch up with the
West. By the mid-1930s, this support had paid off. International recognition of
the Soviet achievements in many disciplines, manifested in holding international
scientific congresses in the Soviet Union and visits by leading Western scientists to
Soviet institutions, obviously led to the perception of the Soviet Union as a world
leader in science as well.

By the mid-1930s, the attitude of Soviet authorities towards "international
science" had acquired a pronounced "patriotic accent." In the summer of 1935,
at the banquet organized for the international physiology congress, Molotov had
praised international science and international scientific relations:

> You, the congress's delegates, could see for yourselves how high is the authority
> of science in our country, how close to their hearts the laborers of the Soviet
> republic take the interests of science, how great is belief in the power of science

among the masses. The very attitude of the masses toward the present congress is an indication that the union of science and labor created in our country makes the interests of genuinely international science close and dear to the laborers of the USSR. The utmost significance of international congresses lay in that they raise the authority of science in the eyes of the peoples of the entire world and give new impulses to the further growth of world science for the benefit of the entire mankind.[17]

But just a year later, in the summer of 1936, the party oracle *Pravda* launched a militant "patriotic" campaign, accusing Soviet scientists of "slavishness and servility" to Western science. The pretext for organizing the campaign was the accusation that the eminent mathematician and member of the Academy of Sciences Nikolai Luzin had published his works in foreign periodicals, instead of Soviet ones.[18] As recently discovered documents have demonstrated, Stalin personally endorsed the campaign,[19] which soon enveloped the entire scientific community.[20]

During the early autumn, the campaign subsided, only to pick up steam a few months later. On the very day *Izvestiia* announced that the genetics congress had been not canceled but merely postponed, *Pravda* carried an article by the president of the USSR Academy of Sciences Komarov, which bitterly attacked two members of the academy—prominent chemists Vladimir Ipatieff and Aleksei Chichibabin—who had refused to return to the Soviet Union from their foreign trips.[21] A week later, the academy's general assembly expelled both of them from its membership, and on January 6, 1937, *Pravda* announced that Ipatieff and Chichibabin had been stripped of their Soviet citizenship.[22]

The emphasis on the "patriotic" duties of Soviet scientists and the value of science as a symbol of the Soviet Union's leadership in the world affairs certainly played a role in the fate of the genetics congress.

From invitation to cancellation

So, what could have happened that induced the Politburo to cancel the genetics congress and, thus, miss the opportunity for extensive propaganda of the sort conducted during the physiology congress? The *New York Times* dispatch of December 14, 1936, that broke the news suggested two possibilities: the first was that the authorities canceled the congress because certain Soviet geneticists were accused of holding views "resembling the racial nonsense of German Fascists"; the second was that the cancellation was related to Lysenko's attack on Mendelian genetics. A third possibility, offered in the Soviet response to the *New York Times* articles a week later on December 21, implied that the congress was somehow "unprepared" and more time was needed for its preparation.

Genetics and race

In his private letter to Mohr of January 4, 1937, Vavilov lent some support to the hypothesis that a major reason for the congress's cancellation had been the inclusion in its program of the session on "genetics in relation to race":

> About seven months ago we received a collective letter from America, signed by many geneticists, asking us to include a discussion of the racial problem in the program of the Congress. Personally I was somewhat in doubt as to its necessity, but other members of the Organizing Committee insisted on its inclusion. The letter of the foreign geneticists was published in our newspapers, and there appeared undesirable commentaries in the German press. The Soviet government disapproved of inclusion of this question in our program.[23]

Vavilov, however, was probably mistaken. He was writing to Mohr under the impression of events, which had happened during the last few weeks, particularly the just-concluded discussion on "issues in genetics" at the VASKhNIL session. On the eve of the session, the mouthpiece of party ideologists *Under the Banner of Marxism* published an article written by the head of the Science Department of the Moscow City Party Committee Ernst Kol'man. The article bore a slashing title, "The black-guard nonsense of Fascism and our medical-biological science," and severely attacked the general secretary of the genetics congress Levit and his co-workers for holding "Fascist views" on human genetics.[24] In addition, the journal's next issue carried a denigrating review of the latest publications by Levit's Institute of Medical Genetics.[25] Furthermore, at the All-Union congress of neurologists and psychiatrists held in late December, several participants also attacked Levit and his co-workers for adherence to "fascist views" on human genetics.[26] During the VASKhNIL session itself, though the name of Levit was not even mentioned, several supporters of Lysenko bitterly criticized Levit's teacher Serebrovskii for his earlier eugenics publications. The critics focused on Serebrovskii's article published in 1929 in a bulletin edited by Levit, in which he had advanced the idea of using the techniques of artificial insemination perfected in the Soviet Union for "positive eugenics."[27] As a result of this attack, on the last day of the session, Serebrovskii delivered a "repentant" speech, acknowledging "a whole number of rude political and antiscientific, anti-Marxist mistakes," he had made in his eugenics work.[28] But all these events took place after the Politburo had already canceled the congress.

During the summer of 1936, when the inclusion of "the racial problem" in the congress's program had actually been discussed in the corridors of power, it had received strong backing from the head of the Central Committee's Science Department, Bauman. In a lengthy memorandum titled "On preparations for the VII International Genetics Congress," which he wrote in late June for Stalin and Molotov, Bauman stressed: "scientific studies in human genetics could not be advanced without criticism of racial theories, and, thus, the congress would have to devote a considerable place to discussing and criticizing these theories."[29] He noted that the initiative for putting this issue before the congress had originated with "a group (33 individuals) of prominent American and British geneticists with anti-Fascist attitudes," and that Huxley and Jennings were to deliver keynote

Plate 14 K. Ia. Bauman (left) and N. I. Vavilov (right), 1935. (From *Nikolai Ivanovich Vavilov. Nauchnoe Nasledie v Pis'makh*, Moscow: Nauka, 2001, vol. 4.)

reports on the subject. Bauman suggested that, "in light of the particular importance" of this discussion at the congress, it was necessary to organize in advance a wide campaign "on the scientific criticism of racial theories" in the Soviet and Western press. Such a campaign, he noted, would serve as a means "to mobilize scientists and the intelligentsia as a whole against Fascism." It is necessary, Bauman emphasized, to put to "maximum use the anti-Fascist feelings of foreign scientists."

It seems that such a campaign "on the scientific criticism of racial theories" was indeed initiated during the summer. On June 18, 1936, *Izvestiia* published a lengthy article by Julius Schaxel. Entitled "The Race Doctrine, Science, and Proletarian Internationalism," the article furiously attacked the Nazis race doctrine and the "biological foundations" of Fascist policies. Citing Franz Boas and Julian Huxley, Schaxel contrasted the views of "progressive Western scientists" with Fascist "nonsense" upheld by many German biologists and politicians. He noted that "American geneticists had proposed that the race doctrine be discussed at the VII international genetics congress" and that this proposal "had been accepted by the Soviet organizing committee."[30] Furthermore, in October, after Muralov and Levit had presented the congress's program to the Science Department, the department's officials again strongly endorsed the proposed discussion of "genetics in relation to race."[31]

The Politburo members probably did not even suspect that their German counterparts had perceived the proposed discussion "on race" as a serious threat and had even considered a boycott of the Moscow congress.[32] As recently-found documents reveal, the Reich Foreign Ministry arranged in August 1936 several meetings on the subject of the Moscow congress with representatives of the Reich Ministry of Propaganda, the Reich Ministry of Science, the Reich Ministry of Education, and the Secret State Police (Gestapo). After the reasons for and against participation had been discussed in detail, all participants came to the conclusion that "the congress would be used by the Soviet side to denounce German racial theory before the world and as a means of Bolshevik propaganda." The officials felt that German delegates should not attend the congress and should convince "friends of Germany and German racial theory" that they "must also stay away from the congress." Only if this collective "boycott" proved impossible, the bosses decided, would German geneticists attend the congress, but even then they insisted: "the German delegation must be comprised only of a small number of exemplary representatives." Prior to the delegation's departure, its members would meet in Berlin "to receive tactical and political instruction for their behavior while at the Moscow Congress," and "the delegation would be ordered to withdraw from the Congress as soon as the behavior of the Soviets or their friends gives cause." In October, the Reich Foreign Ministry again advised the Secret State Police: "There is no doubt that every scientific congress in the Soviet Union will be used directly or indirectly as a propaganda forum against national social-ist Germany." The Politburo decision to cancel the congress thus played directly into the hands of their German opposite numbers.

There is no documentary evidence that the inclusion of the discussion "on race" in the congress program directly influenced the Politburo decision to cancel the congress adopted on November 14. If anything, for the Soviet authorities, "racial genetics" seemed to present a good reason not to cancel, but to hold the congress and to use it to denounce fascism.

Lysenko

In their communications to Western colleagues, Soviet geneticists repeatedly denied the New York Times assertion that the "postponement" of the congress had in any way been related to their disputes with Lysenko and his followers. Indeed, by the time of the *New York Times* publication the debate between Lysenko's disciples and "classic" geneticists had been going on for more than a year, largely on the pages of various agricultural periodicals. The main subject under discussion was Lysenko's doctrine on "the transformation of heredity."[33] Lysenko and his followers rejected the concept of the gene as a material unit of heredity, denied Mendel's laws, and claimed that external conditions could directly affect the "heredity" of plants. Vernalization provided the "experimental" foundation for Lysenko's views.

The basis for vernalization was the fact that a plant's ontogenesis exhibits distinct stages, with every stage requiring specific external and internal conditions—a fact discovered and studied long before Lysenko.[34] In the late 1920s, Lysenko suggested that particular stages in a plant's development could be altered by changing its external conditions. A number of industrial plants, such as wheat and rye, for example, exhibit two different forms—the so-called "spring" and "winter" varieties, and Lysenko thought that such plants had a specific ontogenetic stage, which he called "the stage of vernalization." During this stage young plants (or seeds) require low temperature and high moisture in order to develop normally and produce seeds. According to Lysenko, the spring varieties have a very short stage of vernalization and require relatively high temperature, while the winter forms have a long vernalization stage and require much lower temperature. Under natural circumstances plants cannot "skip" this stage, so the winter varieties could not be sowed in the spring. Lysenko proposed a way of "skipping" the vernalization stage of the winter variety by wetting seeds and exposing them to low temperature in storage. These "vernalized" seeds were then used for spring sowing. Furthermore, he soon expanded this technique to other industrial plants, including cotton, potato, and sunflower.

Although Vavilov and some other geneticists saw vernalization as a useful *laboratory* method for hybridizing plants with different vegetation periods, Lysenko saw it as an *agricultural* technique that could improve the yield of various industrial plants. The winter forms of wheat, for instance, have a potentially much higher yield per acre than the spring ones. But because they are sowed in the autumn, the winter forms are exposed to the uncertainties of winter weather and during a particularly cold winter many sowed seeds do not survive in the soil until spring, resulting in yields not that much higher, and sometimes even lower than that of the spring varieties. If it were somehow possible to sow winter wheat in the spring, it would in theory dramatically improve the yield, and this was exactly what Lysenko proposed to do, using his "vernalization technique." His views were quickly adopted by agricultural officials, who were feverishly searching for suitable means to remedy the disastrous situation in Soviet agriculture created by the forced collectivization of peasantry. They hailed vernalization as a true achievement of Soviet agricultural science and showered its inventor with rewards and honors. In 1932 Lysenko was appointed chair of a special department of vernalization created for him at the Odessa Institute of Genetics and Plant Breeding. In 1934 he was "elected" to the Ukrainian Academy of Sciences. The next year, he was appointed a member of VASKhNIL and head of the Odessa Institute.

Aside from being a popular agricultural technique actively promoted by the party-state apparatus, for Lysenko, vernalization appeared to provide a basis for certain theoretical conclusions as well. The differences between the winter and spring forms are determined by heredity and, Lysenko theorized, the "transformation" of a winter form into a spring one by vernalization actually alters the hereditary characteristics of the winter form: the acquired characteristics of the spring form became hereditary in the progeny of the "vernalized" winter form. Vernalization, thus, became the "experimental foundation" for Lysenko's adherence to the Lamarkian concept of the inheritance of acquired characteristics.

Lysenko also skillfully used the particular culture of Soviet science and quickly capitalized on the growing "patriotic" attitude of its patrons to promote his views. He stated that his doctrine was a direct continuation of works by a Russian amateur plant breeder, Ivan Michurin, who was often portrayed as the Russian Luther Burbank. Michurin died early in 1936 and the Politburo issued a special decree on his commemoration, thus elevating Michurin to the ranks of the sacred "founding fathers" of Soviet science.[35] Lysenko and his followers immediately appropriated "Michurin's legacy" and claimed that they were developing "Michurinist" (i.e. "Soviet") genetics, while their opponents developed "Mendelian" or "Morganist" (i.e. "foreign") genetics. They also accused their opponents of other "mortal sins" incompatible with "Soviet" science—"practical sterility," "contradiction to Marxism," and "anti-Darwinism."

Lysenko's offensive against what he called "formal" genetics spurred its practitioners to launch a counterattack. In July 1936, the VASKhNIL presidium initiated a public discussion on "issues in genetics."[36] At that time, VASKhNIL was a stronghold of genetics that was seen as the scientific basis for "the socialist reconstruction of agriculture." Two vice-presidents of the academy, Vavilov and Mikhail Zavadovskii,[37] were known advocates and supporters of Mendelian genetics. Two leading geneticists, members of the congress's organizing committee, Kol'tsov and Serebrovskii, were also members of the academy. A number of other VASKhNIL members who worked on plant and animal breeding supported Mendelian genetics.

So, in mid-July, VASKhNIL president Muralov appealed to Stalin and Molotov for permission to organize a "public discussion"[38] between "formal" geneticists

Plate 15 A. I. Muralov (left) and N. I. Vavilov (right) at the VASKhNIL session in Moscow, 1935. (From *N. I. Vavilov. Dokumenty i Fotografii*, St Petersburg: Nauka, 1995.)

and Lysenko's followers at a special VASKhNIL session in early December. The commissar of agriculture Mikhail Chernov co-signed the appeal. Muralov and Chernov stressed that such a discussion was particularly necessary in light of the forthcoming international congress, for it would allow Soviet geneticists to present a "united front" at the congress.[39] The discussion was to feature a large number of reports by "practical workers" and a plenary meeting to debate theoretical issues. The composition of the plenary meeting gave geneticists a marked advantage: reports by three leading geneticists—Vavilov, Serebrovskii, and Muller—were stacked against a report by Lysenko. In mid-August the SNK apparatus permitted the discussion and scheduled it for late December 1936.[40] The VASKhNIL presidium promptly compiled a volume entitled *A Collection of Works on Controversial Problems of Genetics and Breeding*, with polemical papers by supporters of both Lysenko and Vavilov, which was to be distributed during the discussion.[41]

Although Lysenko's agricultural nostrums and his quick ascent up the Soviet academic and bureaucratic ladders had been endorsed by various top-level party and state officials, including Stalin himself, there is no documentary evidence that they had at the time actually supported his offensive against genetics and geneticists. On the contrary, there are indications that at least *before* the December VASKhNIL session, top officials of the party apparatus were decidedly neutral in regards to the genetics debate. In his memorandum sent in the summer of 1936 to Stalin and Molotov, Bauman recounted the essence of the controversy. He noted "the impression of many scientists" with whom he had spoken at a meeting in VASKhNIL that "Comrade Lysenko is supported by the government and by the party and [because of that] to argue with him is unbeneficial, despite the fact that he is wrong." Bauman remarked that this "creates an unhealthy atmosphere in the scientific arena." That is why, he continued, "as the head of the Central Committee's Science Department, [in my speech at the meeting] I underlined the necessity and full opportunity for a free discussion on issues in genetics in the USSR."[42]

In his letters to Julian Huxley, which he wrote en route to Spain on March 9 and 13, 1937, H. J. Muller nevertheless intimated that the congress's cancellation was influenced by Lysenko's attack on "formal" genetics. But like Vavilov, Muller was writing under the impression of events at the VASKhNIL discussion and its aftermath, particularly his personal encounters with two party "curators" of the discussion—Bauman and Iakovlev. According to Muller, during the discussion both of them had supported the kind of a Lamarkian view on heredity propagated by Lysenko and that "this . . . represented the view in the highest official circles"—apparently, meaning Stalin himself. Yet, to date, Soviet archives have failed to provide any documentary evidence of Stalin's personal involvement in either canceling the congress or "orchestrating" Lysenko's attack on formal genetics and its leaders.

Furthermore, contrary to the impressions of Western geneticists, judging by its immediate results, Vavilov's supporters won the December discussion. At the end of the session, a resolution adopted by the VASKhNIL presidium endorsed the expansion of experimental work on the "issues in heredity" and provided additional funding for research conducted at Vavilov's institutes—the Institute of Genetics and the Institute of Plant Breeding.[43] The materials of the discussion were quickly published as a special volume.[44] It seems that the December discussion might have actually helped geneticists persuade the Politburo to reconsider its decision on canceling the congress.

"Unpreparedness"

We are left, therefore, with a rather unexpected idea that the reason given in the official Soviet announcement—the need for more time for preparation—perhaps had certain foundations. Indeed, the full text of the November 1936 Politburo decision read: "to revoke the decision of the Central Committee of August 2, 1935, and to cancel the convocation of the VII international genetics congress in the USSR in 1937, due to [its] obvious unpreparedness."[45] But it was the Politburo, not some unidentified scientists, who considered the congress "unprepared" and desired "to have more time for preparations."

The idea to postpone the congress for a year had surfaced at least four months prior to the November Politburo decision, during the discussions of the congress in the SNK apparatus in late July.[46] Perhaps, this idea first emerged as a result of troubles with the international geological congress. On July 7, a deputy-head of the secret police (NKVD) sent Molotov a three-page report by his subordinates from Leningrad "On the failure of preparations for the International Geological Congress."[47] The report listed a number of problems in organizing the congress, particularly "the unpreparedness" of excursion and exhibition programs and of various institutions that were to be visited by foreign delegates. The authors cited pessimistic statements by certain geologists from the Leningrad Geological Institute collected by a secret agent to illustrate the situation and blamed the leading members of the local organizing committee—academicians Ivan Gubkin and Aleksandr Fersman—for the failure. They stated that the organizing committee's actions were "unsatisfactory, which threatens to completely undermine the congress's work and discredits the USSR." Molotov carefully read the report, underlining numerous passages, and forwarded it to his deputy Mezhlauk.

It seems possible that the NKVD report alerted SNK officials to the issues of preparation for not only the geological congress, but also the genetics one. Apparently sometime in late July, Mezhlauk requested a progress report from the organizing committee of the genetics congress. On August 10, Muralov reported to Mezhlauk on the nature and amount of work that his committee had accomplished to date. In this report he noted that, "postponement of the congress till 1938 could provoke a negative reaction abroad."[48] Muralov pointed out that a similar issue had been discussed before the previous, Sixth congress "in relation to the [world] economic crisis, but even under those circumstances, the [American] organizing committee had decided against [the postponement of the congress]." He insisted that August 1937 would be the perfect time for the congress because it would coincide with the opening of the All-Union Agricultural Exhibition, which, according to Muralov, would enable the USSR "to demonstrate all our achievements" to foreigners. At the same time, he continued, the congress would arrange its own exhibition that would represent the latest foreign accomplishments and would be available to many Soviet specialists in plant and animal breeding coming to Moscow for the All-Union Agricultural Exhibition.

Six days later Muralov sent a similar report to Molotov, pointing out "a number of serious difficulties" that could follow a decision to postpone the congress, up to and including "changing the country in which the congress is to be held."[49] He again recounted the benefits the Soviet Union would reap from hosting the congress, particularly "the great importance of informing foreigners about the status and advancements of science in the USSR." Perhaps, Muralov learned that Molotov was on vacation at the Politburo dacha on the Black Sea, for a week later he also sent a copy of this report to two members of the Politburo who were still in Moscow, Lazar' Kaganovich and Vlas Chubar' (who was also a deputy-head of SNK).[50] At this point, his arguments apparently had the desired impact and convinced the party bureaucrats, for no decision on postponement was made in August.

It was Molotov who put the issue of the congress on the Politburo agenda some three months later. On November 14, he wrote a brief note that was circulated among the members of the Politburo: "[I] propose that the [August 1935 Politburo] decision on [holding] the genetics congress in 1937 in the USSR be revoked as inexpedient (due to [its] obvious unpreparedness)."[51] The issue was not discussed at a formal sitting. Other Politburo members—Mikhail Kalinin, Kliment Voroshilov, Vlas Chubar', Andrei Andreev, and Anastas Mikoian—simply put "I agree" on Molotov's note. Kaganovich also agreed to Molotov's proposal, but he also scribbled on it his own notation: "It's not the decision that is inexpedient, but the congress's organizers who are no-good, for first [they] had put forward the proposition, but did nothing. Will have to cancel." Markedly, the signature of Joseph Stalin is absent on the original document. That day the head of the Politburo was not even in the Kremlin, he was at his dacha outside Moscow.[52]

Molotov's note clearly indicates that the initiative to cancel the congress had come from SNK, where it had been brewing since the summer, and not from the party apparatus or even Stalin personally, as Muller later claimed. Had it come from the party apparatus—for instance from the Central Committee's Science Department—it almost certainly would have first been discussed by the Orgburo and probably presented to the Politburo for approval not by Molotov, but by one of the secretaries of the Central Committee, Andreev or Chubar', or by the head of the Science Department Bauman. Molotov's note also undermines the hypothesis that the congress's cancellation was connected with the discussion of the "racial question." SNK was little concerned with scientific issues to be discussed at the congress. These were the prerogative of the Science Department—it was to this department that Levit and Muralov had sent the scientific program and the list of invited speakers in late September 1936, and a few weeks later the department's officials approved both. The SNK apparatus, on the other hand, was first and foremost involved with the congress's funding and various organizational matters, such as accommodations, transportation, excursions, banquets, and exhibitions.

So, what was it exactly that, in Molotov's opinion, was "unprepared"? Molotov was a born bureaucrat. The head of SNK, he worked with papers 14–16 hours a day. (Reportedly, his fellow-members of the Politburo called him "The Iron Butt.") So, one possibility is that what was not prepared was the necessary paperwork for the congress, such as drafts of SNK decrees which should have been agreed upon by all the state agencies involved. Judging by available documents, there were several problems of this sort. For instance, the Commissariat of Finance (expectedly) could not agree with the organizing committee's estimates for the congress budget. Similarly, Gosplan (the State Planning Administration) also raised a number of objections and sent back several drafts prepared by Muralov and his staff.[53] In contrast to the budget for the geological congress, which had been approved in the spring of 1936, during the entire summer the SNK apparatus delayed a decision on the genetics congress's budget, without which the organizing committee could not proceed with preparations.[54] On October 19, Muralov, Vavilov, and Levit paid a visit to a deputy-head of SNK, Ian Rudzutak. As a result of this visit, the SNK apparatus approved the organizing committee's operational expenses for the rest of the year.[55] A discussion in Molotov's SNK office of the congress's entire budget was scheduled for October 23, but Muralov fell ill and the discussion was rescheduled for November 13.[56] The archives did not preserve records of this discussion, but it must have been this discussion that inspired Molotov's note circulated among the Politburo members on the very next day.

It is possible, however, that what was not prepared was not just the paperwork but the entire "genetics show." The major "political" goal of an international congress was to demonstrate to foreign visitors the advances of Soviet science. To achieve this goal a congress's program included numerous excursions to various universities, research institutes, laboratories, and museums, not only in Moscow, but also in the provinces. For instance, the program of the 1937 geological congress included special excursions to the universities, museums, and institutes in Leningrad, Perm', and Sverdlovsk. The organizing committee requested from SNK nearly one million rubles for their remodeling and new equipment, specifically for the purpose of demonstrating these institutions to foreigners.[57] A similar excursion program was planned for the genetics congress, and geneticists addressed to SNK similar requests for necessary funding.

Yet, it was exactly this kind of "showing off" that was not ready for the genetics congress. A centerpiece of the show was supposed to be a brand new Institute of Genetics of the Academy of Sciences, whose construction had begun in Moscow in April 1936. But the construction took much longer than expected. According to a letter the institute's scientific secretary sent to Gorbunov in November:

> The buildings and greenhouses will not be ready on time and this will undermine the major material base of the Congress. The actual work of the congress should be based on the institute, for the congress is held under the Academy

of Sciences auspices. These circumstances "could create a bad impression," namely, that in socialist society science develops "worse" than in capitalist one, and this contradicts the nature of socialist society.[58]

Another very important part of the show was supposed to be the All-Union Agricultural Exhibition designed to present the advancements of the Soviet Union's widely proclaimed "collectivized" agriculture and agricultural sciences, including genetics. The head of the exhibition's scientific program was none other than Vavilov. The exhibition was scheduled to open at the beginning of August 1937, just a few weeks prior to the congress. The opportunity for the congress's participants to visit this exhibition had been widely advertised from the very moment the decision had been made to hold the congress in Moscow.[59] But the exhibition also was nowhere near ready. Other Moscow institutions involved in genetics research, which were on the congress participants' sightseeing tour— notably, the Moscow Botanical Garden and Moscow University's Biology School—also were in a dare need of renovations and thus not ready to accommodate foreign visitors. It is possible that it was the "unpreparedness" of these institutions that Molotov had in mind writing his note to the Politburo. Characteristically, a few days after the Politburo had decided on the transfer of the congress to August 1938, they also approved a new opening date for the All-Union Agricultural Exhibition—August 1, 1938.[60]

The Great Terror

One might suggest, however, that although the "unpreparedness" was probably the major reason for canceling the congress, it was certainly not the only one. If we place the events related to the cancellation in the broader political context of the day, another possible motive for the Politburo decision emerges. On August 19, 1936—that is about the time when the talk of "postponement" was circulating in the SNK apparatus—the first show-trial of the so-called Kamenev–Zinov'ev's block marked the beginning of the Great Terror. A week later, all the accused at the trial were sentenced to death. The Great Terror would ravage the country for more than 2 years, leaving more than eight million people arrested and about one million executed.[61]

The terror took a heavy toll on the entire country and, however indirectly, the genetics congress may well have been one of its victims. Kaganovich's inscription on Molotov's note circulated among the Politburo members indicates that he blamed the situation on the "organizers." Who could Kaganovich have in mind? Probably, Kaganovich was referring to the chairman of the organizing committee Muralov, who in late August had appealed to the powerful member of the Politburo with a request that the congress not be postponed. At the time of the Politburo November decision, Muralov was in trouble. At the beginning of September he had been fired from his post as a deputy-commissar of agriculture. Moreover, Muralov's older brother Nikolai was at the time in prison as an "enemy of the people." Arrested in the summer of 1936 as a Trotskyite, Nikolai Muralov was about to appear at the second Moscow show-trial in January 1937 and would be shot as its result. Perhaps, this connection of the congress's official spokesman to an arrested "enemy of the people" played a certain role in the Politburo decision. Some participants of the events definitely thought so: in his letter to Huxley, Muller stated that this "helped to get [the congress] in disrepute."[62] Aleksandr Muralov indeed would be arrested and executed the next fall.

It is also possible that Kaganovich was referring to the general secretary of the organizing committee Solomon Levit. In November 1936 Levit came under heavy fire from party officials. There are certain indications that the initial stimulus for this attack came from within Levit's institute (from its party cell) and was inspired not by Levit's science, but by his political "affiliations." Prior to joining the Bolshevik party Levit had been a member of the Mensheviks—a faction of the Russian social-democratic party that had parted ways with Lenin's "majority" before the 1917 revolution and had been banned shortly after the end of the civil war.[63] In the early 1920s, after joining the victorious Bolsheviks, Levit became one of the enthusiastic proponents of introducing Marxism in science and medicine: he founded the "Leninism in medicine" society and was very active in various ideological battles of the time. During the mid-1930s, however, many of the 1920s radicals fell victims to the Great Terror, accused of association with Trotsky, Zinov'ev, Kamenev, Bukharin, and other "oppositionists." It seems likely that Levit's troubles came from this quarter.[64] In the atmosphere of the Great Terror, Levit's former association with the Mensheviks, together with his active engagement in the ideological debates of the 1920s (not to mention his friendship with Agol who had been arrested) were more than sufficient for some "vigilant" party member to denounce him to the local party committee. It seems highly probable that that was exactly what happened during the fall of 1936. Furthermore, there are some indications that the attack on Levit was part of a larger plot to implicate high-ranking officials of Narkomzdrav—the commissar Grigorii Kaminskii and head of the Soviet Red Cross Society Khristian Rakovskii—in the "Trotskyist conspiracy."[65]

One of Levit's most ardent critics was the head of the Science Department of the Moscow City Party Committee, Ernst Kol'man, who obviously had been informed about the situation in Levit's institute by a party vigilante. On November 5, 1936, Kol'man sent (outside of channels) an extensive memorandum to Molotov with "information on the situation on the scientific front."[66] The memorandum's central theme was "the recent sharpening of the class struggle on our scientific front." As a major problem, Kol'man listed "the fascisization of scientific theory" and named Levit as one of the main proponents of such "fascisization," noting Levit's previous association with the Mensheviks. Kol'man explained: "This has a particular significance, because Levit is the secretary of the organizing committee of the international genetics congress." "The convocation of this congress here in 1937 is absolutely unprepared," he continued, "the congress's composition promises to be fascist, and there is complete theoretical disarray among our geneticists." Molotov attentively read Kol'man's memorandum and underlined the above quoted passages with red pencil.

Perhaps this denunciation played a role in the appearance in *Izvestiia* some ten days later, on November 16, of a satirical article that portrayed Levit as an overly ambitious scientist who had claimed to have entered the Pantheon of world science, succeeding Darwin and Marx.[67] During November, Levit was several times called to the local party committee for explanations and recantations, which on December 5, resulted in his expulsion from the Communist Party.[68] At that time the attack was directed at Levit personally, and his involvement with human genetics was mentioned only in passing. In early May 1937, when the fate of Levit's institute was discussed in Narkomzdrav, the commissar of public health Grigorii Kaminskii admitted:

> The question of Levit had been decided along lines related not to genetics as such, but to his previous mistakes. These questions need to be separated, as a question about Levit himself and [the] separate questions [about his work]. Aside from his political mistakes, there are questions about his concrete work.[69]

Like Muralov, Levit would be arrested and executed within a year.

The timing and the mechanics of the Politburo decision to cancel the congress, therefore, seem to suggest that the decision was not directly related to Lysenko's attack on genetics, or the controversial issues of relations between genetics and eugenics and between genetics and racism, although these factors perhaps contributed to the cloud of distrust, which, in the eyes of party patrons, engulfed genetics and geneticists in the autumn of 1936. In the atmosphere of the growing Great Terror, the suspicion that some members of organizing committee had ties to the opposition—"Trotskyists murderers," as Stalin called them—probably had much heavier implications than any internal squabbles among Soviet geneticists. Rather, this decision stemmed from the Soviet authorities' concerns with the congress's possible propagandistic impact on invited foreign participants. The Soviet rulers were very anxious about the international image of the Soviet Union as the first socialist society and the world leader in all spheres of life: science, technology, public health, education, and culture writ large. At the time when they decided to cancel the genetics congress, the Politburo members were heavily involved in another international propaganda project, funding and designing the Soviet contribution to the 1937 International Exhibition in Paris.[70] The Soviet government spent an enormous sum of precious hard currency—6,174,000 French francs—and an even larger sum in rubles, on an ambitious pavilion named "The Arts and Technology in Modern Life" and crowned by huge metal figures of a man and a woman bearing a hammer and a sickle.[71] The genetics congress's "unpreparedness" to serve the Politburo's propaganda goals appeared to be the main reason for its cancellation.

From cancellation to re-invitation

Whatever the reasons Politburo members had in deciding the fate of the genetics congress, they clearly did not anticipate either the furious reaction of Western scientists or the stinging comments made by the Western media. The Politburo perhaps considered the whole matter to be their "internal" problem. They canceled one congress, because in their eyes it was not ready, but they still had another one—the geological congress—to display the wonderful achievements of Soviet, socialist science and to conduct a large propaganda campaign.[72]

The adverse reaction in the West clearly forced the Soviet authorities to reconsider their decision. As we have seen, during January through March 1937, various top-level officials of the party-state apparatus, including the commissar of foreign affairs Litvinov, Science Department head Bauman, SNK chairman Molotov, and his deputy Mezhlauk, were involved in the negotiations with the Academy of Sciences officials regarding the issue. And the major motif of these negotiations was Western reaction to the congress's "postponement." In the end, the Politburo decided to permit geneticists to hold the congress in Moscow in August 1938 after all.[73] Available documents indicate that this time the decision was discussed by four of the Politburo members—Stalin, Molotov, Kaganovich, and Voroshilov. Four others—Kalinin, Chubar', Mikoian, and Andreev—simply put "yes" on the draft decision co-signed by the first four.

This decision, however, did not come without cost. The membership of the organizing committee was changed and the entire session on human genetics was excluded from the congress's program.

Human genetics = eugenics = racism

Why, we may wonder, did the attitude of the party patrons change so markedly from endorsing the discussion on race in the summer of 1936, to abandoning the entire issue of human genetics a few months later?

Perhaps a major reason was the campaign against Levit and human genetics writ large.[74] Although initially the attack on Levit had been spurred by his "political mistakes," his science soon became construed as one of them. During the 1930s, in the minds of many people in the Soviet Union, human genetics still resonated strongly with its earlier incarnation—eugenics. Students of human genetics tried insistently to distance themselves from the discredited predecessor, inventing new names for their studies, such as "anthropogenetics" or "medical genetics," and publishing numerous diatribes against "bourgeois eugenics." Yet, as one of the participants in the Narkomzdrav discussion of Levit's institute noted: "Now genetics is considered by the masses of physicians from the point of view of eugenics."[75]

Perhaps, the attack on Levit was not the only event that made human genetics suspect in the eyes of the Soviet leadership. In his letters to Huxley, Muller confided that, in a way, he might have been personally responsible for the troubles, for he himself had inspired Stalin's unfavorable attitude toward genetics in general and human genetics in particular.[76] Indeed, on May 5, 1936, Muller sent Stalin a copy of his recently published book *Out of the Night*, which advanced his long-held ideas on "positive eugenics."[77] In a letter sent along with the book, Muller urged Stalin to implement his ideas in practice in the Soviet Union.[78] Castigating "the evasions and perversions of this matter . . . seen in the futile mouthing about 'Eugenics' current in bourgeois 'democracies', and in the vicious doctrine of 'Race

Purity' employed by the Nazis as a weapon in the class war," Muller suggested that the well-being of the nation could be radically improved through the artificial insemination of willing women with the sperm of "gifted individuals."

The rhetoric and particularly the timing of Muller's letter to Stalin—just two weeks after the Academy of Sciences presidium had acceded to the request of Western geneticists to include the issue of race in the congress' program—suggests that Muller perhaps deliberately timed his appeal to Stalin as part of the anti-fascist campaign planned by the geneticists in the summer of 1936. Muller told Huxley that he had received no response to his letter, but had learned unofficially that Stalin "has been reading the book, is displeased with it, and has ordered [an] attack against it." He implied that the attack on Serebrovskii (whose ideas had laid a foundation for Muller's own program) at the December VASKhNIL session had been a result of Stalin's order.

Stalin might well have been displeased with Muller's ideas, but Muller was likely exaggerating his own importance in the whole affair. It seems much more probable that the assault on Serebrovskii was linked to the attack on his pupil and collaborator Levit. In accordance with the norms of Soviet scientific culture, many scientists (and not just Lysenko's supporters, as the congress of neurologists made clear) perceived publications against Levit in the central newspapers as the beginning of a new public campaign against eugenics and hurried to join the witch hunt. Even before the direct attack on Serebrovskii at the VASKhNIL session on December 19, Levit's editorship of the journal where Serebrovskii's infamous article of 1929 had appeared was cited as one of Levit's "grave mistakes." Lysenko's supporters simply capitalized on the ongoing campaign to draw Serebrovskii (and later Kol'tsov) into the camp of condemned "bourgeois eugenics."

But what appeared even more damaging for human genetics was that since Hitler's ascent to power, the very name "eugenics" (particularly its German variant—"Rassenhygiene") in Russia had become strongly associated, if not equated, with the explicit racist policies of the Nazis.[79] Again, despite the consider-able effort of Soviet geneticists to "expose" Rassenhygiene and to dissociate, in the words of one of them, "real genetics" from its "perversions" in the Nazi propaganda and policies, human genetics, in the minds of many, had Fascist connotations.[80] Even its methods, such as twins studies, came to be labeled "Fascist" (as happened, for instance, during the earlier mentioned discussion of Levit's institute in Narkomzdrav).

This "association" of human genetics with Fascism became particularly poisonous as the relationship between the Soviet Union and Germany deterio-rated. In the fall of 1936, the onset of the Spanish civil war brought the two coun-tries to the brink of open conflict: the USSR was the only state openly supporting the Republicans, while Germany backed Franco's insurgents. The Soviet press launched an extensive campaign of anti-Fascist propaganda, portraying Nazi Germany as the Soviet Union's worst enemy. Furthermore, a number of the accused at the show-trials of the Great Terror were charged with spying for Germany. The deterioration of Soviet–German relations perhaps "sensitized," as it were, both the Soviet authorities and Soviet geneticists to the alleged links between human genetics and racism.

This may explain why the inclusion of the discussion "on race" in the congress program became an issue *after* the congress's cancellation. Obviously, the suspicion that human genetics had "links to Fascism" reinforced the Soviet authorities' fear that the congress could become a vehicle for pro-Fascist propaganda. As we have seen, it was a major point in Iakovlev's assessment of the organizing committee's "mistakes." He stated that the proposed discussion "would have given upper-hand to <u>the supporters of fascist genetics</u>."[81] It is unlikely that the members of the organizing committee knew the contents of Iakovlev's letter sent to Stalin and Molotov on January 30. However, the December campaign against Levit and his institute, together with the attack on Serebrovskii's "eugenic mistakes" at the VASKhNIL session, made it clear that the very subject of human genetics had become entangled in a "racial" and "eugenic" muddle and was politically dangerous. This is why, in their memo to Molotov sent a week after he had received Iakovlev's assessment, Komarov and Gorbunov themselves suggested that the entire session on human genetics be removed from the congress's program. Characteristically, the reason given by the Academy of Sciences officials was that "discussion of the racial problem in light of genetics" was the prerogative of "special eugenics congresses," which were "to address questions of eugenics."[82] Thus, even the academy officials involved with the preparation of the genetics congress conflated human genetics with eugenics and racism.

Agricultural genetics and Darwinism

By the end of 1936, in the eyes of party patrons (and "party scientists") human genetics had become an unsuitable subject for the congress aimed at "demonstrating our achievements to foreigners." Not surprisingly, in the proposals for a new program, it was replaced with several other subjects.

In his report to Stalin and Molotov, Iakovlev suggested that the congress program focus on several topics in agricultural genetics in which, he claimed, Soviet scientists held the leading position in the world. His first choice was his pet project—Lysenko's vernalization. While occupying the post of the USSR commissar of agriculture, Iakovlev had actively promoted Lysenko's nostrums.[83] It was largely through his efforts that vernalization had been introduced and was widely practiced on millions of acres on collective farms throughout the country. Iakovlev's second choice was "distant hybridization." Initially, distant hybridization had attracted considerable attention from geneticists and cytologists as a useful laboratory method in studying the chromosomal mechanisms of heredity. In 1927, it was Karpechenko who obtained the first ever, fertile inter-generic hybrid between cabbage and radish—*Raffanobrassica*. Although Karpechenko's hybrid had no practical value, during the early 1930s in the Soviet Union, several plant breeders, notably Georgii Meister and Nikolai Tsitsin, attempted to apply the technique for more practical purposes. They tried to produce hybrids between wheat and rye and to create perennial forms of wheat and rye by crossing them with a perennial weed (couch grass).

Vernalization, wheat–rye hybrids, and perennial crops promised quick results in fixing the problems of Soviet "collectivized" agriculture and thus commanded particular attention from agricultural officials. Furthermore, these two subjects—vernalization and distant hybridization—were indeed studied almost exclusively by Soviet researchers, and thus, from the patrons' viewpoint, were particularly appropriate for demonstrating the advances in Soviet agricultural genetics.

In their variant of a new program, Komarov and Gorbunov also stressed Soviet achievements in agricultural genetics. But along with vernalization and distant hybridization, they also included research conducted at Vavilov's Institute of Plant Breeding on the world's variety of cultivated plants and the centers of their origins. However, this research was presented under the rubric of "evolutionary theory in light of genetics." Unlike Iakovlev, who, together with his protégé Lysenko, considered genetics "anti-Darwinist"[84] and suggested that the entire subject of "evolution in relation to genetics" be dropped along with human genetics, Komarov and Gorbunov highlighted it in their proposal. They stated that Darwinism was truly advanced only in the Soviet Union and thus presented an appropriate subject for "demonstrating our achievements to foreigners."

This difference in opinion regarding Darwinism between Iakovlev and academy officials is noteworthy. As I have argued elsewhere, in the Soviet Union in the 1930s, Darwinism became a powerful cultural resource employed by both scientists and party ideologists to justify their own agendas. While geneticists tried to claim Darwinism for themselves in order to protect their research, their opponents (both Lysenko's followers and their party supporters) claimed that genetics was "anti-Darwinist."[85]

Scientists and bureaucrats

The differences in the proposals advanced by Iakovlev on one hand and Gorbunov and Komarov on the other illuminate an important feature of the negotiations between Soviet geneticists and their party-state patrons: geneticists had limited access to the upper level of the party-state apparatus, where decisions on the congress had been made. Practically all the negotiations between geneticists and their patrons were conducted through intermediaries. A number of people directly involved with the organization of the genetics congress in Moscow had only "administrative" ties to the field. Even within the first organizing committee approved by the Politburo in early 1936, nearly one-third of its members—most importantly, VASKhNIL president Muralov, Academy of Sciences vice-president Komarov, and the academy's permanent secretary Gorbunov—were not geneticists, but administrators appointed to their positions by the party apparatus.[86] The organizing committee proposed by Iakovlev in his memorandum to Stalin and Molotov in January 1937 was composed almost exclusively of party and science officials (the only exceptions being Vavilov and Muller). And even the majority of the organizing committee nominated by Komarov and Gorbunov consisted of administrators, not geneticists.

Of course, geneticists tried to influence the decision-making process, sending numerous letters to the party bosses and carefully editing information fed to the decision makers. For instance, it is almost certain that Julius Schaxel himself provided Bauman with the copies of his correspondence with Walter Landauer in January 1937, obviously hoping to convince the party bosses to reconsider their decision on the congress's cancellation. Geneticists also mobilized their contacts with various party appointees to the scientific community: Vavilov had drafted practically all letters that Gorbunov sent to the party apparatus.

But geneticists were not the only ones providing party officials with information on the issues of the congress. An illustrative example is the scientific secretary of Vavilov's Institute of Genetics, Mikhail Prokhorov. A member of the party, during the early 1930s Prokhorov headed agricultural departments in several provincial party committees. In October 1936, he was appointed to the Institute of Genetics.[87] Just after a month in his new job, Prokhorov notified Gorbunov of the institute's "unpreparedness" to host the congress. What is more, Prokhorov was the first who openly announced that "at the Congress, we would be forced to allow a disproportionately large number of reports by foreign scientists, and obviously to a large degree we would have to give the Soviet stage to <u>Fascists</u>."[88] It is possible that, given his long-time association with the party apparatus in charge of agriculture, Prokhorov was the source of information for the assessment of the organizing committee's "mistakes" by the head of the Central Committee's Agricultural Department Iakovlev.

Prokhorov was not the only informant among people associated with the congress. The executive secretary of the organizing committee's technical apparatus, a certain G. I. Bankin, played a similar role. For instance, on June 7, 1937, Bankin sent a long memorandum to Gobunov, Iakovlev, and officials of the Commissariat of Foreign Affairs.[89] The memo's subject was the visit by Otto Mohr, which at that time was strongly endorsed by Komarov and Vavilov. Bankin, however, was deeply concerned with the possible consequences of such a visit. Noting that all the official announcements regarding the congress's postponement referred to "the desire of many scientists to have more time for preparations," Bankin warned the bosses:

> Naturally, during his visit to Moscow, Prof. Mohr would like to examine all the materials of the Organizing committee, and the committee, having invited him to discuss the congress, would not be able to refuse. However, the committee had not received any letters with a request to postpone the congress and hence such letters are absent in its files. Furthermore, since the question of the postponement had not been discussed at the committee's meetings, there are also no protocols confirming the information that the congress had been postponed as a result of such letters.

Bankin also worried that, while in Moscow, Mohr would certainly hold private discussions with such members of the original organizing committee as Vavilov, Kol'tsov, Levit, Navashin, and Karpechenko. In Bankin's opinion, "some of them would give him information radically different from what he had received officially and would in general try to present the entire issue in a very unfavorable light." Mohr did not come to Moscow, so Bankin's worries proved unjustified, but his memo illustrates the kind of information the party apparatus was receiving. Administrators, "party scientists," and low-level bureaucrats associated with the preparation of the genetics congress, unlike geneticists, did not have a personal stake in holding the congress in Moscow and were mostly concerned with their own survival and careers. They appeared much more susceptible to political currents and followed the official party line much more closely.

Nevertheless, although they had to sacrifice a few items on the congress agenda and cope with the new membership of the organizing committee, Soviet geneticists managed to convince their patrons in the party-state apparatus that the benefits of hosting the congress in the Soviet Union would far outweigh the negative consequences of its unilateral cancellation. What they failed to achieve was to convince their foreign peers that holding the congress in Moscow was imperative for the further development of Soviet genetics.

From Moscow to Edinburgh

In November 1937, following the official announcement of the IOC decision to relocate the congress to Britain, the academy presidium decided to petition SNK for permission to organize the "All-Union conference on genetics" in 1938 and to invite a number of foreign geneticists, "whose works present particular interest for Soviet genetics," to participate.[90] One reason for such a move was that Soviet geneticists were afraid that they would not be allowed to go to Britain. As early as June 1937, at the meeting of the organizing committee, Komarov had emphasized that "if the congress were held not in the USSR but in Britain, then, of course, our geneticists would not be there."[91] So, in November, at Vavilov's prompting, the academy presidium started preparing for a "separate congress" to be held in Moscow in 1938. In late November 1937, a draft of the SNK resolution on the conference, together with the conference budget and a list of thirty foreign participants, was sent to Molotov.[92]

In February 1938, the letter from the British organizers inviting a large Soviet delegation to come to the congress in Edinburgh occasioned a change in Soviet geneticists' plans. Soviet geneticists clearly considered participation in the international congress vital to the well-being of their discipline. Apparently, the plan of a "separate congress" in Moscow was dropped and Vavilov began immediately to lobby the party patrons for permission to go to Edinburgh.

To a large degree, Vavilov's efforts were prompted by the considerable worsening of geneticists' position during the time that had lapsed since the spring of 1937. A number of people associated with the preparations for the congress in Moscow had fallen victim to the Great Terror for their alleged involvement with various political oppositions. Several members of the original organizing committee, including Gorbunov, Levit, Meister, and Muralov, as well as their party "curators" Bauman and Iakovlev, had been arrested as "enemies of the people" and executed. Moreover, exactly at the time when Crew's invitation arrived, the notorious opponent of "Mendelian" genetics Trofim Lysenko was appointed the VASKhNIL president, seizing administrative control over geneticists' former bastion and forcing geneticists to migrate from agricultural institutions to those of their only remaining base—the USSR Academy of Sciences.

Vavilov carefully crafted his appeals to the authorities. In his letter to Molotov, he notified the head of SNK that he had been elected president of the forthcoming congress and that a number of Soviet geneticists, including Lysenko, had been asked to deliver keynote reports at its various sections.[93] He asked Molotov for permission to accept the presidency over the congress, "for it honors not myself, a humble scientist, but my country; such honor is not often bestowed on Soviet scientists." Vavilov also tried to dispel his patrons' worries about possible "Fascist links" of genetics by emphasizing that "there is every reason to believe that Fascist Germany would not allow its geneticists to take part in the congress, because . . . a Swedish geneticist, stringent antifascist, [Gunnar] Dalhberg, had been appointed the chair of the section on human heredity." Supported by a letter from the trusted president of the USSR Academy of Sciences Komarov,[94] Vavilov's appeal apparently proved effective, for during the following months he and his colleagues were busily preparing for the congress.

However, in May 1938, there came another blow: after a discussion of the academy's plan for that year, SNK decided to completely reorganize the academy—to increase the number of its divisions, enlarge its membership, and "strengthen" the academy with "young scientific forces."[95] The proposed plan dissatisfied SNK, especially in the fields of geology and genetics. As a member of the USSR Supreme Soviet and the VASKhNIL president, Lysenko participated in the fateful SNK meeting that discussed the academy's plan and some historians have suggested that it was his comments that instigated the SNK dissatisfaction with genetics.[96] Whatever the case, as a result of this SNK meeting, the Academy of Sciences presidium created a special commission headed by Lysenko's ally, academician Boris Keller, to "evaluate" research at Vavilov's Institute of Genetics. On the basis of the commission's evaluations, a special session of the presidium severely criticized Vavilov's research and invited Lysenko to work in the institute.[97] Lysenko organized his own department in the institute and staffed it with his closest disciples from Odessa.

In the face of this advance by his opponents, Vavilov decided to use the opportunity afforded by the international congress to remove certain "blemishes" on the image of genetics propagated by Lysenko and his allies. One of the most dangerous accusations against genetics advanced by Lysenko's supporters was its "practical sterility"—the inability of geneticists to provide quick fixes for the "collectivized" agriculture. This apparently inspired Vavilov's letter to Crew in October 1938 with a request to expand the representation of agricultural genetics in the congress program. Vavilov stressed that "there is a great need of connecting the present genetic understanding with the practical achievements of plant and animal breeding, and, of course, this can be done especially well in your country."[98]

During the rest of 1938, preparations of Soviet geneticists continued at full speed. At the beginning of the following year, however, the situation in Soviet genetics deteriorated even further. In January 1939, Lysenko was "elected" to the USSR Academy of Sciences and appointed member of its presidium. Following the election, Lysenko and his cohort launched a new attack on "Mendelian" genetics.[99] Their first target was Kol'tsov's Institute of Experimental Biology.[100] The academy presidium again created a special commission to "examine" the institute's work: Lysenko's most active ideologist, Isaak Prezent, carried out the inspection. As a result, Kol'tsov was dismissed from the directorship.[101]

Geneticists again attempted to organize a counteroffensive. In seeking to improve their position, as they had done at the 1936 discussion, geneticists sought to use the format of a "public discussion." In summer 1938, after the SNK criticism of the Academy of Sciences plan for genetics, the academy presidium had decided to organize a new discussion on "issues in genetics." The impending reorganization of the academy and the subsequent elections delayed the matter, but in March 1939, the general assembly of the academy returned to this issue, deciding that "in 1939 the [academy's] Biology Division will hold a discussion on the main issues in genetics on the basis of debates over the results and research plans of the Institute of Genetics [headed by Vavilov] and the [Odessa] Institute of Genetics and Breeding [headed by Lysenko]."[102]

Shortly thereafter, the newly appointed vice-president Otto Shmidt began to prepare the discussion. He consulted with almost all the geneticists who worked in the academy, including corresponding members Levitskii and Serebrovskii, and collected a large dossier of materials against Lysenko and his team. Serebrovskii even wrote a preliminary draft of the presidium resolution, "On the Genetics Discussion," for adoption at the forthcoming discussion.[103] He also prepared a thirty-page "Short Review of the Practical Applications of Genetics" for Shmidt. Geneticists clearly hoped that "a decisive improvement on the biological and agricultural fronts can come from an authoritative elucidation of the [present] situation by [a discussion on genetics in] the USSR Academy of Sciences."[104] They anticipated that such a discussion would, in Vavilov's words, "dispel the prevailing unhealthy atmosphere."[105]

Meanwhile, their opponents expanded their assault by launching a campaign aimed at changing the syllabi for genetics courses in educational institutes.[106] On June 12, Narkomzem's major newspaper, *Sotsialisticheskoe Zemledelie*, published a letter signed by twenty-four students from the Timiriazev Agricultural Academy, which demanded the complete removal of "formal" genetics from their curricula (including the suppression of existing textbooks on plant breeding) and its replacement with Lysenko's "Michurinist" genetics. Alarmed by the apparent advance by critics of genetics and its possible repercussions for Soviet geneticists' attendance of the international congress, the same day Vavilov fired off a letter to Muller, asking him for help in securing the participation of Soviet geneticists in the Edinburgh congress. A month later, on July 15, Vavilov also sent a long letter to the Secretary of the Central Committee in charge of agriculture Andrei Andreev, asking him to speed up the decision on Soviet geneticists' participation in the Edinburgh congress.[107]

Vavilov's efforts were in vain. What he did not know was that already at the beginning of June, Komarov had sent a special memorandum on the congress to SNK.[108] After recounting the history of the congress's organization in the USSR and its subsequent relocation to Britain, Komarov referred to the decision that had allegedly been adopted by the academy presidium in September 1937 "not to take part in the congress." The academy president stated that there were no "sufficient reasons" to revise this earlier decision. And party bosses obviously agreed with him.

On July 23, the recently appointed deputy-commissar of foreign affairs Andrei Vyshinskii (notorious for his role as the Prosecutor General during the Great Terror and newly "elected" member of the USSR Academy of Sciences) presented the head of the commissariat Viacheslav Molotov a draft of the letter that was to be sent to Edinburgh in the name of Vavilov and his Soviet colleagues, announcing their withdrawal from the congress.[109] Judging by available documents, Vavilov had been asked to prepare a draft cable to Crew, but Vyshinskii found it unsatisfactory and presented Molotov his own version of a longer letter.[110] Molotov approved Vyshinskii's variant and two days later it was forwarded to the Academy of Sciences. Vavilov translated the approved version into English and on the next day it was sent to Edinburgh.[111]

All hopes of Soviet geneticists to attend the congress were shattered.

5　Soviet geneticists and their peers

The convocation of the international genetics congress in Moscow entailed continuous interaction between Soviet geneticists and their foreign peers, as well as among the world's geneticists. In the end, the international genetics community reached a conclusion that, ironically, echoed the Politburo November 1936 decision—Russia was not ready to host an international genetics congress—and moved the congress to Britain. But, of course, the international community's reasons for such a conclusion differed substantially from those of the Politburo. The IOC decision to withdraw the congress from Russia was based on the perception the international genetics community had of what was going on in Soviet genetics and why the Soviets had "postponed" the congress in the first place. But why and how was this perception translated into the decision to relocate the congress?

The international community and its Soviet branch

In the mid-1930s, Soviet geneticists occupied a leading position in world genetics. In quantitative terms—the number of departments, researchers, and publications—it was second only to the United States. According to Robert Kohler's calculations, in 1936–37 Soviet scientists working on Drosophila genetics published more articles than their colleagues in all other European countries and Japan combined and only slightly fewer than US drosophilists.[1] In certain subfields, such as human genetics, Soviet genetics was second to none. As Davenport once admitted: "I have told many students of human genetics of the United States that Russia is taking the lead away from the United States in this subject, which it formerly held."[2] Similarly, in agricultural genetics, the international community regarded research at Vavilov's Institute of Plant Breeding on its worldwide collection of cultivated plants to be outstanding.

By the mid-1930s Soviet geneticists had built networks of close contacts with many foreign, particularly American, colleagues. Vavilov maintained correspondence with hundreds of geneticists throughout the world, in addition to extensive personal travel that brought him in touch with leading geneticists in various countries.[3] During their American tenures, Agol, Dobzhansky, Karpechenko, Levit, and Navashin had established contacts not only with the members of the groups with

Plate 16 During the Fifth international genetics congress in Berlin, September 1927. Left to right: Leslie C. Dunn, Bruno Duringen, and Aleksandr Serebrovskii at Duringen's Poultry Museum in Berlin. Courtesy of APS.

whom they had been associated as Rockefeller fellows, but also with specialists in their respective fields all over the United States. Dobzhansky, after his Rockefeller stipend had ended, stayed with Morgan's group at Caltech and became a kind of unofficial "ambassador" for his compatriots.[4] Agol and Levit worked not only at Muller's department in Texas, but also spent the summer of 1931 at Davenport's lab in Cold Spring Harbor. While working at Babcock's department in Berkeley, Navashin and Karpechenko spent much time at Morgan's lab at Caltech in Pasadena. Similarly, the visits to the Soviet Union of leading Western geneticists, including Baur, Bridges, Darlington, Dunn, Goldschmidt, Huxley, and Muller, introduced them to a large number of their Russian colleagues. Muller's move to the Soviet Union in 1933 further strengthened the international community's connection to its Soviet "branch." It was the personal contacts and authority of Karpechenko, Kol'tsov, Levit, Muller, Navashin, Serebrovskii, and Vavilov, combined with the tremendous amount of work done by Soviet geneticists, that made Moscow a natural, though not for all foreign geneticists equally appealing, choice as the place for an international genetics congress.

The news of the congress's cancellation activated a small group of Western geneticists, which included Darlington, Demerec, Dunn, and Mohr. This group spearheaded all the activities on "saving the congress." They regularly corresponded with each other and with Soviet geneticists. They in turn mobilized a number of their colleagues to join them in the action. As Dunn reported to Demerec the next day after the *New York Times* announcement:

> We did the following things here today: I sent a telegram to Morgan giving him news of cancellation of the Congress and of arrest of Vavilov and Agol and asked him to telegraph the Soviet ambassador at Washington and inquire [of] the status of Vavilov, Agol and Levit. Conklin, as president of the American Association [for the Advancement of Science], sent a similar telegram and says that if the news is true he will have a resolution prepared for the whole Association to vote on. I wired Emerson the same and asked him to get [the Secretary of Agriculture] Henry Wallace to see somebody in the Soviet Embassy.[5] . . . Blakeslee got in touch with President [John C.] Merriam[6] for the same purpose and [Franz] Boas wired direct to the Soviet ambassador. I expected to do these things in conjunction with you, but since you were in Washington I went ahead after talking with [Franz] Schrader, [Walter] Landauer and [Alexander] Weinstein. I suppose that you would also make some inquiries as representative of the Genetics Society.[7]

The first concern of Western geneticists was the "safety of the three men"[8] mentioned in the *New York Times* dispatch. Dunn thought that "the really serious aspect [of the whole affair] seems to be that two members of the organizing committee, Vavilov and Agol, are accused of treason and Levit, the secretary, is under suspicion." He opined: "I think most geneticists would agree that the three men accused are sound scientists and that their offenses, if any, have to be judged apart from their activities as geneticists or as organizers of the congress."[9] In the following campaign on behalf of their Soviet colleagues, Western geneticists were generous with their praise, particularly for Vavilov. As Demerec put it in his letter to Troyanovskii:

> Professor Vavilov is one of the leading biologists of the world. His name and his work are known in every corner of the globe. His contributions to science as a whole and particularly to theoretical and applied science in Russia are outstanding. It is a great shock to all scientists to learn that a man of whose scientific accomplishments every other nation would be proud is arrested because of his scientific work.[10]

Davenport used almost the same language in his letter to the US Secretary of State:

> Vavilov have been regarded by geneticists everywhere as the leading geneticist of the USSR. His great learning, his broad ideas, his tremendous energy are of incalculable value not merely to the USSR but to agricultural science all over the world. Owing to the relation between the progress of genetics and that of national wealth in agriculture and other basic departments of national life, to interfere with the work of a man like Vavilov is committing not only national suicide but dealing a blow in the face of civilization.[11]

Davenport also gave a similar praise for Levit.

In a few days, the *Izvestiia* editorial, followed by responses of Soviet diplomats and Vavilov's cable to the *New York Times*, assured Western geneticists that Vavilov and Levit were (at least for the moment) safe and that they could do nothing to help Agol. At this point, Western geneticists turned their full attention to the question of what to do about the congress.

The personal

The news of the congress's cancellation caused quite a commotion among the members of the international genetics community. But their reaction to the news varied significantly, according to their individual political sympathies, scientific interests, and institutional agendas.

First of all, the cancellation opened an opportunity for some other national group to step in and to host the congress. Several national communities tried to seize this opportunity. For instance, the secretary of the Dutch Genetics Society A. L. Hagedoorn suggested to Mohr that the congress be held in Holland.[12] However, the Dutch representative on the IOC, Tine Tammes, did not share Hagedoorn's optimism about organizing the congress in Amsterdam, largely due to the impossibility of raising sufficient funds, and Mohr did not pursue the issue.[13]

Francis A. Crew's offer to host the congress in Edinburgh proved much more successful. At least initially, many British geneticists were unwilling to take up the burden of organizing the congress. As a staunch supporter of socialist ideas at the time, the British representative on the IOC, J. B. S. Haldane, was strongly in favor of having the congress in Moscow. As he put it to Mohr in January 1937, "if the congress can be held in the USSR next year, we had better wait till then."[14] (Indeed, he voted for Moscow even after the British Genetical Society had extended its invitation to host the congress.) Haldane was not very optimistic about holding the congress in Britain, if it proved impossible to have it in Russia, largely due to the lack of institutional support. Indeed, although numerically the British Genetical Society was probably the fourth largest in the world, institutionally British genetics was not very strong. There were practically no specialized genetics departments within the British university system.[15] The largest establishment involved in genetics research was the John Innes Horticultural Institution, where, after Bateson's death in 1926, Haldane became a consulting geneticist. However, in 1936 Haldane resigned from his position there and was working exclusively as the chair of genetics at University College, London. Furthermore, in the summer of 1937, the chair was eliminated, as Haldane remarked, "probably because I discovered linkage in man when I should have been asking millionaires for money."[16] Haldane became the College's chair of biometrics, where, as he admitted in one of his letters to Mohr, he did not even have a secretary.

Crew did everything he could to convince Mohr that Edinburgh was the only place for the congress. In his first letter of February 20, 1937, Crew lamented that other British geneticists would perhaps prefer the congress to be held in London. But, he continued: "London, in my own opinion and experience, is one of the worst places to have a congress in. It is so full of people that the members of the congress never seem to meet and they are swallowed up in the hugeness of the Metropolis."[17] To show that he was not alone in considering Russia an inappropriate place for the congress, Crew also persuaded his friend R. Ruggles Gates to write Mohr a letter. "Since the debacle of the Russian attempt to hold a Genetical Congress this year I feel, as one of the British Government representatives at the last congress,[18] a certain responsibility in connection with the next," explained Gates and asked Mohr to keep him posted on "further steps" regarding the matter.[19]

Mohr was, of course, delighted to have an offer from Britain,[20] and Crew kept courting the IOC chairman. In early April, he invited Mohr to come to Britain.[21] As current President of the Zoology Section of the British Association for the Advancement of Science, Crew had the privilege of inviting distinguished foreign guests to the association's annual meeting. So he put Mohr's name (the second invitee was Raymond Pearl) on the list: "Do come across. You will have a very good time, and, of course, I hope you will bring Mrs. Mohr with you. You will be suitably entertained, and I think that you will enjoy the meeting." Crew also began lobbying his fellow-members of the British Genetical Society for supporting the idea of holding the congress in Britain.

Crew's efforts to have the congress in Edinburgh were almost certainly motivated by his desire to improve his own and his institute's rather modest and peripheral standing within the British genetics community.[22] (This he accomplished. Indeed, shortly before the congress opened in Edinburgh, Crew had been elected to the Royal Society.) Crew was undoubtedly a very able administrator.[23] In 1929 he had managed to obtain a large Rockefeller grant to convert a small Experimental Station for Animal Breeding loosely affiliated with Edinburgh University into an Institute of Animal Genetics, which soon became the second largest genetics institution in Britain.[24] He also managed to bring in a number of talented young refugee geneticists from Europe, including Peo Koller, Charlotte Auerbach, and Guido Pontecorvo (in 1937), which strengthened the institute's staff considerably. Alas, the leading "lights" of British genetics, including Fisher, Punnett, Haldane, Huxley, and Darlington among others, all worked in the South—in Cambridge, Oxford, or London. Although all of them occasionally visited Edinburgh, not a single meeting of the British Genetical Society was ever held there. Crew certainly felt that neither he himself nor his institute got the credit and appreciation they rightly deserved. The prospect of hosting the congress in Edinburgh promised to change that. Indeed, in late June of 1937, as Crew excitedly informed Mohr, "for the first time in history [the society] has left the South and crossed the border to hold its meeting here."[25] It was at this meeting that British geneticists decided that "if, in the opinion of the International Committee, it be impossible to hold the Congress in Russia in 1938, then the Genetical Society Committee will welcome the invitation from the International Committee to hold the Congress in this country in 1939."

A person favoring a conspiratorial reading of history might even suggest that the rumor of Kol'tsov and Serebrovskii's arrests, which so profoundly affected the fate of the congress, had originated all too conveniently with Crew's right-hand man—Peo Koller. Haldane, for one, considered it wholly inappropriate to have the congress in

Edinburgh, exactly because of that.[26] Similarly, one could easily imagine that Crew invited Muller to come to work at his institute with a goal of ensuring that the congress meet in Edinburgh and not in Cambridge, Oxford, or London. Initially, Crew was not at all taken with the idea of having Muller in Edinburgh. As he remarked in a letter to Mohr in June 1937: "Huxley now writes to me to find Muller a job, but I doubt very much that I can, and I am not quite sure that I particularly want to."[27] But apparently Crew soon realized that Muller's presence in Edinburgh would greatly enhance his chances of convincing his colleagues to hold the congress there. Conversely, Muller's rather drastic change of mind about having the congress in Russia during that autumn might well have been connected to Crew's timely offer to come to Edinburgh, for after Muller's decision to leave Russia, his attempts to secure a position elsewhere proved absolutely fruitless.[28]

The attitude of the largest group in the discipline—American geneticists—to the events in Russia varied considerably. Being a conservative with strong anti-Soviet feelings, Robert Cook was opposed to accepting the Soviet invitation from the start and he deliberately used his control over the *Journal of Heredity* to convey to the world's geneticists his personal opposition. Characteristically, many Soviet and Western geneticists considered Cook's actions improper.[29] Other members of the American Genetics Society, however, were more concerned with the state of their discipline than any political events in Russia. In his capacity as the society's secretary-treasurer, Milislav Demerec took upon himself the task of keeping his colleagues apprised of the Soviet developments, he regularly circulated all available information through his extensive mailing list, which included not only US geneticists, but also secretaries of genetics societies in Germany, Britain, Japan, Sweden, and other countries.[30] Demerec's personal support for holding the congress in Moscow almost certainly stemmed from his deep involvement in Drosophila genetics: in 1934 he and Bridges had founded the DIS—Drosophila Information Service—and Soviet geneticists were the largest group outside the United States contributing to this field of studies.[31] In May 1937, after receiving Mohr's first memorandum, the US representative on the IOC Emerson questioned more than sixty of his colleagues on the subject. The results of his poll were revealing. A majority of US geneticists (forty-five) were "definitely opposed to accepting the invitation of Russia to hold the Seventh Congress in Moscow in 1938." Less than one-third of them (eighteen) were in favor of having the congress in Moscow. Emerson himself felt that he should join the minority, largely because he considered it important to lend "moral support" for Soviet geneticists in times of trouble.[32]

But, of course, the key person behind the IOC decision was its head Otto Mohr. His attitude to the issue underwent a striking transformation—from a firm intention to remedy the situation by personally coming to Moscow to an elaborate effort to relocate the congress to Britain. It seems that Mohr's change of mind was brought about mainly by political events in the Soviet Union. Being a liberal with a favorable attitude towards socialist ideals, Mohr was dismayed by the show-trials of the opposition conducted in Moscow in 1936–37, as were many other left-leaning intellectuals in the West. Shortly before the *New York Times* report on the cancellation of the congress, Mohr wrote to Dunn: "The killing of Zinov'ev,

Kamenev and the others was a terrible blow to all us who looked to Russia for hopes in the future. Not the least here in Norway where we have Trotsky as our guest."[33] Furthermore, exactly at the time when Mohr learned about the troubles with the congress and offered to come to Moscow to help the Soviet organizers with settling the issue, the second Moscow show-trial began. As he noted in another letter to Dunn on January 25, 1937:

> Just now everything is upset by the equally abhorrent and tragic Radek trial. Isn't it fantastic and incredible? For me who really believed in a sound development in [the] USSR, the Zinov'ev–Kamenev trial and now this has been a terrific blow.[34]

Not all Western geneticists agreed with Mohr's assessment of the Soviet situation. The British representative on the IOC Haldane, for one, wrote to Mohr in February 1937:

> I'm afraid I don't share your gloom about the recent trials in Moscow. I think it is very remarkable that the people who made the revolution in 1917 didn't start shooting one another for 17 years. This is at least a record time![35]

Nevertheless, the "blow" of the unfolding Great Terror profoundly shaped Mohr's attitude towards the possibility of holding the congress in Moscow and moved him to project his own adverse opinion on to the IOC members through his memoranda.

The collective

Despite the plausibility of all these individual reasons and actions as a source of the IOC decision, to concentrate exclusively on the "personal" dimensions of the story would lead us to overlook a larger issue—the collective response of the international genetics community, which was shaped not only by individual political preferences, research and institutional agendas, as well as personal likes and dislikes, but also by Western geneticists' perceptions of what was going on in Russia and why the Soviets had cancelled the congress in the first place. In trying to understand how these perceptions were formed we need to examine what information was available to foreign geneticists, how it was communicated, and how it shaped their views.

First of all, during the entire debacle with the congress in Moscow (from December 1936 through September 1937) foreign geneticists had no person-to-person contacts with their Soviet colleagues. In fact, not a single Soviet geneticist had been allowed outside the country since 1933. Only H. J. Muller had been allowed to work in the Soviet Union and travel outside of it, which made him a key "ganglion" in all the actions regarding the congress there.

But Muller's position in the whole affair was dubious at best. On the one hand, he actively lobbied his colleagues for holding the congress in Moscow. On the other hand, even before the congress's cancellation, in the fall of 1936, he had privately let his friends know that he "was not overenthusiastic about recent developments in the USSR" and "if he could get a decent job somewhere else after the congress, he would be glad to accept."[36] When in early December 1936, Muller sent out his letters announcing that it was "found impracticable" to hold the congress in Russia next summer, many Western geneticists were quite uncertain of what to make of them. As Dobzhansky stressed in a letter to Darlington written on January 1, 1937:

> Muller's explanations are undoubtedly humbug, and he cannot be expected to tell the truth. The fact is that he wants to extract himself from the socialist paradise, and I have what seems to me a good guess why. But the evidence is inconclusive, so I keep silent.[37]

Furthermore, in March 1937 Muller left Russia for Spain, which was promptly reported in *Science*, and, although the report mentioned that Muller was planning "later to resume his work in Moscow," for many this was a clear sign that he was fleeing the Soviet regime.[38]

Aside from information coming through Muller, Soviet geneticists maintained contacts with their Western counterparts through correspondence only. However, during the 1930s the flow of letters between Soviet and Western scientists was

Plate 17 C. Bridges (standing) delivers a lecture at the Laboratory of Genetics in Leningrad in November 1931. (From *N. I. Vavilov. Dokumenty i Fotografii*, St Petersburg: Nauka, 1995.)

steadily diminishing. This trend became particularly pronounced with the beginning of the Great Terror, when any foreign contact became a dangerous liability for a Soviet citizen. Many Soviet scientists (not only geneticists) simply stopped responding to their colleagues' letters, which caused much anxiety to their correspondents. For instance, Babcock told Mohr that he had not received a single letter from his friend Navashin for almost a year, though he himself had regularly written to Moscow and even sent Navashin a Christmas present.[39] Similarly, Dobzhansky noted in a letter to Darlington: "my friends [in Russia] are afraid to write me letters even about their children, the weather, and such other state secrets."[40]

For a majority of Western geneticists, then, the main source of information on the Soviet events was the *New York Times*: the initial dispatch from Moscow on December 14, the editorial "Science and Dictators" on December 19, the translation of the *Izvestiia* editorial on December 22, and Vavilov's telegram on December 23, accompanied by yet another sarcastic editorial comment.[41] Furthermore, the newspaper continued the coverage of events in Soviet genetics beyond the cancellation of the congress. On December 27, it described the continuing attack on Levit at the Congress of Neurologists,[42] and on the next day, its correspondent cabled in a large article on the discussion between Soviet geneticists and Lysenko's followers.[43] European newspapers seemed to have kept a total silence on the subject,[44] but several of the *New York Times* publications were reprinted in *Science, Nature,* and *Journal of Heredity,* which made them available to scientists outside the United States.

Although some Europeans did not take the *New York Times* publications seriously, commenting that it was "well known with what readiness newspapers, and especially American ones, publish the most fantastical information,"[45] apart from the blunder with Vavilov's arrest, the *New York Times* dispatch of December 14 was surprisingly accurate. The dispatch was not signed, but most likely its author was a *New York Times* correspondent Harold Denny: he was covering Soviet science and culture for the paper.[46] The content of the cable suggests that Denny obtained his information from someone closely related to the congress and its organization and privy to Soviet geneticists' inside information, as Agol's arrest was not public knowledge at the time. Denny knew personally several Soviet geneticists, for instance, Levit. In 1935, he had even published a story about research at Levit's institute.[47] But given Levit's recent troubles, it seems highly unlikely that he would have made contact with the American correspondent. Furthermore, given the atmosphere of the Great Terror, with its suspicion of everything foreign, it seems unlikely that any Soviet citizen would have made such a contact.

Denny, however, also knew H. J. Muller and had even interviewed him for the newspaper.[48] Most likely it was Muller who gave Denny another "interview," for he was certainly one of the very few people in the know of all the events reported in the *New York Times* dispatch. At the beginning of December, Muller had already informed his closest friends that "it was found impracticable to hold the congress" in Moscow. He certainly knew that the congress had been cancelled by the "order of the Soviet government." He definitely knew about the ongoing attack on Levit and the forthcoming discussion with Lysenko and his supporters.

He probably knew about the arrest of his former student Agol. The blunder with Vavilov's arrest may well have been "an inadvertent mistake in transmission," but more likely it was a misunderstanding on the part of the correspondent. It is safe to assume that after telling Denny about Agol's arrest, Muller might have mentioned a possibility that Vavilov was in danger of being arrested as well. Given the unfolding Great Terror, Muller perhaps even felt threatened himself.

Muller undoubtedly thought that a publication in the leading American newspaper would help remedy the situation, dispelling the personal danger for his friends. Furthermore, the timing of the "interview" suggests that Muller perhaps hoped that it could force the government officials to reconsider their decision on the cancellation. He was aware of Vavilov's efforts in this direction, notably the draft letter Vavilov wrote for Gorbunov to be sent to Molotov, which warned the head of the Soviet government that "a complete abandonment of the congress could provoke undesirable speculations and declarations undermining the prestige of Soviet science."

Whether it had been Muller who "spilled the beans," and whatever his motives might have been, the *New York Times* publications definitely prodded the members of the international genetics community to appeal for clarification to Soviet representatives abroad, as well as to Soviet scientists. By the end of January 1937, the Soviet organizing committee had received more than twenty letters from geneticists from all over the world asking "whether the holding of the Seventh International Congress of Genetics in Russia in 1937 has been definitely cancelled."[49] At the time, Soviet geneticists themselves did not know the answer and hence simply did not respond to their colleagues' inquiries.

The answers Western geneticists did receive—from Soviet diplomats, the *Izvestiia* editorial, and Vavilov's cable—created confusion over the question of who had been responsible for the "postponement." The *New York Times* had stated that it was the Soviet government, but the *Izvestiia* official announcement shifted the blame to scientists who had allegedly needed "more time for preparations." Soviet geneticists, first of all, Vavilov, repeated the official version in their communications with Western colleagues. As a result, although a few Western geneticists who had received private messages from Moscow knew (and many others suspected) that the congress had been "postponed" by the Soviet government, some Western geneticists seemed (or perhaps wanted) to believe the official statement. Hagedoorn even decided to rebuke Vavilov:

> I do not doubt your statement that several letters have been received from scientists requesting the postponement of the Congress in order better to prepare for it, but I must say I am rather surprised that your Committee has yielded to those requests, as I know from experience that one of the chief difficulties in organizing such a Congress lies rather in the excess of papers presented than in their dearth! You must not be surprised if you will find that most of the non-Russian geneticists have the impression that your Committee or your government or where ever the blame rests, have let us down very badly.[50]

Similarly, Crew felt it necessary to declare to Mohr that,

> if [Soviet geneticists] bowed the knee to political pressure, then I think this is
> blameworthy, and if they have acted, as the published explanation seems to
> suggest, entirely without reference to the International Committee, then I
> think such conduct is entirely damnable.[51]

Many Western geneticists wanted to get reliable information on what had
happened in Moscow before they would make any decision. They understood
that such information "can only be obtained through personal contacts," and that
was why they urged Mohr to undertake his trip to Moscow.[52] As Dobzhansky
lamented in March 1937: "If Mohr has been in Moscow the whole situation may
be now known from an authentic source."[53] However, after postponing his trip for
several months Mohr finally decided not to go, thus cutting off the opportunity to
learn first-hand what had happened and what was happening in Moscow.

Soviet geneticists did communicate with their foreign colleagues through
"official" channels: Vavilov's cable to the *New York Times* was reprinted in *Science* and
the Soviet organizing committee's letters were circulated by Mohr and thus were
available to the IOC members and the international community as a whole. In
addition, in the spring of 1937 the organizing committee sent out a number of
letters signed by all the leading Soviet geneticists to the IOC members and other
influential foreign geneticists, trying to assure their colleagues that there "were all
necessary conditions for holding the congress in Moscow." Furthermore, Soviet
geneticists deployed their own personal networks to transmit the same information to their foreign colleagues: they sent a number of "confidential" letters to
their personal friends and acquaintances.[54] Yet, all these letters failed to change
decisively the opinion of the international community, because of a widespread
distrust of all communications from Russia. As Haldane opined in one of his
letters to Mohr: "You must remember that the news reaching many members of
the committee from the Soviet Union is entirely unreliable."[55]

To a large degree, this distrust was a by-product of a particular culture developed by Soviet scientists in adaptation to the heavy political pressure from the
party-state apparatus.[56] When they did correspond with their colleagues abroad,
they often used doubletalk, saying one thing in their private messages and another
in their "official" letters, as illustrated by Vavilov's correspondence with Mohr.
Soviet geneticists often peppered even private messages with official slogans and
clichés. For instance, in his letter to Babkock, Navashin repeated the official cas-
tigation of Agol as "an enemy of the people."[57] While in the Soviet Union this
doubletalk was imperative for survival and was well understood by all "native
speakers," it contributed considerably to the confusion in the West. As Mohr
lamented in a letter to Muller: "Not to be able to trust the information you receive
creates a feeling that is unbearable. And not to dare to write openly, even to
friends, for fear that the letter may bring them in difficulties, feels still worse."[58]
But, personal feelings aside, this mistrust forced Western geneticists to place much
greater trust than was ever warranted on the "eyewitness" accounts of

fellow-travelers and journalists like Roald Lund and on the advice of "experts" in the matters Soviet like the Norwegian ambassador to the Soviet Union, who advised Mohr that it would be unsafe for him to go to Moscow.[59]

The lack of reliable information from the Soviet Union, and the distrust of what little information was available, paved the way for wild rumors and speculations. For instance, Dobzhansky wrote to Dunn in March 1937:

> I have heard a rumor, allegedly based on an information coming from Moscow, that Dr. Muller has been arrested and kept in a socialistic jail (which of course exists in order to re-educate the "criminals" rather than to punish them). I hope this is nonsense, but do you know anything to prove that it is?[60]

As we have seen, in May 1937, the story of the Serebrovskii and Kol'tsov arrests circulated in Britain and made its way to Norway, while similar rumors of mass arrests of Soviet geneticists surfaced in the United States.

It was these rumors and the assumptions Western geneticists made on the basis of available information that guided their actions and opinions. Many Western geneticists assumed that the Soviet authorities were somehow ill-disposed towards genetics and geneticists. Dunn, for instance, thought that the Soviet authorities saw "something inherently counterrevolutionary in Mendelian genetics."[61] Despite the numerous declarations of Soviet geneticists to the contrary and despite the fact that the Soviet government did extend a new invitation for the congress, this assumption held many Western geneticists captive and profoundly shaped their perceptions of events in the USSR. For instance, Vavilov sent Mohr the bulletins of the December VASKhNIL session in order to show him that Soviet geneticists could freely discuss their "disagreements" with Lysenko's followers, but Mohr read them as a proof of "a marked tendency towards political coloring of facts as well as of opinions."[62]

The political

The story of the genetics congress illuminates not only the importance of available information and the ways it was communicated through the international community, but also the even greater importance of the political context in which that information was perceived. In September 1939, in his report on the congress's work in Edinburgh, Crew observed: "The chief qualifications demanded of those who undertake the organization of an international scientific conference in these days would seem to be an unwarrantable optimism and a complete disregard for current political events."[63] Yet in their attempts to set up the international congress, geneticists found themselves continuously caught in the "force field" of political tensions among Hitler's Germany, Stalin's Russia, and Western democracies.

Many Western geneticists viewed the situation in Soviet genetics through the prism of German genetics and considered the situation in both countries to be very similar. As Cook noted in one of his letters to the Soviet ambassador Troyanovskii: "We cannot avoid expressing our regret that Soviet Union scientists seem in danger of being exposed to the same kind of mental crucifixion that German scientists have recently suffered under the Nazi regime."[64] Not only did many Western geneticists see the political regimes in both countries as dictator-ships under which "academic freedom" did not and could not exist, but in both countries they also saw their discipline becoming a "red-hot political issue."[65]

Since Hitler's ascent to power, the persecution of left-wing intellectuals combined with the anti-Jewish legislation forced many geneticists to leave Germany. At the very time when the troubles with the congress began, in November 1936, even the German representative on the IOC, Richard Goldschmidt, moved to the United States to join Babkock's genetics department at Berkeley. Their colleagues, particularly in Britain and the United States, spared no effort in helping German émigré geneticists to find jobs outside of Germany.[66] Yet, despite the attempts by sev-eral German émigrés (notably Landauer and Schaxel) to induce the international genetics community into waging an organized campaign against the persecution of their colleagues in Germany, the community as a whole appeared reluctant to take a collective action.[67] As Davenport remarked in his answer to Landauer's solicitation in November 1935:

> Though science is international and the advancement of any scientific worker is of interest to all the workers in the same field, still I am in some doubt as to how far the scientific workers in one country should interfere in the public policy of another country, even though that policy affects the scientific work of a colleague in that country.

He deemed any action on the part of world geneticists fruitless: "You, like me, know of many . . . cases in which scientific colleagues have been cruelly handled. We are glad to help them individually in any way we can, but there is no use to write protests to Hr. Hitler."[68] (A year later, after the report on Vavilov's alleged arrest, Davenport apparently changed his mind and decided that writing protests to "Comrade Stalin" might be of some use.)

Geneticists all over the world had watched in alarm the growing deployment of "genetics language" in Nazi propaganda and political pronouncements, as well as the mounting usage of the Nazi rhetoric of Aryan racism by certain German col-leagues. As Mohr confided to Dunn, a colleague of Mohr's who had recently spent a month in Berlin "was perfectly horrified at the wild and barbaric spirit down there."[69] This explains why, when German émigrés Julius Schaxel and Walter Landauer initiated the request in the spring of 1936 that the program of the Moscow congress include a discussion on "genetics as related to race theo-ries," more than thirty leading American geneticists eagerly supported this initia-tive, as did some of their Soviet and British colleagues. Obviously geneticists wanted to dissociate their discipline from "Fascist nonsense."

In the eyes of many people abroad (and not just geneticists), the situation in the Soviet Union during 1936–37—the growing Great Terror with mass arrests and executions of "oppositionists"—was very similar to that in Hitler's Germany. Exactly at that time, genetics also became a politically charged issue in the Soviet

Plate 18 Julius Schaxel in his laboratory in Moscow, 1935? (From Dieter Fricke, *Julius Schaxel, 1887–1943: Leben und Kampf eines marxistischen deutschen Naturwissenschaftlers und Hochschullehrers*, Leipzig: Urania-Verlag, 1964.)

Union, largely for two reasons: the attack on Levit (and human genetics writ large) and Lysenko's attack on "formal" genetics. The apparent similarity of the general situations in Germany and the Soviet Union led many Western geneticists to believe that the reported arrests of Soviet colleagues had been related to their scientific views. At the same time, many Western geneticists attributed the congress's cancellation to the Soviet authorities' negative attitude towards their field as a whole, which had been inspired to a certain degree by the Nazi abuses of genetics.

Many Western scientists actually believed the *New York Times* headline— "Nazi Racial Theories Ascribed to Some Scientists Causes the Dropping of World Congress." And this caused some of them much anguish. As Jennings confessed in a letter to Dunn: "I fear that the movement which was made to press upon the Congress the desirability of a discussion of race problem (I signed the letter) was an unfortunate one."[70]

When in the spring of 1936 Landauer had undertaken the initiative to request that the Soviet organizing committee include in the congress's proceedings a discussion on race, not all US geneticists had been of the same mind about the proposal. For example, a leading US specialist in human genetics, Davenport, refused to add his signature to the request, because he thought it had been formulated in too vague terms and hence "it might arouse just an angry, political debate and bring genetics into bad repute."[71] Although they supported the necessity of such a discussion as a matter of principle, some geneticists thought that an international congress, particularly one held in the USSR, was not the best place for the discussion.

One geneticist suggested that it would be better if the issue were discussed instead at a meeting of the American Genetics Society, "though even in this gathering," he surmised, "it will be hard for some members to avoid letting personal factors influence their scientific opinions."[72] Nevertheless, he was certain that the society was "big enough and cosmopolitan enough" to express a weighty opinion on its own, and it would be "politically safe for its members to follow their scientific data to whatever conclusions they may lead," while, he was certain, "neither Russian, German, Italian, nor Japanese geneticists <u>dare</u> do this."[73] He further suggested that the society:

> might ask for its report to be included in the Proceedings of the International Congress, and that it would be wisest to ask for this inclusion without public discussion of it, but perhaps accompanied by an individual secret vote, with the total recorded, to indicate to what extent the International Congress approved of it.

Other US geneticists, however, thought that the whole idea was a bad one. As Demerec put it to Landauer: "As a geneticist I would hate to see our congress involved in a question which borders on politics and which would stir up a great deal of both desirable and undesirable publicity."[74] Some geneticists were concerned that the proposed discussion would put their German colleagues in an awkward position:

> At the forthcoming congress is it not probable that any geneticists present who may have political opinions favorable to the present German government will automatically be driven into a defensive attitude (whatever their real scientific opinion may be) on practices adopted by Germany? If German official delegates are there, they will certainly have to support their Government's practices. On the other hand, if German representatives are not present, it would be claimed by German propagandists that any conclusion unfavorable to them, which might be reached by the congress, was biased and not an international one.[75]

Others worried that the request could bring Soviet colleagues into trouble. Demerec, for example, warned Landauer:

> As you know, there is less freedom for discussion in Russia than in any other country, including both Germany and Italy. The idea of inequality among individuals of the human species is against the doctrine of those now in power and a discussion on this subject may not be tolerated. I recall that a few years ago one of the prominent Russian geneticists was in trouble because he expressed his view on this subject too freely.

Demerec's worries were certainly confirmed by private messages from Soviet colleagues, who claimed that among the reasons for the congress's cancellation:

> some influence had the inclusion of the question on racial problems which was included according to the request of thirty-two American geneticists. The Soviet government found it not reasonable to have the discussion of this problem in our country, where this problem does not exist at all.[76]

Characteristically, as a way to remedy the situation, Dobzhansky suggested in December 1936: "It might be good if some American geneticists would compose a sort of short popular treatise on the subject 'genetics is the opposite of a Nazi theory', and send such a treatise to Moscow."[77] However, he was not very hopeful about the success of such an action.

After December 1936, it was clear to many scientists involved that even if the congress were to meet in Moscow, the discussion of "race in relation to genetics" would not be possible. They evidently deemed such a situation unacceptable. As Jennings remarked:

> I have something of a feeling that [the congress] should not meet in a country where free and open discussion is not permitted, and it was [this] consideration that induced me to sign the letter [asking for the inclusion of the discussion in the congress's program].[78]

The suspicion that the proposed discussion on race might have led to the congress's cancellation weighed heavily on Western geneticists' minds.

However, what appeared even more important in shaping Western geneticists' reaction to the events in the Soviet Union was Lysenko's attack against Mendelian genetics. The December discussion between Vavilov's and Lysenko's supporters proved to be a decisive factor in moving the congress to Britain. Accounts of the discussion, which appeared in the *New York Times* and *Nature*, characterized it as "an attack on modern genetic theory."[79] This raised doubts regarding the viability of holding the congress in Moscow, even though Soviet geneticists persistently tried to convince their colleagues that there were no problems anymore. As Cook pointed out to Dunn: "What assurances are there that the Congress would be held if Mr. Lysenko did some more yarovizing?"[80] These doubts certainly played an important role in shaping the attitude of many Western geneticists. As Mohr candidly admitted in one of his letters:

> the only thing which gave me a real base for the course taken was the Bulletin from the [VASKhNIL] congress of which Vavilov sent me a copy. When I had had it translated I realized that Moscow could not possibly be the proper place for a congress now.[81]

But why, we should ask ourselves, did Lysenko scare Mohr so much? Obviously, not all Western geneticists shared this fear. Emerson, for one, suggested to Mohr that: "It would be perfectly proper to have both sides of the dispute presented in the papers and discussions at the Congress."[82] The answer, I believe, lay in what, for many geneticists, Lysenko's attack signified, namely—the infringement by the Soviet political authorities on the sacred territory of science.

As Nils Roll-Hansen has demonstrated convincingly, Lysenko's work on vernalization, for which he was primarily known outside of the Soviet Union, fitted well within the framework of contemporary plant physiology.[83] Lysenko's ideas on manipulating stages in plant development attracted favorable attention from a number of plant physiologists, particularly in Britain and the United States, who tried to repeat his experiments.[84] They confirmed that vernalization actually worked: it was indeed possible to "skip" certain stages and speed up the development of plants in the laboratory. Some Western scientists shared Vavilov's opinion that vernalization could be a useful tool in plant breeding. Lysenko's claims that vernalization was a very practical and profitable agricultural technique were received with much more caution. As the head of the Cambridge Imperial Bureau of Plant Genetics, P. S. Hudson, asserted in 1936: "It is in the application of vernalization to practical agriculture that doubts remains."[85] Lysenko's claims that changes induced by vernalization could become inherited (that is, the winter wheat could be "transformed" into the spring one, and vice versa), as well as his "critique" of Mendelian genetics, were summarily dismissed by Western geneticists as a naive Lamarkism.

The prominence given to Lysenko and his agricultural nostrums in the Soviet Union led Western geneticists to assume that Lysenko's position vis-à-vis genetics was also supported by the Soviet authorities and represented an "official view" on genetics. As Jennings put it: "It is a real disaster that [the Soviets] have decided to join Germany in prescribing official doctrines to science."[86] In the wake of the "troubles" with the congress in December 1936, the American Society of Naturalists voiced this concern in a special resolution that lamented "an increasing tendency in certain parts of the world to require of investigators the conformity of their research to officially prescribed doctrines."[87] Despite Soviet geneticists' numerous declarations to the contrary, Western geneticists perceived Lysenko's attack on genetics as instigated by the Soviet authorities.

In the summer of 1937, Muller pleaded with his US colleagues:

> Let us do what we can to stand behind worthy colleagues like Vavilov, Karpechenko, Levit, Navashin, Serebrovskii, Kolt'sov, in an effective way, at a time that is critical for them and for our science. We cannot be hurt by it, we are not entering a firing line ourselves, we have only a chance to do good, to further the concepts for which we all—regardless of political shade—have worked and fought all our lives.[88]

But his passionate plea could not overcome the international community's mode of operations. As Mohr wrote to Dunn at almost the same time:

> One main point remains: Ought we to go to Moscow in order to give support to the decent geneticists who are in a critical situation? This argument carries

Plate 19 H. J. Muller (second on the left in the first row) with his co-workers at the Institute of Genetics in Moscow, 1936? Courtesy of Lilly Library, Indiana University, Bloomington, Indiana.

for me a heavy weight. But, do you know Dunn, as far as I am able to judge, the situation is such that open support to them may well bring them into great difficulties. I have just discussed this point with our Moscow ambassador, an old liberal whom I know well, and he thinks that the last mentioned eventuality is the most probable one.[89]

Once again, the advice of a "specialist in Soviet affairs" proved more effective than the plea of a person who knew the situation from the inside.

In the end, the fate of the congress was formally decided by the IOC vote. In the spring of 1937, Vavilov calculated that out of fifteen IOC members, the representatives of Austria (Tschermak), Britain (Haldane), Denmark (Winge), Finland (Federley), France (Vilmorin), Norway (Mohr), Sweden (Nilsson-Elle), and, of course, he himself would vote for holding the congress in Moscow, while the representatives of Germany (Wettstein[90]), Italy (Ghigi), and Switzerland (Schlaginhaufen) would certainly vote against it.[91] We can only speculate on what was the basis of Vavilov's calculations. But it seems likely that he thought that the German, Italian, and Swiss votes would be determined by the political relations of these countries to the Soviet Union.[92] On the other hand, he counted on the votes of Vilmorin, Haldane, Tschermak, Federley, Mohr, Nilsson-Elle, and Winge largely on the basis of their personal connections to Soviet geneticists, first of all, to himself.[93] He knew them all personally, and had particularly close working relations with Tschermak, Winge, Federley, Vilmorin, and Nilsson-Elle, all of whom worked in Vavilov's own field—plant genetics. Haldane was a personal friend and a strong supporter of the Soviet Union, and Vavilov obviously counted on Mohr's vote not only because of Mohr's well-known left-wing sympathies, but also because of his close friendship with Muller. If Vavilov's calculations proved correct, the IOC would support the new Soviet invitation with a majority of one vote, even if all the other representatives of "oscillating" countries (Holland, Belgium, Japan, and the United States) voted against it. Nevertheless, not leaving anything to chance, Vavilov sent personal letters to all the IOC members whom he counted among his friends, as well as to the secretary-treasurer of the American Genetics Society Demerec, asking them to vote in favor of Moscow.

The actual IOC vote, however, showed that Vavilov miscalculated. Only Vilmorin and Haldane cast their votes for Moscow, for reasons both personal and political. All the others voted against it, (with the exception of the representatives of Japan and Belgium whose votes never came). A letter from Tschermak to Mohr written on May 5, 1937 clearly illustrates the reasons behind such an outcome:

> Vavilov has written to me too, in favor of delaying the international genetics congress for a year. Although I would follow his wishes in <u>normal times</u>, I do believe that during one year situation will hardly change so much that one can count on a visit by foreigners to Moscow and Leningrad.[94]

Like other IOC members, Tschermak felt that the congress should be held on some neutral territory. He personally favored Sweden or Finland. In a world strained by tensions among Hitler's Germany, Stalin's Russia, and Western democracies, the troubled political situation had outweighed personal friendships.

The "apolitical"

The reluctance of Western geneticists to see their discipline entangled in a political controversy appeared to be the major reason for the congress's withdrawal from Moscow. Yet, even though the IOC moved the congress to the "neutral" ground in Britain, the international community still had to deal with "red-hot political issues": Lysenko's doctrine and "racial and eugenical questions in relation to genetics." The British organizers discussed thoroughly the composition of the congress's scientific program with their colleagues at home and abroad and these two items caused them much anxiety. Western geneticists had to decide how to deal with the very subjects that they thought had caused the "postponement" of the Moscow congress.

But, first of all, the British organizers needed to somehow soften the blow that the congress's withdrawal from Moscow had delivered to their Soviet colleagues. They were very concerned that Soviet geneticists would not attend the congress.

As Crew put it: "it would be a thousand pities to have a congress and no Russian delegation."[95] He felt that:

> we should do everything we possibly can to make it clear that we are very sympathetic to our Russian colleagues, not blaming them for the breakdown of the Congress at Moscow and . . . that the Congress shall become as much theirs as ours.

To accomplish this task Crew suggested an unprecedented gesture—that Vavilov be elected the congress's president, contrary to the custom of international congresses to elect a national of the host country as president. He asked for opinion a number of his colleagues, who enthusiastically supported his suggestion. As Dunn summarized the views of American geneticists:

> We think that it would be a very graceful and wise move to elect Vavilov as President, not only to help the position of our colleagues in Russia by paying them this compliment but to help smooth the waters that were so troubled after the decision of the International Committee not to meet in the Soviet Union.[96]

The plan was immediately put in motion and the congress's first official notice distributed at the beginning of April 1938 duly announced that "the Organizing Committee have elected as President of the Congress Dr. N. I. Vavilov."[97]

Crew also consulted with a number of geneticists both inside and outside of Britain on the best possible course of action regarding representation of Lysenko's "Michurinist" genetics at the congress.[98] As the newly-elected secretary-treasurer of the American Genetics Society, E. W. Lindstrom, advised him in the summer of 1938:

> Whether we should encourage a section on genetico-physiology with the Lysenko school leading, is quite debatable. They are still submerged in a wordy misunderstanding, I suppose. The same is true of Goldschmidt's recent splurges.[99] Both of these topics are "green" as now debated but might be crystallized better by 1939.[100]

In the end, the organizers decided not to stage a special session to discuss Lysenko's ideas. Instead they extended an invitation to Lysenko personally to deliver an evening lecture on his "doctrine of heredity."[101]

This decision to a large extent was guided by Western geneticists' appreciation of a precarious position of their Soviet colleagues in disputes with Lysenko. They thought that open criticism of Lysenko at the congress could have negative repercussions for Soviet geneticists. As Muller advised one of his correspondents in April 1939, geneticists outside of the Soviet Union should refrain from publicly saying anything "which could be regarded as implying that the geneticists in the USSR had not given Lysenko due credit." Muller was quite sure that this "will be immediately seized upon inside Russia as a vindication of the attack on genetics itself."[102] And obviously, the congress's organizers wanted to avoid such developments.

The organizers dealt with the "issues of race and eugenics in relation to genetics" with the same deftness. In November 1937, Mohr heatedly advised Muller on the organization of the congress in Edinburgh:

> Look out for one thing. Don't mix the genetics congress with a eugenics congress!! Keep the two apart. A letter from eugenics circles made me a little afraid. They of course want to join. The International Committee doesn't want [anything] of the sort, I am sure. Human genetics at our Congress should rank with genetics in other animals.[103]

Knowing that Crew had long-standing relations to the Eugenics Education Society (as a member of its governing Council), Mohr also asked Muller to relay this advice to Crew. The organizers apparently heeded Mohr's counsel.[104] Gunar Dahlberg was put in charge of the congress's section "F" that dealt with the issues of human heredity. Furthermore, on Dahlberg's invitation, Mohr himself delivered one of the major reports at the section's plenary meeting. Not surprisingly, though German geneticists were in the majority among the contributors to the section "F," none of its six sessions even mentioned the "questions of race in light of genetics," or eugenics.

However, shortly before the congress opened in Edinburgh an opportunity presented itself for those geneticists who felt the need to express their opinion on the issue. On August 4, the same day he received Vavilov's letter announcing the Soviet withdrawal, Crew also received a cable from the chief-editor of Science Service, Watson Davis, asking him and the congress's "representative participants" to provide Science Service with "several hundred words discussing how could [the] world['s] population [be] improve[d] most effectively genetically."[105] Crew, of course, was far too busy and turned the request to Muller, who enthusiastically attended to the task. Muller wrote a long memorandum and sent it to Darlington, Huxley, Lancelot Hogben, Haldane, and Joseph Needham asking them to add their signatures.

Muller carefully worded the memorandum that soon became known as the "geneticists' manifesto."[106] He did not even use the word "eugenics." Neither German "Aryanism," with its emphasis on the hereditary superiority of the "Nordic" race, nor Soviet "Lysenkoism," with its explicit belief in the Lamarkian inheritance of acquired characteristics, was mentioned directly. Although the main thrust of the manifesto was that "the effective genetic improvement of mankind is dependent upon major changes in social conditions, and collective changes in human attitudes," both German and Soviet "attitudes" towards genetics received ample attention. "The second major hindrance to genetic improvement," stated the manifesto, "lies in the economic and political conditions, which foster antagonism between different people, nations, and 'races'." It stressed:

> The removal of race prejudices and of the unscientific doctrine that good or bad genes are the monopoly of particular people or of persons with features

of a given kind will not be possible, however, before the conditions, which make for war and economic exploitation have been eliminated. This requires some effective sort of federation of the whole world, based on the common interests of all its people.

As the fifth major point in improving the world's population genetically, the memorandum listed:

a far wider spread of knowledge of biological principles and of recognition of the truth that both environment and heredity constitute dominating and inescapable complementary factors in human well-being, but factors both of which are under the potential control of man and admit of unlimited but interdependent progress.

It further stated:

It must . . . be understood that the effect of bettered environment is not a direct one on the germ cells and that the Lamarkian doctrine is fallacious, according to which the children of parents who have had better opportunities for physical and mental development inherit these improvements, biologically, and according to which, in consequence, the dominant classes and peoples would have become genetically superior to the underprivileged ones.

Muller did not attempt to make his memorandum an "official statement" of the congress or even make it a subject for public discussion at one of the sessions. Instead he personally asked a number of participants to add their signatures to those of their British colleagues. His quest met almost universal approval: "with very few exceptions all those asked to sign it did so." Fourteen geneticists added their signatures to the original seven. But, of course, Muller obviously approached only those who, he knew, shared his views.[107]

The sudden withdrawal of the Soviet delegation presented another problem for Western geneticists. They knew that Vavilov's letter was "merely the official excuse for non-participation,"[108] because on the same day Crew received Vavilov's "official excuse," Muller received from Vavilov a "confidential letter": "I am very sorry to inform you that none of us will go to Edinburgh. It was definitely decided only today, and I am hastening to write to you unofficially."[109] Of course, Western geneticists could not even imagine that the official letter they received had actually been written by a deputy-commissar of foreign affairs, Vyshinskii, and edited personally by the newly-appointed commissar of foreign affairs and head of SNK Molotov.[110] But certainly, no one among Western geneticists took seriously the reasons given for the withdrawal of the Soviet delegation. As Crew remarked in his letters to Darlington and Haldane: "though the signature is Vavilov's, the substance of which the letter is composed in no way represents his actual views."[111]

Western geneticists suspected that, as one observer put it, "the turn of international events has had some bearing on the fact that the Russians had not received their passports."[112] The abrupt reversal of the Soviet Union's militant anti-fascism to alliance with Hitler's Germany during that summer certainly lent support to this suspicion. But Western geneticists were also well-aware of a new attack on genetics launched by Lysenko and his followers, and they thought that the sudden withdrawal of the Soviet delegation was related to a renewed debate between geneticists and their opponents, which had flared up in the Soviet Union during the summer.[113]

The organizers felt that they had to be very careful in their response to the withdrawal of their Soviet colleagues from the congress. Crew drafted a courteous letter of acknowledgement to be sent to Moscow and circulated it among leading British geneticists to get their approval. He certainly did not "wish to do anything that might in any way deleteriously affect" Vavilov and other geneticists in the Soviet Union.[114] Many Western geneticists shared Crew's concern. At the congress itself, its participants "decided against sending a message to Vavilov on the ground that any gesture of friendship from non-communist biologists would be dangerous to him."[115] Even publishing in the congress's proceedings the abstracts of Soviet papers that had been received by the organizers was ruled out for the same reason.[116] Western geneticists obviously thought that distancing themselves from their Soviet colleagues was the best way to help them in their current troubles.

It would take World War II and the death of their dear friend Vavilov in Stalin's prison for many Western geneticists to realize that they might have been mistaken.[117]

6   International science

Ideologies, patrons, and networks

The story of the Seventh international genetics congress illuminates complex interactions between national and international "forces" that profoundly affected geneticists' attempts to organize the congress first in Moscow and then in Edinburgh. It suggests that the long debate on whether science, in some Platonic sense, is truly "international" (the notion arduously advocated by scientists and some historians[1]), or ultimately "national" (the notion studiously propagated by many social historians[2]), is basically unproductive. The real question is rather why and how national and international "dimensions" interact in scientists' activities at certain times and in certain places, what forces compel scientists to seek "internationalization," "nationalization," or "denationalization," and how scientists affect, mediate, exploit, or resist these processes.

In December 1936, in a letter to the US Secretary of State, Davenport elegantly described the dual nature of scientists' position: "Men of science have two loyalties, one to their country and one to their science." For Soviet geneticists, these dual loyalties were embodied in relations to their domestic patrons and their foreign peers, with whom they had to negotiate the terms of hosting (and later attending) the Seventh international genetics congress. Yet, during the entire negotiations, Soviet geneticists also served as intermediaries and interpreters in an ongoing "dialogue" between their patrons and their peers. On one hand, they translated (both literally and figuratively) requests and expectations of their foreign colleagues for party officials, and, on the other, they interpreted actions and statements of their patrons for their peers.

This translating process was almost never direct. During the entire period of preparations for the congress in Moscow (most importantly during the "times of trouble" from December 1936 through July 1937) and then in Edinburgh, Soviet geneticists had no opportunity to meet personally either with their Politburo patrons or with the key members of the international genetics community. In both directions, practically all communications went through correspondence and intermediaries, which made the translating process ever more difficult.

Ultimately, Soviet geneticists failed in their role as interpreters for their patrons and for their peers. The major reason for such an outcome was that, though Soviet geneticists' concrete negotiations with their patrons and their peers concerned the arrangements for the congress, the "dialogue" they were mediating actually revolved around several interconnected issues in science policy and ideology, such as "academic freedom," scientific internationalism, and relations between "pure" and "applied" science and between science and the state, which underpin scientists' dual loyalties. The different understanding of these issues by their patrons and their peers put Soviet geneticists in an impossible position: they could not reconcile the opposing views and thus find a compromise between their dual loyalties, a compromise that would at the same time be satisfactory for their patrons and for their peers.

Dual loyalties

In his letter to the Secretary of State Davenport insisted that scientists' loyalty "to their science" takes precedence over loyalty to their country: "It is by loyalty to their science that they are best able to make discoveries and advance knowledge which is of so much value to their country."[3] The Soviet authorities obviously thought differently. During the second half of 1936, through a series of public "patriotic" campaigns—first against Luzin and then against Chichibabin and Ipatieff—the government unambiguously demonstrated to its scientists that loyalty to the Soviet Union was of much greater importance than loyalty to their science.

Muller was free to choose which loyalty he wished to uphold and left Russia to pursue his science in Edinburgh.[4] His Soviet colleagues had no choice but to adhere to the official line. As Vavilov stated in his cable to the *New York Times*: "I more than many others am indebted to the government of the USSR for the great attention it pays to the organization of which I am the leader and to my own work. As a true son of the USSR I consider it my duty and good fortune to work for the benefit of my fatherland and to give all of myself to science in the USSR."[5] Although many Western readers perhaps perceived Vavilov's cable as pragmatic (or even opportunistic) lip service to the authorities, there are many indications that he was quite sincere in his, using Paul Forman's fitting expression, "patriotic political posturing."[6] Vavilov often expressed similar sentiments not only in public statements, but also in private letters that were never meant to be public.[7] He certainly tried hard to find a suitable compromise between loyalty to his country and loyalty to his science.

For many Western geneticists, loyalty to their country simply meant allowing that country to share in the fruits and glory of their scientific exploits. Loyalty to their science, however, meant adherence to certain ideals embodied in their current practices and ideology, such as "academic freedom," "scientific internationalism," and "separation of science and politics." And, in their views, by "postponing" the international genetics congress, the Soviet authorities violated every one of these ideals.

The story of the Seventh international genetics congress makes it clear that the Soviet authorities indeed did not subscribe to the ideals upheld by the international scientific community. In their view, science had to serve the aims of its patrons—the party-state apparatus—and hence, was inseparable from their politics. For them, the main criterion of validity of scientific research was not its "objectivity," that is its confirmation by other researchers, but its approbation in the "practice of socialist construction." And the main goal of scientists' international contacts was to serve the patron's objectives, first of all, as a vehicle for propaganda.

Science and politics

The contention that science and by extension its practitioners are "above" and "beyond" politics had long been upheld by many scientists. During and immediately after World War I, however, a number of scientists began to play active roles as political actors on both domestic and international fronts. In the postwar years, some German scientists, in an apt observation of Paul Forman, were even "sacrificing the interests of German science and their personal interests as scientists, for the sake of patriotic political posturing."[8] Yet, at the same time, scientists wanted to keep their *professional* pursuits separate from political entanglements.

Of course, the international scientific community was in no sense a monolith and not every single member of the community unvaryingly subscribed to this ideal. During 1935 and particularly 1936, largely in response to events in Germany and Spain, a number of left-wing scientists in Britain and the United States began to question the separation of science and politics, calling for much closer attention to the interrelations of science and society, science and the state.[9] Yet, although several prominent geneticists, notably Haldane and Huxley, played leading roles in this movement, their advocacy of scientists' more active engagement in the political issues of the day did little to change the conviction of the majority of Western geneticists that science should be kept separate from politics of any kind, and particularly the kind that could affect their discipline directly: the politics of the Nazis racial programs and the politics of Soviet agricultural debates.

Certain members of the international genetics community, however, did try to stir their fellow-geneticists into taking up the most notorious "political" issue of their discipline—Nazi "racial" genetics—by proposing a special discussion on the subject at the Moscow congress. And, initially, it met with approval from the Soviet organizers. But, as we have seen, many geneticists had opposed this proposal from the start. After the reported "postponement" of the congress, which many observers and participants of events attributed at least in part to the proposed discussion on "race," this opposition to "mixing" science with politics was greatly reinforced.

The majority of Western geneticists' were reluctant to see their discipline embroiled in a political controversy. As the secretary of the Dutch Genetics Society Hagedoorn warned Mohr in the spring of 1937: "Your committee would do wise to eschew any of the violently politically-minded countries, such as Germany, Italy or Russia." Similarly, the Italian representative on the IOC Alessandro Ghigi declared in his response to Mohr's memorandum:

> I perfectly agree with you in considering it convenient to hold the congress in another country than in [the] USSR if the postponement of the congress should have been caused by extra-scientific reasons, because I am of the opinion that the scientists of all the world ought to prevent that science could

serve as a basis for contrasting political-social points of view. This would be a rather dangerous precedent.[10]

Haldane, on the other hand, asserted in a letter to Mohr that genetics was not free of politics even in Britain: "It is incorrect to suppose that political conditions [do] not interfere with genetical work in this country. It is very difficult to explain certain recent appointments and dismissals except on political grounds."[11] He saw no "political" obstacles to holding the congress in Soviet Russia. Haldane, however, was obviously in a minority.

In December 1936, Jennings mused: "Will men wish to go [to Russia] to discuss a subject which is considered a red-hot political issue?"[12] A few months later, the international genetics community answered this rhetorical question with a definitive "no." Even a long-time admirer of the Soviet Union and Soviet genetics, Leslie C. Dunn, refused to lend support to the campaign waged by Muller in the summer of 1937 to convince Western geneticists that it was imperative to hold the congress in Moscow. As he pondered in a letter to Landauer in July:

> Muller's letter has some good reasoning in it but I'm afraid does not persuade me to [engage into] active propaganda in favor of Congress in [the] USSR. For myself I should vote for it so, and should go, but to persuade others somehow seems to involve promising something and I haven't faith enough to do that in this case.[13]

Many Western geneticists apparently felt that if the congress were held in the Soviet Union, it would be automatically drawn into the political muddle, and that was an eventuality they tried to avoid. As Mohr quite openly stated in his second memo to the IOC members:

> The science of genetics comes in an exceptional position in so far as some of its principles and practical bearings are apt to be interpreted in a political light. This relation has during recent years been brought to the very foreground of public attention. Several members of the International Committee have expressed in their letters the view that under the conditions prevailing in Europe at present it would be advisable to hold the next congress in a country where this situation is least likely to be felt.[14]

Yet, even after the relocation of the congress to the "safe ground" in Edinburgh, the organizers chose to keep the congress clear of the politically charged issues of both Lysenkoism and race in relation to their discipline.

Academic freedom

Although some Western scientists thought they had the right to have a say in politics, they denied the right of politicians to interfere in science, consistently guarding what they regarded as their most precious asset—"academic freedom." The international community perceived the "postponement" of the congress in Moscow as a clear sign of the absence of such freedom in the Soviet Union.

This perception was shaped not so much by what Western geneticists actually knew about the relations between scientists and political authorities in the Soviet Union, as by Western geneticists' experience in dealing with their own governments. At this time, the attitude of the majority of Western governments to their scientists' international activities is perhaps best described as encouragingly indifferent. During the 1930s, most governments (with the notable exceptions of Germany and the USSR) considered such activities to be scientists' private affairs.[15] Unlike international gatherings on public health, the state's involvement in the organization of international scientific congresses was minimal. As best, some states appointed symbolic "representatives" to international congresses.[16] As we have seen, even when geneticists in Britain and the United States tried to induce their own government officials to support their efforts of "saving" the congress, state agents on both sides of the Atlantic politely refused.[17]

For Soviet scientists, situation was entirely different. Since the 1917 Bolshevik revolution, the state had been the sole patron of Russian science, liberally funding and strictly controlling scientists' international activities. Western scientists were well-aware of the fact that the remarkable growth of science under the Soviet regime resulted from the lavish funding the regime afforded its scientists and the astonishing progress of Soviet genetics was the best illustration of this generous support. Many Western scientists cited the Soviet example in their lamentations about the meager conditions in which they themselves often worked and wanted their own governments to support their scientific pursuits.[18] But they could not accept what they perceived as the Soviet government's interference with their "academic freedom."[19]

Despite the total dependence of Soviet science on the government's funding, however, both its practitioners and its patrons tried, for the benefit of foreign peers, to maintain the appearance of Soviet scientists as citizens of "the free republic of letters." In preparing the congress in Moscow, and later negotiating their participation in the congress in Edinburgh, Soviet geneticists had to comply with the strict control and stiff rules their patrons set for the Soviet science system. They had to obediently follow the party line in their "official" statements. But at the same time they tried to keep members of their personal networks apprised of the real situation through "confidential" messages. In their turn, while constantly monitoring, editing, and approving Soviet geneticists' communications with their foreign colleagues, the party patrons carefully kept their hand in the whole affair "hidden" from the international community, removing all mention of "the government" from Soviet geneticists' "official" statements. Even the congress's "postponement" was presented to the Western public as an act of the Soviet organizing committee made under the request of scientists, and not as a consequence of a Politburo decree. The party patrons thus also cultivated the appearance of the "academic freedom" of Soviet scientists.[20]

But, as the December 1936 *Izvestiia* editorial clearly demonstrated, the Soviet government's understanding of what "academic freedom" meant differed considerably from that of Western scientists. In its resolution adopted in the wake of the "troubles" with the congress in December 1936 and published in *Nature* a few weeks later, the American Society of Naturalists emphasized that "intellectual progress is compatible only with perfect freedom in the conduct of investigation."[21] In his response to British geneticists' inquiries published in the next issue of the same journal, the Soviet Ambassador to Britain Ivan Maiskii clearly articulated the differences: "The prevailing view in the USSR is that science must not consider itself a demi-god with the right to choose its own course without any reference to the needs and requirements of the people [read 'the state'—N. K.]. On the contrary, the primary object of science is to serve as faithfully as possible the needs of the people."[22] From the point of view of its patrons, the freedom of Soviet science was to serve their own agendas.

Scientific internationalism

Although, of course, some of them were quite enthusiastic about it, for the majority of Western geneticists, holding the congress in the Soviet Union was just one among possible options. For their Soviet colleagues, it was imperative. They desperately wanted to have the congress in Moscow, particularly after its initial cancellation by the Politburo and the December 1936 VASKhNIL discussion with Lysenko and his followers. In addition to bringing considerable extra funding and to further strengthening their ties to the international community, the congress might have been their best hope in countering Lysenko's attack on their discipline. Geneticists clearly expected that their foreign colleagues would help them expose Lysenko and his disciples in the eyes of party-state patrons for what they really were—incompetent and ignorant demagogues.

This expectation was grounded in the main tenet of the ideology of scientific internationalism—the "universality" of scientific knowledge embodied in the disciplinary consensus over research methods, tools, agendas, concepts, and explanatory hypotheses. Such "universality" requires that knowledge obtained in a particular locale must be true anywhere and implies the necessity of a free exchange of ideas and results. It also implies that scientists in other locales serve as independent, neutral, uninvolved in local affairs—be it competition for resources or political struggles—"verifiers" of such knowledge. This status of foreign scientists as such neutral "judges" was what Soviet geneticists counted on, expecting that party-state officials would defer to the opinion and authority of their Western colleagues, and hence would support geneticists in their struggle against Lysenko's "Michurinist" genetics. As Vavilov wrote to Muller in April 1937, asking him for help in persuading Western geneticists to support the congress's convocation in Moscow: "Of course, you understand that it is very important for the benefit of genetics to have [the congress] in the USSR. There are 220 experiment stations [here] engaged in plant and animal breeding, and they all need [a] firmer theory for their work."[23] Characteristically, in June 1937, when Soviet geneticists learned of the possibility that the congress might be relocated to Britain, they began immediately preparing for this contingency by planning for 1938 an All-Union genetics conference with the participation of a large number of those foreign geneticists who were in favor of holding the international congress in Russia.[24] Alas, this plan was never realized.

For their part, many Western geneticists suspected that the congress's withdrawal from Moscow might have "disastrous consequences" for their Soviet colleagues and might in a certain way even aid the Soviet critics of genetics. As Darlington saw it: "Vavilov, Levit and the rest will become identified with bourgeois principles while Lysenko will appear, as he claims to be, the Soviet champion."[25] In their letters and cables to various Soviet representatives Western geneticists indeed wore the mantle of "impartial judges" of events in Soviet genetics: they praised their Soviet colleagues' contributions and denied the legitimacy of Lysenko's critique.

Many Western geneticists clearly understood the precarious position of their Soviet colleagues. As Dunn warned Jennings in December 1936:

> I think it particularly important that the tone of any publicity should not be anti-Soviet but based on an understanding of conditions in Russia. This is just as difficult for us to recognize as it was for Europeans to understand our monkey trial in Tennessee. The two cases, being based on heresy hunts, seem quite analogous to me.[26]

Western geneticists' stern reaction to the reported arrests of their colleagues and the congress's "postponement" certainly helped Soviet geneticists persuade the Politburo to permit the congress's convocation in Moscow a year later, in 1938. But the IOC's subsequent decision to withdraw the congress from the USSR played into the Soviet authorities' "patriotic" attitude toward international scientific relations, which was rapidly developing during the mid-1930s. As demonstrated by the letter sent in July 1939 to the congress's organizers in Britain, the Soviet authorities perceived the congress's relocation to Edinburgh as an affront.

The congress's withdrawal from Moscow reinforced the Soviet authorities' already mounting suspicion of a major premise of "scientific internationalism"—the free exchange and cross-validation of ideas and results. Already during the Luzin affair of summer 1936, when the prominent mathematician had been castigated for publishing his works in foreign periodicals instead of Soviet ones, the explicit message the Politburo had sent to its scientific community was that publishing research abroad was no longer an accepted way of validating scientific results through their review by independent peers. Such publications were now considered not as recognition of the scientist's achievements—which enhanced the nation's international prestige—but as ideologically unacceptable "slavishness to the West." It implied that foreign scientists no longer could serve as peers for the adjudication of Soviet scientific research. The congress's relocation to Britain helped reinforce this attitude, by demonstrating that the international community appeared unwilling to pick a fight with the Soviet critics of genetics on their own territory in Moscow, thus giving up foreign scientists' role as "neutral judges." As a result, the Soviet authorities delegated this role to the party officials and Marxist "philosophers": the next round of the Vavilov–Lysenko debate in October 1939 was conducted before a panel of "judges" chosen by the Politburo from among party-ideologues. No wonder, in such a situation (even though his most poignant argument—genetics' links to fascism—had been annulled by the

Molotov–Ribbentrop pact), Lysenko's staple arguments against "formal" genetics—incompatibility with Marxism, practical sterility, and foreign origins—proved much more effective than geneticists' critique of the numerous flaws in Lysenko's experiments.[27] One can only speculate that if the congress had been held in Moscow, the position of Soviet geneticists would have been greatly fortified and they perhaps would have been able to fend off Lysenko's attack.

"Academic" versus "applied" genetics

The conflict inherent to Soviet geneticists' dual loyalties was perhaps best manifested in the differences of opinion between their patrons and their peers regarding the relationship between "pure" and "applied" genetics. Two areas of genetics' applications were of particular salience in this respect—eugenics and agriculture.

As many historians have persuasively demonstrated, the early association of genetics with eugenics and agriculture was crucial for its institutionalization, providing the fledging discipline with suitable arguments for establishing its "external" legitimacy in the eyes of prospective patrons.[28] In the early years, would-be-geneticists in various countries utilized their links to agriculture or eugenics or both to foster the establishment of their field as an *academic* discipline. They referred extensively to possible contributions their discipline would make both to improving agriculture and to "bettering humankind" to justify its right for existence and to claim their share of resources available for research in eugenics and agriculture.

Of course, the relative significance of the patronage coming from each of these two areas to the institutionalization of genetics differed from country to country. In some, like Germany, geneticists' links to eugenics far outweighed those to agriculture; in others, like Sweden and the Soviet Union, agriculture appeared to be the leading source of support; in still others, like the United States and Great Britain, eugenics and agriculture played perhaps equally important roles.

Furthermore, entrepreneurial "founders" of genetics differed significantly in their personal attitudes to the importance of their discipline's involvement with eugenics and agriculture.[29] As we have seen, Bateson was quite determined to keep genetics separate from too close an association with eugenics (or agriculture, for that matter). In the Galton lecture delivered to the Eugenics Education Society in February 1921 he declared forcefully: "Alliances between pure and applied science are [as] dangerous as those of spiders, in which the fertilizing partner is apt to be absorbed."[30] Bateson's friend Erwin Baur, to the contrary, worked very hard to forge extensive links between genetics and eugenics, as well as between genetics and agriculture.[31] One of the principal founders of the German Genetics Society, Baur became the first professor of genetics at the Berlin Agricultural College and the first director of the Kaiser Wilhelm Institute for Breeding Research. He also was a life-long member of the German Society for Racial Hygiene and co-authored (with Eugen Fisher and Fritz Lenz) the notorious two-volume *Outlines of Human Heredity and Racial Hygiene*.[32] Similar differences could be observed in the attitudes of other "founding fathers" of genetics, such as, to pick at random, Morgan, Correns, Filipchenko, Davenport, Goldschmidt, Punnett, Vavilov, de Vries, Kol'tsov, Johannsen, and Vilmorin.

After genetics had been firmly established as an academic discipline, however, its practitioners' need for "external" justifications receded dramatically. Geneticists quickly developed their own research programs—the chromosome and cytoplasmic mechanisms of heredity, developmental and population genetics, the gene, its mutability and expression, to name but a few—which had very little (if any) relevance to the concerns of their early partners and patrons in the fields of both agriculture and eugenics. A new generation of geneticists, which came into the field in the 1920s, was predominantly engaged in pursuing these new exciting avenues of research—mapping chromosomes, searching for mutagenes, deciphering biochemical intricacies of the gene's actions, or uncovering the distribution of various genes in wild populations—and paid scant attention to anything else. They adopted a few model organisms suitable for laboratory exper-imentation, notably *Drosophila* and mice, as their primary research tools. As a result, geneticists became even further distanced from their "foster parents"— eugenics and agriculture. One might even suggest that in the 1930s, the relation-ship between genetics and eugenics became in a certain sense reversed, as compared to that in the 1900s and 1910s: now eugenicists sought to justify their various claims by reference to the newest genetic data and concepts.[33]

This developing rift between "applied" and "pure," "basic," "academic" genetics was particularly pronounced on the international scene. Even a cursory glance at the proceedings of the seven international genetics congresses held between 1899 and 1939 reveals a dramatic decline in the number of reports dealing with "applied" genetics, particularly in the 1920s and 1930s. To be sure, researchers interested in applied topics organized their own international conferences and many geneticists attended such gatherings, be it international eugenics congresses, world's poultry congresses, or international congresses for studies on population. But at their own meetings, geneticists focused more and more on "academic" research.

The situation at domestic gatherings, particularly in the two "troubled" com-munities—Soviet and German—was somewhat different. The distribution of papers among "basic," "agricultural," and "eugenic" topics[34] at these meetings clearly reflected existing patronage and institutional patterns, with a heavy emphasis on the version of "applied" genetics supported by their state patrons. The First All-Russia congress on genetics held in 1929 was concerned predomi-nately with "agricultural" genetics. Reports on animal and plant breeding occupied four out of the six volumes of the entire proceedings, while reports on "pure" research far outnumbered those dealing with "eugenic" issues.[35] The December 1936 VASKhNIL session on "issues in genetics" dealt almost exclu-sively with agricultural subjects, with only six out of seventy-two reports devoted to "academic" issues and a few denigrating remarks about eugenics in the discus-sion that followed.[36] In contrast, the Tenth meeting of the German Genetics Society held in 1934 was dominated by reports dealing with various aspects of "rassenhygiene," while reports on "basic" issues outnumbered those on "agricultural" subjects.[37] The contrast is even more striking in comparison to the annual meet-ing of the American Genetics Society held the same year, which was almost totally devoted to "pure" research, with less than one quarter of the presentations dealing with agricultural subjects, and only two (out of fifty-two) reports touching upon those of eugenics.[38]

Obviously, on the international scene geneticists pursued their intellectual interests in "pure" science without much regard for anything, but research agendas promoted by their peers, while on the domestic one they also had to accommodate specific interests of their patrons.

In contrast to the situation, for instance, in the United States, where geneticists were able to tap a variety of private and public sources of funding, the patronage of genetics in both Germany and the USSR in the mid-1930s rested exclusively with the party-state apparatus (though German geneticists managed to maintain certain links to other patrons in private foundations and industry). Both Soviet and German state patrons were particularly interested in "applied" genetics, albeit in its different versions. German patrons were mostly involved with eugenic applications of genetics, while Soviet patrons were concerned predominantly with agricultural ones. These governmental concerns created a favorable atmosphere for some scientists engaged in "applied" genetics in both countries to begin advancing certain theoretical constructs—the genetic supremacy of the "Nordic race" in Germany and "the transformation of heredity" in the USSR—which many geneticists in other countries considered seriously flawed.

Both German "racial" genetics and the Soviet "Michurinist" version posed a challenge to the international genetics community, threatening to undermine the disciplinary consensus and, together with it, the major tenet of scientific internationalism—the universality of genetics knowledge. To be sure, a number of American, British, and Soviet geneticists published critiques of German "racial" genetics and racial policies.[39] And, as we have seen, some of them wanted to meet the "German challenge" by organizing a special discussion on "eugenical and racial questions in light of genetics" at the Moscow congress, thus trying to build up the disciplinary consensus regarding "racial" genetics. Their efforts, however, were unsuccessful. After the congress's "postponement" and relocation to Britain, geneticists decided to abstain from any direct confrontation with the proponents of "racial genetics," and the international genetics community, as a whole, stayed clear of the issue throughout the 1930s. Even the American Genetics Society, unlike the American Anthropological Society, chose to remain silent.[40]

The international genetics community failed completely to realize the challenge posed by "Michurinist" genetics and simply dismissed it as "Lamarkian." Although they recorded their "astonishment" at Lysenko's attack on Mendelian genetics, Western geneticists abstained from any serious consideration of its sources and decided to avoid any direct confrontation with "Michurinist" genetics and its proponents either in Moscow or in Edinburgh. The first detailed analysis of Lysenko's genetic concepts in the West would appear only after World War II.[41]

Because both Soviet and German "national" versions of genetics were backed by their respective state patrons, the international community chose to treat both "racial" and "Michurinist" genetics as artifacts of political pressure by their governments on German and Soviet scientists and as such "pseudoscientific," beyond the purview of the community. As the resolution of the American Society of

Naturalists reiterated in December 1936: "the scientific world can place no reliance upon reports of research carried on under conditions which limit its freedom by an enforced agreement with any preconceived views or dogmas."[42] The international genetics community as a whole appeared unwilling to engage proponents of both "racial" and "Michurinist" genetics into an open fight, fearing that it would, in Davenport's words, bring their discipline into "a bad repute," or, as Demerec put it, "stir up a great deal of both desirable and undesirable publicity."[43]

In his address as the AAAS retiring president in December 1937, Edwin G. Conklin searched for reasons of such passivity on the part of scientists and called on them to take a more active stance:

> In spite of a few notable exceptions it must be confessed that scientists did not win the freedom which they have generally enjoyed, and they have not been conspicuous in defending this freedom when it has been threatened. Perhaps they have lacked that confidence in absolute truth and that emotional exaltation that have led martyrs and heroes to welcome persecution and death in defense of their faith.... The spirit of science does not cultivate such heroism in the maintenance of freedom. The scientist realizes that his knowledge is relative and not absolute, he conceives it possible that he may be mistaken, and he is willing to wait in confidence that ultimately truth will prevail. Therefore, he has little inclination to suffer and die for his faith, but is willing to wait for the increase and diffusion of knowledge. But he knows better than others that the increase and diffusion of knowledge depend entirely upon freedom to search, experiment, criticize, proclaim. Without these freedoms there can be no science.[44]

If Western geneticists could for a time afford "to wait in confidence that ultimately truth will prevail," their Soviet colleagues were in no position to do so. They could ill afford to ignore Lysenko's challenge, because it involved not merely intellectual issues of their discipline (and hence, the "internal" disciplinary consensus), but also its institutions and patrons (and hence, its "external" legitimacy). In response to this challenge, Soviet geneticists initiated two public discussions with the proponents of "Michurinist" genetics in 1936 and in 1939. As I have argued elsewhere, although these disputes revolved around the intellectual content and methodology of "Michurinist" versus "Mendelian" genetics, the actual issues at stake were control over genetics institutions and relations to their patrons.[45] And the crucial issue in scientist–patron relations in the Soviet Union was the "practicality" of science.

Many Russian scientists had long-internalized the belief that scientific pursuits must yield practical results important for the nation's economy, technology, agriculture, and medicine.[46] In part, it was this belief that helped Russian scientists overcome their initial hostility to the Bolshevik regime and made viable their collaboration with the new pragmatic rulers.[47] As we have seen, in the early years of the regime, geneticists capitalized on "practical applications" of their studies in both eugenics and agriculture to build an institutional foundation for their field. When during the Great Break, their patrons deemed eugenics as politically unacceptable "bourgeois" science, Soviet geneticists quickly disposed off the Russian

Eugenics Society and other eugenics institutions (though their earlier association with eugenics would haunt them for years to come), and sought to strengthen their links to agriculture. But, as did many of their foreign colleagues, Russian scientists also believed in the primacy of "pure," "academic," "theoretical" research in developing practical applications.

Their Bolshevik patrons, however, believed in the primacy of "practical work" in the advancement of "theory." This belief gained particular currency among the Bolshevik leadership and was actively promoted in the course of the crush industrialization and collectivization campaigns of the early 1930s.[48] How deeply this belief was ingrained in the conscience of Soviet leaders could be illustrated by a discussion in December 1935 among the members of the Politburo of the idea of a "Soviet Hollywood," a discussion quite remote from science and scientists. Presenting the idea of building the Soviet "city-of-dreams," the head of the State Committee on Cinematography Boris Shumiatskii described the requirements for its location: a large number of sunny days a year, low yearly precipitation, the presence of sea, rivers, and mountains, and temperate climate. He informed the Politburo that his committee was mounting a special expedition with the participation of prominent scientists to search for such an ideal location. At this moment, Molotov interrupted the presentation with a pointed remark: "Do not trust scientists too much. They had often failed, because they rarely know practice."[49]

This distrust of science and scientists as "theoretical," and thus removed from practical concerns of the state, contributed considerably to the rise of Lysenko as the spokesman for a new and "practical" agricultural science that was ready to fulfill any order of its patrons—"Michurinist" genetics. Not incidentally, Lysenko labeled Mendelian genetics as "formal," using a contemporary Soviet epithet clearly connoting the "abstract," "theoretical," "academic" nature of his opponents' work. At the same time, the actual inability of Soviet geneticists to provide quick solutions to the permanent crises that plagued Soviet "collectivized" agriculture, despite the state's heavy investment in genetics research and institutions, fueled their patrons' suspicion of genetics as "academic," and hence useless for "the construction of socialism," undermining the "external" legitimacy of Mendelian genetics in the eyes of its party patrons. Vavilov and his co-workers incessantly tried to dispel this image of Mendelian genetics as "nonpractical" and continuously tried to enlist the assistance of their foreign colleagues for this venture. Vavilov's appeal to Crew in the autumn of 1938 to expand the representation of agricultural genetics at the congress in Edinburgh was an undisguised cry for help: "many breeders and even geneticists feel that there is a real gap between the most interesting genetical work on the chromosome theory, etc. and the needs of practical breeding work.... There is a great need of connecting the present genetic understanding with the practical achievements of plant and animal breeding."[50] Vavilov's plea clearly reflected not only his worry about the standing of Soviet genetics in the eyes of its party patrons, who seemed inclined to agree with Lysenko's claims about the "practical sterility" of genetics, but also genuine dissatisfaction with Mendelian genetics on the part of many practical workers in plant and animal breeding, the dissatisfaction that led them to flock to Lysenko's

Plate 20 Russians in Pasadena, 1930. Left to right: Th. Dobzhansky, N. Dobzhansky, N. Vavilov, G. Karpechenko. (From *Nikolai Ivanovich Vavilov. Nauchnoe Nasledie v Pis' makh*, Moscow: Nauka, 1997, vol. 2.)

line.[51] But as we have seen, at the time the international genetics community was moving farther and farther away from "practical" applications of their research and did not take the challenge of "Michurinist" genetics seriously.

In the spring of 1939, in the wake of Lysenko's renewed attack on Mendelian genetics, Vavilov told a meeting of his co-workers: "[We] will go to the stake, we will burn, but we will not give up our principles."[52] His arrest the following summer and subsequent death in Stalin's prison became an international symbol of scientists' loyalty to their science.[53]

Networks of trust

International congresses played a seminal role in establishing the discipline of genetics in both local and international settings, largely because they fostered the emergence of close-knit networks of personal contacts among its practitioners. Consider just a few names from the list of invitees to the London conference on hybridization and plant breeding in 1906, where the very word "genetics" was publicly introduced for the first time: Bateson, Baur, Correns, Davenport, de Vries, East, Emerson, Johannsen, Lotsy, Nilsson-Elle, Punnett, Sutton, Tschermak, Vilmorin. They are easily recognizable as the "national founders" of genetics in Austria, Britain, Denmark, France, Germany, Holland, Sweden, and the United States. But these "founders" not only spearheaded the intellectual development and institutionalization of genetics in their various home countries, they also led its "internationalization." At the next congress in Paris, eight persons from this list became members of the first permanent committee for genetics congresses.

A network of personal contacts among the "national founders" of the new discipline, which had been consolidated in London and Paris, quickly expanded, branched out, and multiplied to include their students, co-workers, friends, relatives, and even casual acquaintances. The combined multitude of such personal networks formed a kind of a "hidden" substructure of the international genetics community and the discipline of genetics as a whole. These networks became major channels for domestic and international exchanges of ideas, methods, results, publications, tools, honors, students, and even funding (for instance, in the form of Rockefeller fellowships and grants). As we have seen, the ability of Russian scientists to tap into such international networks was a critical factor in the tremendous progress of genetics in the Soviet Union during the 1920s.

Furthermore, one can argue that the major function of international congresses in genetics was exactly the perpetuation and "maintenance" of such international networks. Networks' "interests" defined, to a large degree, arrangements made for the congresses. In the 1930s, the Soviet branch of the international networks represented the second largest and most active group of geneticists in the world and as such was very important to the well-being of the genetics community. It was the need to further contacts with Soviet colleagues that lay behind the IOC decision to hold the congress in Moscow in the first place. And it was the need to maintain the contacts with Soviet geneticists that guided much of Western geneticists' efforts after the announced cancellation of the congress in the Soviet Union. As Dunn put it: "their numbers and contributions are too important to overlook their convenience in settling the place for the next congress."[54] As he also pointed out in his letter to Muller in early January 1937:

> We all know that the main thing for us all [is] to stick together and that genetics will go on regardless of the congress. Especially the two most active centers, the U.S.A. and the U.S.S.R. ought to be chiefly concerned with contact and continuity and ought to try to influence the decision of the international committee to hold the congress in a place acceptable to these large groups.[55]

In July 1937, Haldane advised Mohr against the congress's withdrawal from Moscow: "I realize that the postponement of the congress was a serious blunder on the part of someone in Russia. But I cannot think that this blunder can justify an action which is likely to affect adversely the whole future development of genetics."[56]

The genetics networks were first and foremost disciplinary networks. Of course, geneticists did cultivate contacts with various individuals outside their discipline: in response to the congress's "postponement," Western geneticists mobilized such contacts with their local political and scientific establishments, as did their Soviet colleagues. But although the networks' "external" reach was quite impressive, it was clearly limited. In July 1937, that is, exactly at the time when the IOC was considering the congress's relocation to Britain, the international geological congress was being held in Moscow. Yet, as far as I was able to determine, searching for information

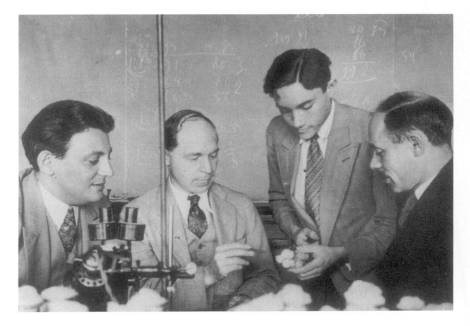

Plate 21 Russians in Texas, 1931. Left to right: S. Levit, H. J. Muller, C. Offerman, I. Agol. Courtesy of the Lilly Library, Indiana University, Bloomington, Indiana.

on the state of affairs in the Soviet Union, Western geneticists did not contact their countrymen who were going to the geology congress. They also did not even consider postponing their decision to relocate the genetics congress until the "outcome" of the geology one in Moscow would become clear. It is possible that the all-out effort by the Soviet authorities to make the geology congress a success would have convinced Western geneticists that holding their congress in Moscow was quite possible, as witnessed by a letter Vavilov received in September 1937 from George H. Shull, a professor of genetics at Princeton University: "It seems that present times are not very favorable for holding international congresses, but I learned from my colleagues geologists that they had had a great time at their congress this summer and had been received by your government and your people in a truly royal fashion."[57]

Geneticists' personal networks played a crucial role in disseminating available information, debating possible actions, forming opinions, and making decisions. The networks' composition, however, was neither uniform, nor rigidly defined. It was more like a "fluid crystal," assuming particular configuration in response to a particular "signal." One signal, say a proposal "to put to discussion the national-socialist race theory," stirred to action only a certain group of geneticists, but left others indifferent. Another signal, say a *New York Times* report of Vavilov and Agol's arrests, set in motion a different group. Furthermore, not all members of the networks played the same role in their operations. Some individuals, by virtue of their temperament, research interests, institutional positions, political sympathies, or moral authority, acted as "nodes" or "ganglions" in the networks' activities. They maintained much broader contacts than "ordinary" members and often played the role of "triggers" in the networks' response to particular incoming signals. In the networks' reaction to the events surrounding the congress one can easily identify such "nodes" among the members of national networks: Vavilov, Kol'tsov, Levit, and Muller in the Soviet branch, Dunn, Demerec, Emerson, and Landauer in the US branch, Haldane, Huxley, Darlington, and later Crew in the British branch, and Mohr in the Norwegian one.

The administrative barriers the Soviet authorities erected to curb foreign travels of Soviet scientists in the 1930s, however, severely limited direct contacts of the international networks with their Soviet members and, hence, the flow of information. The lack of face-to-face contacts with their Soviet colleagues and insufficient information on the state of affairs in Moscow were key factors in the IOC decision to move the congress to Britain. By the mid-1930s, the virtual isolation of Soviet geneticists made Muller the principal "ganglion" in their contacts with foreign colleagues. But Muller's growing doubts about his own future in the Soviet Union, which he quite openly shared with Mohr and Huxley, his trip to Spain at the crucial time in the early spring of 1937, and his ultimate decision to leave Moscow for good, cut off even this limited channel of communications.

Even more important, however, appeared the distrust of what little information Soviet geneticists did provide to their foreign colleagues. A network is more than a sum of individuals who form it. It is an entity with its own holistic characteristics and operating procedures. The major principle of a network's operation is trust. Network members share and act upon certain information that may, but more often may not, be a part of public knowledge. Yet, discrepancies between Soviet geneticists' private and "official" public messages undermined this trust and forced the international genetics community to rely on information and advice proffered by "eye-witnesses" and "Soviet experts." For instance, a letter signed among others by Karpechenko, Kol'tsov, Levit, Navashin, Serebrovskii, and Vavilov, and widely distributed by the Soviet organizing committee among Western geneticists in the summer of 1937, failed completely to convince them that the situation was quite favorable for holding the congress in Moscow. Mohr's letter to Dunn offers an explanation of why and how this happened:

> The other day I had a visit from an English scientist who came straight from Moscow. He had seen quite a few of the geneticists—he was a neurologist interested in genetics—but it was absolutely impossible for him to talk to any of them (Gershenzon, Levit, a[nd]. o[thers].) without an "interpreter" being present all the time. He had made several attempts but in vain. Suspicion everywhere, and all conversations started with cliché declaration about the Marxist science being the only science, etc. etc. I showed him the letter I got, which was signed by all the geneticist[s]. He said: "you couldn't trust it at all, they simply <u>had</u> to."[58]

The issues of trust also greatly affected the distribution of available information. Muller, for instance, was very selective in his correspondence with Western colleagues. In early March 1937, writing to Huxley on the situation in Russia, he specifically instructed his correspondent who can and who cannot be included into the circle of people in the know:

> Haldane, especially, must <u>not</u> be informed—not now, anyway—for I judge from the tone and content of his letters to me that he is at present having his political opinions impressed upon him with a rubber stamp (greatly as I admire his intellect and person), and could be influenced in the reverse direction from which I intended. He would think I had gone to the conservative or Fascist camp, which is the very impression I am trying to disprove.[59]

Relocating the congress to Britain, Western geneticists certainly hoped that their Soviet colleagues would be able to attend the congress in Edinburgh and thus to break down their isolation. After all, in 1937, Soviet–British relations were markedly better than a mere decade earlier, and for a time it seemed that Britain and the Soviet Union could even form a "united front" against Fascism. And for a while these hopes appeared to be well-founded. The sudden withdrawal of the Soviet delegation from the Edinburgh congress dealt a heavy blow to the international networks and deepened profoundly the distrust of information coming from the Soviet Union through open, public channels.

The importance of trust and face-to-face contacts in a network's operations could be further illustrated by the reintroduction of the Soviet branch into international genetics networks during and immediately after World War II.[60] Three events proved critical in this process: a year long stay in 1944–45 in the Soviet Union of a prominent British plant physiologist, Eric Ashby, as a scientific attaché of the Australian legation; a two-weeks visit by Julian Huxley to Moscow on the occasion of the 220th anniversary of the USSR Academy of Sciences in June 1945; and a two-months visit to San Francisco by a Soviet geneticist, Anton Zhebrak, as a member of the Soviet delegation to the UN founding assembly in June–July 1945.

In Moscow, Huxley and Ashby met with all leading Soviet geneticists who had survived the war, notably Aleksandr Serebrovskii and Nikolai Dubinin. In San Francisco, Zhebrak promptly contacted geneticists at the University of California in Berkeley, first of all, Ersnt Babkock (almost certainly bringing him personal greetings from Babkock's old friend Mikhail Navashin) and Richard Goldschmidt (probably sharing with him memories of the last years of Goldschmid's life-long friend Nikolai Kol'tsov). Zhebrak also entered into correspondence with many other geneticists in the United States, including his one-time mentor Leslie C. Dunn, his former compatriot Theodosius Dobzhansky, and his Moscow acquaintance H. J. Muller.

Information brought by Ashby, Huxley, and Zhebrak spread like fire through international genetics networks. It confirmed what many Western geneticists had long suspected: Vavilov's arrest in the summer of 1940 and his subsequent death in Stalin's prison. Western geneticists also learned that several of Vavilov's eminent co-workers, notably Georgii Karpechenko and Grigorii Levitskii, shared his fate. But there was also the good news that "Lysenko's position is less secure than it has been, and Russian geneticists are hoping to get [out] from under."[61] And now it seemed that Western geneticists could make a difference, because, they learned, "the Soviet Government at the moment is definitely disposed toward giving considerable weight to the opinion of American scientists."[62] When Western geneticists found out that their Russian friends "personally and <u>confidentially</u> ask for support of those American colleagues who are known to be friendly to Russia,"[63] they enthusiastically responded to the call and organized a virtual "second front" against Lysenko in the West. Four US geneticists—Dunn, Demerec, Dobzhansky, and Muller—orchestrated the American part of the campaign, while Huxley coordinated the British part.[64]

Western geneticists even attempted once again to schedule an international congress in Russia. During his stay in the Soviet Union, Ashby discussed this idea with Dubinin and Serebrovskii, who enthusiastically approved it. He also discussed the matter with Leon Orbeli, a vice-president of the USSR Academy of Sciences and a long-time supporter of genetics. Orbeli "too was quite interested, but indirectly made it clear that, so long as Lysenko was in a strong position, he would not be willing to incur Lysenko's hostility by pushing the matter actively."[65] Ashby suggested to his colleagues that they coordinate the anti-Lysenko campaign in influential Western journals and make a "formal approach" to Academy of Sciences authorities regarding the future congress. He supposed that publications indicating "the views of foreign biologists on the worthless[ness] of Lysenko's work" would carry "at least considerable weight" in some quarters in the USSR and therefore would facilitate the organization of the congress there.[66]

Western geneticists eagerly attended to this project. Demerec, who had been elected the US representative to the IOC at the Edinburgh congress, wrote to the Norwegian representative Mohr: "It would be well if the next Congress could be held in Russia, and I sincerely hope that this can be arranged. It might tip the balance in favor of the real geneticists as against the Lysenko school."[67] The IOC's new chairman Crew used an international genetics conference that convened in London in October 1945 to solicit the opinion of other geneticists on the subject. Although Soviet invitees, including Serebrovskii and Dubinin, did not come to the conference, most of those attending approved the idea of holding the next international congress in Russia. As Crew informed his US colleagues, "it would be a very gracious gesture, and [a] helpful one, if we took appropriate steps to make it possible for our Russian colleagues to invite the next Congress to meet in the USSR."[68] Crew discussed the "appropriate steps" with those members of the IOC who attended the conference and consulted with Ashby and Huxley.

The first step was to invite a Soviet representative to join the IOC to fill the slot made vacant by Vavilov's death. Crew wrote a letter to the Soviet Ambassador to Britain Ivan Maiskii "telling him of the existence of this Permanent International [Organizing] Committee and of the desire of its members" to include a representative of the USSR "for the completion of its composition." He stated that "Zhebrak, well-known to all of us, would be regarded as a very welcome reinforcement," and asked the ambassador "to forward this request to the appropriate body in the USSR." Crew noted that the committee would have to decide before the end of March 1946 which of the invitations it received for the holding of the next congress should be accepted and that, therefore, "the Russian nomination must be made immediately."[69] In February 1946 Crew informed the Soviet embassy that the committee was still awaiting the Russian answer: "We are so eager to have the help and support of our Russian colleagues and so reluctant to come to any decision about the next Congress without having heard their views that we are willing to wait until the end of March before taking any final step."[70] The embassy forwarded Crew's letters to the Academy of Sciences, but the plan fell victim to Soviet bureaucratic delays. The correspondence over this project between the Academy of Sciences and the Central Committee dragged on until May 1946, far beyond the announced deadline.[71]

Western geneticists anticipated the possible failure of their project, but they hoped to at least make it possible for their Soviet colleagues to attend the next congress. They considered the international congress "a very effective way to break down the isolation that now exists between us and the Russian geneticists."[72] As Demerec advised his fellow-members on the IOC:

> It seems to me that it would be of the utmost importance, if the Congress could not be held in Russia, to hold it at a place where we could meet the greatest possible number of Russian geneticists. In that case, Sweden might be a much better location than the United States.[73]

Demerec's suggestion was apparently met with approval: the congress was scheduled for Stockholm and Soviet geneticists were invited to participate.

The campaign waged by Western geneticists certainly helped their Soviet colleagues to greatly improve their position vis-à-vis Lysenko's clique in the immediate postwar years. But what neither Soviet geneticists, nor their Western colleagues could anticipate was the coming Cold War. In just two years after the revival of Soviet geneticists' foreign contacts in the summer of 1945, the Cold War once again turned these contacts from an indispensable asset into a dangerous liability. In the autumn of 1947, Zhebrak was put on a show-trial—the honor court—for his "lack of patriotism" and "servility to the West."[74] Dubinin barely escaped the same fate. Understandably, not a single Soviet geneticist appeared at the Eighth international genetics congress held in July 1948 in Stockholm. Furthermore, just a few weeks later, in early August, with Stalin's personal blessings, "Mendelian" genetics was officially banned at a special session of VASKhNIL and "Michurinists" led by Lysenko seized total control over genetics institutions.[75]

Upon learning of Lysenko's final triumph, Western geneticists came to the conclusion that Soviet genetics had "died." They mourned the fate of their Soviet colleagues, and published grieving obituaries for Soviet genetics and angry philippics against its "murderers."[76] But, of course, genetics as an international discipline survived the "amputation" of almost one-third of its ever-growing body of researchers. The international congresses in genetics continued.

Epilogue
Another forty-year long road

An international genetics congress did eventually come to the Soviet Union. But this happened more than forty years after the ill-fated Seventh congress was supposed to have met there and thirty years after genetics had been officially banned in the Soviet Union at the August 1948 VASKhNIL session.

In August 21–30, 1978, almost 3,500 delegates from some sixty countries attended the Fourteenth international genetics congress in Moscow. The congress proceedings included three plenary sessions, twenty-four symposia, thirty-two sections, thirteen invited lectures, and three exhibitions and featured more than 1,800 reports, nearly one-third of them delivered by the hosts—Soviet geneticists.

In a way, the same man who had spearheaded the efforts to arrange the Seventh congress brought the Fourteenth congress to Moscow—Nikolai Vavilov. The congress's first plenary session was devoted to "Vavilov's legacy in modern genetics." Five speakers—one American, three Russian, and one Swedish—joined their voices to praise Vavilov's contributions to the science of genetics and to highlight their importance in contemporary research. None of the speakers mentioned Vavilov's failed attempt to organize the Seventh congress in Moscow or his absence from the president's chair at the congress in Edinburgh. Yet, a huge portrait of Vavilov that hung on the backcloth of the meeting hall testified to the congress organizers' appreciation of his role in fostering international relations in genetics. A special exhibition mounted in the lobby chronicled Vavilov's research and institution-building activities, including extensive coverage of his travels and contacts with researchers throughout the world. Clearly, Vavilov's name had come to symbolize Soviet geneticists' ties to their foreign counterparts.

But, there ought to have been two more portraits on that backcloth—Nikolai Kol'tsov's and Iurii Filipchenko's. For it was mostly their students (and the students of their students), including Sos Alikhanian, Dmitrii Beliaev (the congress's general secretary), Nikolai Bochkov (chairman of the Soviet organizing committee), Nikolai Dubinin (member of the Soviet organizing committee), Vladimir Efroimson, Sergei Gershenzon, Aleksandra Prokof'eva-Bel'govskaia, Isaak Rapoport, and Vladimir Strunnikov, who actually made it possible for the congress to come to Moscow in 1978.

Contrary to the impressions of Western observers, Soviet genetics did not "die" in 1948—rather, it went "underground." Its survival was assured by the very factor

Plate 22 The Fourteenth international genetics congress, Moscow, 1978. (From *Vestnik Akademii Nauk SSSR*, 1979, no. 10.)

that caused its official abolition at the infamous August 1948 VASKhNIL session—the Cold War. The importance of genetics research in the new atomic age combined with the fierce competition between the superpowers in the development of biological weapons, space exploration, and biomedical research helped Soviet geneticists once again win the ear of their party patrons and gradually restore and then expand genetics' institutional base in the Soviet Union.[1]

Furthermore, although in 1948 the Cold War erected the Iron Curtain between the two blocs—East and West—a mere decade later, geneticists were able to part that curtain and, albeit on a limited scale, reestablish Soviet genetics' representation within international networks. Despite the fact that in August 1958, only representatives of "Michurinist" genetics came to the Tenth international congress in Montreal, a month later, in September, several Soviet "Mendelists," including Prokof'eva-Bel'govskaia and Alikhanian, appeared at the Second international conference on the peaceful uses of atomic energy in Geneva. There, after more than twenty years of separation, they met with their one time mentor H. J. Muller, as well as a number of other Western geneticists.

It took another decade and the fall of Lysenko's principal supporter among the new Soviet leadership—Nikita Khrushchev—for Soviet geneticists to arrange for their attendance at the Twelfth international congress. In 1968, in Tokyo, a sizable delegation headed by Dubinin demonstrated to the world community that Soviet genetics was very much alive and striving to make up for the time lost while Lysenko and his cronies dominated their discipline. Ten years later, Soviet geneticists'

Plate 23 Soviet "Mendelists" in Geneva, September 1958. Left to right: B. Glass, Taylor, S. Alikhanian, A. Prokof'eva-Bel'govskaia, Copal-Ayengar, H. J. Muller, Swaminathan, Gustafsson. Courtesy of Lilly Library, Indiana University, Bloomington, Indiana.

efforts to reintegrate into the international community culminated in the convocation of the Fourteenth congress in Moscow.

The forty years since the failed attempt to hold a genetics congress in the Soviet Union had witnessed not only the considerable quantitative growth and geographical expansion of genetics as an international discipline, but also the strengthening of its institutions. Various national genetic societies were now united into the International Genetics Federation. The Federation's Executive Board and Council of National Representatives assumed the functions of the Permanent International Organizing Committee for Genetics Congresses. It was the Executive Board's decision at the Thirteenth congress in Berkeley, CA in August 1973 to accept the invitation of the Soviet delegation that brought the next congress to Moscow.

But the new institutional structures did not free international genetics from contemporary politics. The Moscow congress clearly reflected a new geopolitical context: the triangle of political forces that had dominated the 1930s—Hitler's Germany, Stalin's Russia, and Western democracies—had been replaced by the Cold War confrontation between the superpowers—the Soviet Union and the

United States. The host of the previous congress—the American Genetics Society—boycotted the Moscow congress, as did the Israel Genetics Society. Nor did official representatives of these countries appear at the business meetings of the International Genetics Federation held during the congress. This, however, did not prevent the attendance of more than two hundred American geneticists at the congress in Moscow, demonstrating that even in the thoroughly polarized world of the Cold War many scientists were able to uphold loyalty to their science.

In the 1970s, paraphrasing Mohr's earlier concern, genetics was once again "brought to the very foreground of public attention."[2] But this time, in contrast to the situation in the 1930s, genetics generated mostly "desirable publicity." The breaking of genetic code had inaugurated the "molecular revolution" and precipitated advances in genetic engineering and biotechnology, which came to define what modern genetics was all about.

The congress's official motto—"Genetics and the well-being of mankind"— embodied the new reality: the dichotomy between "applied" and "academic" genetic research in local and international settings had all but disappeared. To a certain degree, this reflected significant changes in the patronage of genetics. The growth of state patronage of science stimulated in many countries by the Cold War made "applied" subjects particularly important for maintaining the external legitimacy of genetics in local settings. On the other hand, the emergence of a number of international agencies, particularly under the umbrella of the United Nations (including UNESCO, the Food and Agricultural Organization, and the World Health Organization), which took an interest in, and partially funded research in agricultural and medical genetics, legitimized "applied" genetics on the international scene.

No less important, however, was the fact that after World War II genetics finally began to deliver on its early promises to contribute to the improvement of agriculture and the "betterment of mankind." New high-yield varieties of industrially important plants, animals, and microbes (including yeasts and antibiotic-producing molds), the development of technologies for screening genetic disorders and for monitoring mutagenic effects of environmental pollution, these and many other highly publicized achievements displaced the image of genetics as a purely "academic" discipline. At the congress in Moscow, almost 20 percent of presentations addressed the "genetic basis of breeding" in plants and animals,[3] while more than one hundred reports dealt with "genetic security," highlighting the mutagenic danger of various environmental pollutants.[4]

At the same time, in the wake of the revelation of the Nazi atrocities that had thoroughly undermined the public and scientific support for eugenics, geneticists were able to finally dispose of the "undesirable publicity" that for a long time marred the practical applications of human genetics. From the 1950s through the 1970s, a number of geneticists took to rewriting the history of their discipline in such a way that did not even mention eugenics.[5] Human genetics became a major subject of international discussion: one of the four volumes of the congress proceedings dealt entirely with various issues in medical applications of genetics.[6]

The congress also attested to the profound changes in genetic methods and research agendas that had been prompted by the "molecular revolution." A special volume of the congress proceedings was devoted to "molecular foundations of genetic processes," heralding advances in deciphering the internal organization of chromosomes and biochemical analysis of gene expression, transcription, and reparation.[7] The new techniques also invited renewed discussions of the old problems of "evolution in light of genetics research."[8]

In the best tradition of its predecessors, the Soviet leadership headed at the time by Leonid Brezhnev spared no expense to show the world their respect for international science. The congress opened in the Kremlin Palace of Congresses with a deputy-head of the USSR Council of Ministers, former head of the Central Committee Science Department V. Kirillin, delivering the government's greetings to the participants. The central newspapers *Pravda* and *Izvestiia* carried almost daily interviews with eminent foreign and Soviet delegates, reports, and feature articles on the congress proceedings, hailing the achievements of genetics and the need for international cooperation among its practitioners.[9]

For their part, neither Soviet geneticists nor their foreign guests missed an opportunity to emphasize the need for international congresses. As one would have expected, their major concern was the propagation and continuity of international networks. The congress's general secretary Dmitrii Beliaev stressed in his interview to *Izvestiia*: "no correspondence, no exchange of reprints can substitute for an immediate, live dialogue, when scientists look into each other's eyes."[10] Interviewed by *Pravda*, the French vice-president of the congress Jean Lejeune echoed Beliaev's sentiment: "The Moscow genetics congress demonstrates the importance of personal contacts, exchange of ideas, [and] open discussions to the normal development of science .... No exchange of scientific publications or letters can replace personal contacts among scientists."[11]

Although not recorded in any official accounts of the congress, one event epitomized perfectly the continuity of international genetics networks—the appearance at the congress of Nikolai Timofeeff-Ressovsky, after more than thirty years of absence on the international scene.[12] Ever since Timofeeff-Ressovsky moved to Germany in 1925, he was an active member of international networks. During the 1920s and 1930s, hardly any international event in genetics went without his participation—he attended the Berlin, Ithaca, and Edinburgh congresses, as well as a number of smaller conferences held during the 1930s, like the one organized by Niels Bohr in November 1936 on relations between physics and genetics. In early 1937, in the wake of the "patriotic" campaign against Chichibabin and Ipatieff, the Soviet embassy approached Timofeef-Ressovsky with an invitation to come back to the USSR, but he declined and stayed in Berlin continuing his research through the war years.[13] After the war, in October 1945, Timofeeff-Ressovsky was arrested by the Soviet secret police and transported to a Moscow prison. A year later, he was sentenced to ten years of hard labor in the Gulag for his refusal to return to the Soviet Union, qualified as "high treason." But within a year, half-dead from starvation and pellagra, Timofeeff-Ressovsky was moved to a special "prison" laboratory in the Southern Urals, which was established for him

Plate 24 Timofeeff-Ressovsky at the Fourteenth international genetics congress, Moscow, 1978. (From V. V. Babkov and E. S. Sakanian, *Nikolai Vladimirovich Timofeev-Resovskii, 1900–1981*, Moscow: Pamiatniki Istoricheskoi Mysli, 2002.)

as part of the Soviet atomic bomb project. In 1951, thanks to his contribution to the studies of genetic effects of radiation, the prison sentence was revoked, but for the rest of his life Timofeeff-Ressovsky was officially forbidden to even visit Moscow.[14] His appearance at one of the congress sessions was clandestinely arranged by his pupil and co-worker, Nikolai Vorontsov, and produced an unprecedented furor. Charlotte Auerbach—who in the early 1930s had known Timofeeff-Ressovsky in Berlin and had not seen him since the Edinburgh congress—burst into tears. Timofeeff-Ressovsky was immediately surrounded by a number of foreign geneticists, who wanted personally to greet one of the legendary "founders," who, together with Max Delbruck and Karl Zimmer, had laid the foundation for radiation genetics and biology. The KGB and party "curators" of the congress were beyond themselves at such a breach of rules, but could not interfere for fear of an international scandal.

For Timofeeff-Ressovsky, the congress presented a chance to reunite with his long-lost friends; for hundreds of Soviet geneticists, it was the first opportunity to meet their foreign colleagues face to face. The Soviet branch of the international networks initiated by the founders of Soviet genetics was greatly expanded.

Just thirteen years later, following the dissolution of the USSR and the collapse of the Soviet science system in 1991, these personal contacts forged during the congress would play a crucial role in the migration of a disproportionately large number of Soviet geneticists (considerably larger than, for instance, the number of Soviet physiologists) to the centers of their discipline in Europe, North America, and Australia. In 1937, Robert Merton noted pointedly: "as long as scientists themselves are uncertain of their primary loyalty, their position becomes tenuous and uncertain."[15] The end of the Cold War enabled Soviet geneticists to overcome that uncertainty and to choose freely between their dual loyalties—to their country or to their science.

Notes

Preliminaries

1 Davenport to the Secretary of State, December 17, 1936, Manuscript collections at the American Philosophical Society Library (hereafter—APS), Ch. Davenport Collection. B: D 27, (hereafter—Davenport Papers).
2 Robert K. Merton, "Science and the social order," *Philosophy of Science*, 1938, vol. 5, 321–37.
3 See Nikolai Krementsov, *Stalinist Science*, Princeton: Princeton University Press, 1997.
4 See Nikolai Krementsov, "A 'second front' in Soviet genetics: The international dimension of the Lysenko controversy," *Journal of the History of Biology* (hereafter—*JHB*), 1996, vol. 29, 229–50.
5 See Mark B. Adams, *Networks in Action: The Khrushchev Era, the Cold War and the Transformation of Soviet Science*, Trondheim: Trondheim Studies on East European Cultures and Societies, 2000.

Prologue

1 Alas, it was never sent. It is preserved among Darlington's documents at the Department of Western manuscripts, Bodleian Library, Oxford (UK), (hereafter—Darlington Papers), C. 98. H. 52. Unfortunately, I was unable to identify three of the fourteen signatories.
2 A comprehensive bibliography of publications in the history of genetics would include several thousand works. A simple search with the keyword "genetics" in the Eureka database for the history of science, technology, and medicine produces more than 2,500 references, and this database is far from complete.
3 Compare, for instance, Leslie C. Dunn, *A Short History of Genetics: The Development of Some of the Main Lines of Thought, 1864–1939*, New York: McGraw-Hill, 1965; and Jonathan Harwood, "National styles in science: Genetics in Germany and the United States between the World Wars," *Isis*, 1987, vol. 78, 390–414; also, idem., *Styles of Scientific Thought: German Genetics Community, 1900–1933*, Chicago: University of Chicago Press, 1993.
4 For instance, only recently, the role of international congresses in setting certain agendas of genetic research has been explored by Robert H. Haynes, "Heritable variations and mutagenesis at early international congresses of genetics," *Genetics*, 1998, vol. 148, 1419–31.
5 On Mendel and the rediscovery of his laws, see an excellent work of Jan Sapp, "The nine lives of Gregor Mendel," in H. E. Le Grand (ed.) *Experimental Inquiries*, Dordreht: Kluwer Academic Publishers, 1990, pp. 137–166.
6 On this production system, see, for instance, Robert Kohler, *Lords of the Fly*, Chicago: University of Chicago Press, 1994; and Karen A. Rader, "Of mice, medicine, and

genetics: C. C. Little's creation of the inbred laboratory mouse, 1909–1918," *Studies in History and Philosophy of Biology and Biomedical Sciences*, 1999, vol. 30C, 319–43; idem., " 'The mouse people': murine genetics work at the Bussey Institution, 1909–1936," *JHB*, 1998, vol. 31, 327–54. All of these works, however, focus on developments in particular locales, notably the United States, and barely mention the international dimension of this particular mode of production.

7 On the particular history of French genetics, see Richard M. Burian, Jean Gayon, and Doris Zallen, "The singular fate of genetics in the history of French biology, 1900–1940," *JHB*, 1988, vol. 21, 357–402.

8 For support of the first point of view see, for instance, Brigitte Schroeder-Gudehus, "Nationalism and internationalism," in R. Olby *et al.* (eds) *Companion to the History of Modern Science*, London–New York: Routledge, 1989, p. 909; Jean-Jacques Solomon, "The 'internationale' of science," *Science Studies*, 1971, vol. 1, p. 24. For support of the latter viewpoint see, for instance, Elisabeth Crawford, "Internationalism in science as a casualty of the First World War," *Social Science Information*, 1988, vol. 27, 163–201; Elisabeth Crawford, *Nationalism and Internationalism in Science, 1880–1939: Four Studies of the Nobel Population*, Cambridge: Cambridge University Press, 1992; and David N. Livingstone, *Putting Science in its Place: Geographies of Scientific Knowledge*, Chicago: University of Chicago Press, 2003.

9 See, for example, George W. Gray, *Education on an International Scale: A History of the International Education Board, 1923–1938*, Westport: Greenwood Press, 1978; Marcos Cueto (ed.) *Missionaries of Science: The Rockefeller Foundation and Latin America*, Bloomington: Indiana University Press, 1994; Elisabeth Crawford, *The Beginnings of the Nobel Institution: The Science Prizes 1901–1915*, Cambridge and Paris: Cambridge University Press, 1984; C. G. Bernhard, Elisabeth Crawford, and Per Sorbom (eds) *Science, Technology and Society in the Time of Alfred Nobel*, Oxford: Pergamon Press, 1981; Robert M. Friedman, *The Politics of Excellence: Behind the Nobel Prize in Science*, New York: Times Books, 2001; Ellen C. Lagemann, *The Politics of Knowledge: The Carnegie Corporation, Philanthropy, and Public Policy*, Middletown: Wesleyan University Press, 1989; Tore Frangsmyr (ed.) *Solomon's House Revisited: The Organization and Institutionalization of Science*, Canton: Science History Publications, 1990; Patrick Petitjean, Catherine Jami, and Anne Mari Moulin (eds) *Science and Empires: Historical Studies about Scientific Development and European Expansion*, Dordreht: Kluwer Academic Publishers, 1992; John Krige (ed.) *History of CERN*, Amsterdam: Elsevier, 1987–1996, vol. 1–3; F. W. G. Baker, "The International Council of Scientific Unions (relations and reflections)," *Transnational Associations*, 1997, vol. 49, 304–10; Frank Greenaway, *Science International: A History of the International Council of Scientific Unions*, Cambridge: Cambridge University Press, 1996; James Trefil and Margaret H. Hazen, *Good Seeing: A Century of Science at the Carnegie Institution of Washington, 1902–2002*, Washington, DC: Joseph Henry Press, 2002; Giuliana Gemelli and Roy MacLeod (eds) *American Foundations in Europe: Grant-Giving Policies, Cultural Diplomacy, and Trans-Atlantic Relations, 1920–1980*, Bruxelles, New York: P. I. E.-Peter Lang, 2003.

10 See, for instance, Brigitte Schroeder-Gudehus, *Deutsche Wissenschaft und Internationale Zusammenarbeit, 1914–1928*, Geneva: Dumaret & Golay, 1966; Harry W. Paul, *The Sorcerer's Apprentice: The French Scientist's Image of German Science, 1890–1919*, Gainesville: University of Florida, 1972; Paul Forman, "Scientific internationalism and the Weimar physicists: the ideology and its manipulation in Germany after World War I," *Isis*, 1973, vol. 64, 151–80; Brigitte Schroeder-Gudehus, *Les scientifiques et la paix: La communauté scientifique internationale au cours des ânes 20*, Montréal: Presse de l'Université de Montréal, 1978; George Magyar, "Science and nationalism," *Scientia: Rivista di Scienza*, 1978, vol. 113, 867–84; R. W. Home and S. G. Kohlstedt (eds) *International Science and National Scientific Identity: Australia between Britain and America*, Dordreht: Kluwer Academic Publishers, 1991; Elisabeth Crawford, Terry Shinn, and Sverker Sorlin (eds) *Denationalizing Science: The Contexts of International Scientific Practice*, Dordreht: Kluwer Academic Publishers, 1993.

11 See, for instance, Paul Hoch's essay review of several publications on the subject, which was provocatively entitled "Whose scientific internationalism?", but did not even raise the issue of science patrons' attitude towards international activities. See Paul Hoch, "Whose scientific internationalism?" *British Journal for the History of Science*, 1994, vol. 27, 345–9.

12 See Mark B. Adams, *Networks in Action: The Khrushchev Era, the Cold War and the Transformation of Soviet Science*, Trondheim: Trondheim Studies on East European Cultures and Societies, 2000, here—pp. 11–12.

13 Consider just one much studied example—the creation of the International Research Council (IRC) in the aftermath of World War I. There is little doubt that the IRC's original statutes, agendas, and membership were profoundly affected by its principal architects—the French Emile Picard, the Belgian Georges Lecointe, the British Arthur Schuster, the Italian Vito Volterra, and the American George E. Hale—who continuously communicated with each other.

14 On the role of networks in advancing certain experimental practices see, for instance, Jean-Paul Gaudilliere, "Molecular biologists, biochemists, and messenger RNA: the birth of a scientific network," *JHB*, 1996, vol. 29, 417–45.

15 See, for instance, Rolv P. Amdam, "Professional networks and the introduction of research in the British and Norwegian pharmaceutical industry in the inter-war years," *History and Technology*, 1996, vol. 13, no. 2, 101–14.

16 See, for instance, Seigfried Grundmann, "Zum Boykott der deutschen Wissenschaft nach dem ersten Weltkrieg," *Wissenschaftliche Zeitschrift der Technischen Universitat Dresden*, 1965, vol. 14, 799–906; Daniel J. Kevles, "Into hostile political camps: the reorganization of international science in World War I," *Isis*, 1970, vol. 62, 47–60; Brigitte Schroeder-Gudehus, "Pas de Locarno pour la science: La coopération scientifique internationale et la politique étrangère des Etats pendant l'entre-deux-guerres," *Relations Internationales*, 1986, vol. 46, 173–94; and Elisabeth Crawford, "Internationalism in science as a casualty of the First World War," *Social Science Information*, 1988, vol. 27, 163–201.

17 For an analysis of scientific relations between the two blocs, see, for instance, Linda L. Lubrano, "National and international politics in US–USSR scientific cooperation," *Social Studies of Science*, 1981, vol. 11, 451–80; for a perfect example of the historical analysis of physicists' relations within the Western bloc, see John Krige (ed.) *History of CERN*, Amsterdam: Elsevier, 1987–96, vol. 1–3; for a comparable account of physicists' relations within the Eastern bloc, see N. N. Bogoliubov (ed.) *Nauchnoe Sotrudnichestvo Sotsialisticheskikh Stran v Iadernoi Fizike*, Moscow: Energoatomizdat, 1986. On a more general theme of the formation of "academic regime" within the Eastern bloc, see Michael David-Fox and Gyorgy Peteri (eds) *Academia in Upheaval: Origins, Transfers, and Transformations of the Communist Academic Regime in Russia and East Central Europe*, Westport, London: Bergin & Garvey, 2000.

18 See, for instance, Kazimiera Prunskiene and Elmar Altvater (eds) *East-West Scientific Co-operation: Science and Technology Policy of the Baltic States and International Co-operation*, Dordrecht: Kluwer Academic Publishers, 1997.

19 A telling example of this neglect of the interwar period in historical studies of scientific internationalism is the history of international cooperation in geophysics and meteorology. There are several historical accounts of the First international polar year, 1882–83: see, for instance, William Barr, "Geographical aspects of the First International Polar Year, 1882–1883," *Annals of the Association of American Geographers*, 1983, vol. 73, 463–84; W. Schröder, "The First International Polar Year (1882–1883) and international geophysical cooperation," *Earth Sciences History*, 1991, vol. 10, 223–26; and F. W. G. Baker, "The First International Polar Year, 1882–83," *Polar Record*, 1982, vol. 21, 275–85. There are also several historical studies of the International geophysical year, 1957–58; see, for example, contributions to Roger D. Launius, John M. Logsdon, and Robert W. Smith (eds) *Reconsidering Sputnik: Forty Years Since the Soviet Satellite*, Amsterdam: Harwood Academic Publishers, 2000. However,

the history of the Second international polar year, 1932–33, remains to be written; see V. Laursen, "The Second International Polar Year (1932/33)," *Bulletin of the World Meteorological Organization*, 1982, vol. 31, 214–22. In contrast, historians of medicine and public health have been much more active in the exploration of the interwar international relations in their fields of inquiry. See, for instance, Paul Weindling (ed.) *International Health Organizations and Movements, 1918–1939*, Cambridge: Cambridge University Press, 1995; William H. Schneider (ed.) *Rockefeller Philanthropy and Modern Biomedicine: International Initiatives from World War I to the Cold War*, Bloomington: Indiana University Press, 2002.

20 Of course, the challenges are not limited to these two factors. Daniel Aleksandrov, for instance, has recently suggested that one of the major factors defining scientists' attitudes towards "nationalization" and "internationalization" is the size and the development of internal structures—the "self-sufficiency"—of a local community. See D. A. Aleksandrov, "Pochemu sovetskie uchenye perestali pechatat'sia za rubezhom: stanovlenie samodostatochnosti i izolirovannosti otechestvennoi nauki, 1914–1940," *Voprosy Istorii Estestvoznaniia i Tekhniki* (hereafter—*VIET*), 1996, no. 3, 3–24.

21 For accounts of the role of Rockefeller philanthropies in promoting international scientific relations see, for instance, George W. Gray, *Education on an International Scale: A History of the International Education Board, 1923–1938*, Westport, Conn.: Greenwood Press, 1978; and Marcos Cueto (ed.) *Missionaries of Science: The Rockefeller Foundation and Latin America*, Bloomington: Indiana University Press, 1994; Reinhard Siegmund-Schultze, *Rockefeller and the Internationalization of Mathematics between the Two World Wars: Documents and Studies for the Social History of Mathematics in the 20th Century*, Basel, Boston: Birkhäuser Verlag, 2001; William H. Schneider (ed.) *Rockefeller Philanthropy and Modern Biomedicine: International Initiatives from World War I to the Cold War*, Bloomington: Indiana University Press, 2002.

22 The literature on the role of Rockefeller philanthropies in fostering international relations in genetics is quite extensive. Unfortunately, most of this literature focuses on the post-World War II period. See, for instance, Robert E. Kohler, "The management of science: the experience of Warren Weaver and the Rockefeller Foundation program in molecular biology," *Minerva*, 1976, vol. 14, 279–306; Paul Weindling, "The Rockefeller Foundation and German biomedical sciences, 1920–40: from educational philanthropy to international science policy," in Nicolaas A. Rupke (ed.) *Science, Politics and the Public Good: Essays in Honour of Margaret Gowing*, London: Macmillan, 1988, pp. 119–40; Lily E. Kay, *The Molecular Vision of Life: Caltech, the Rockefeller Foundation, and the Rise of the New Biology*, New York: Oxford University Press, 1993; idem., "Rethinking institutions: philanthropy as an historiographic problem of knowledge and power," *Minerva*, 1997, vol. 35, 283–93; Pnina Abir-Am, "The discourse of physical power and biological knowledge in the 1930s: a reappraisal of the Rockefeller Foundation's 'policy' in molecular biology," *Social Studies of Science*, 1982, vol. 12, 341–82; idem., "Converging failures: Science polity, historiography, and social theory of early molecular biology," in Tamara Horowitz and Allen I. Janis (eds.) *Scientific Failure*, Lanham: Rowman & Littlefield, 1994, pp. 141–65; Diane B. Paul, "The Rockefeller Foundation and the origins of behavior genetics," in Keith R. Benson *et al.* (eds) *Expansion of American Biology*, New Brunswick: Rutgers University Press, 1991. pp. 262–83; Jean-Paul Gaudillière, "Rockefeller strategies for scientific medicine: molecular machines, viruses and vaccines," *Studies in History and Philosophy of Biological and Biomedical Sciences*, 2000, vol. 31C, 491–509.

23 In the post-World War II period, when science became a matter of "national security," scientists' international activities came under strict governmental control in practically every country. See, for instance, Ronald E. Doel and Allan A. Needell, "Science, scientists, and the CIA: balancing international ideals, national needs, and professional opportunities," *Intelligence and National Security*, 1997, vol. 12, 59–81; Jessica Wang, *Science in an Age of Anxiety: Scientists, Anticommunism, and the Cold War*, Chapel Hill: University of North Carolina Press, 1999; and Krementsov, *Stalinist Science*.

24 The difference in governmental attitudes towards international relations in science and public health was readily evident even in the Rockefeller philanthropies' different strategies in these two fields. When fostering international activities in science, Rockefeller agencies—both IEB and the Rockefeller Foundation—dealt directly with members of various scientific networks: the award of an IEB fellowship required only recommendations of leading scientists in the fellow's discipline. But when promoting international relations in public health, the Rockefeller International Health Board (IHB) worked exclusively through governmental agencies: the award of an IHB fellowship required approval of a governmental agency (usually, the ministry of public health or its equivalent) of the country from which the fellow applied. For an account of how these different strategies played out in Rockefeller philanthropies' activities in Soviet Russia see, Susan G. Solomon and Nikolai Krementsov, "Giving and taking across borders: the Rockefeller Foundation and Russia, 1919–1928," *Minerva*, 2001, no. 3, 265–98.

25 For a comparative analysis of governmental attitudes towards international science, see Ronald E. Doel, Dieter Hoffmann, and Nikolai Krementsov, "State limits on international science: a comparative study of German science under the Third Reich, Soviet science under Stalin, and U.S. science in the early Cold War," *Osiris*, 2005 (forthcoming).

26 Davenport to the Secretary of State, December 17, 1936, Manuscript collections of the American Philosophical Society Library (hereafter—APS), Ch. Davenport Collection. B: D 27, (hereafter—Davenport Papers).

27 Forman, "Scientific internationalism and the Weimar physicists," p. 152.

28 See, for instance, David Joravsky, *Soviet Marxism and Natural Science, 1917–1932*, London: Routledge and K. Paul, 1961; Loren R. Graham, *Science and Philosophy in the Soviet Union*, New York: Vintage Books, 1974; Dominique Lecourt, *Proletarian Science? The Case of Lysenko*, London: NLB, 1977; Monika Renneberg, *Science, Technology and National Socialism*, Cambridge: Cambridge University Press, 1994; Robert Bowen, *Universal Ice: Science and Ideology in the Nazi State*, London: Belhaven Press, 1993; Mark Walker, *Nazi Science: Myth, Truth, and the German Atomic Bomb*, New York: Plenum Press, 1995.

29 For instance, at a special symposium on the influence of politics on studies in human heredity, participants have concentrated exclusively on events within the national communities—Russian, German, and Scandinavian—while the international "dimensions" of the described events have largely been ignored, see, *Genome*, 1989, 879–1137.

30 For a brief survey of the state of genetics in the 1930s, see James F. Crow, "Genetics in the thirties," *Advances in Cancer Research*, 1994, vol. 65, 1–15. Characteristically, this account does not even mention the contradictions between "national" and "international" variants, which plagued the discipline during this period.

31 See, for example, Robert N. Proctor, *Racial Hygiene: Medicine under the Nazis*, Cambridge: Harvard University Press, 1988; Peter Weingart, Jürgen Kroll, and Kurt Bayertz, *Rasse, Blut und Gene: Geschlichte der Eugenik und Rassenhygiene in Deutchland*, Frankfurt am Main: Suhrkamp, 1988; and Paul Weindling, *Health, Race, and German Politics between National Unification and Nazism, 1870–1945*, Cambridge: Cambridge University Press, 1989.

32 On the rise of "Michurinist" genetics in the Soviet Union, see Zhores Medvedev, *The Rise and Fall of T. D. Lysenko*, New York: Columbia University Press, 1969; David Joravsky, *The Lysenko Affair*, Cambridge: Harvard University Press, 1970; Douglas R. Weiner, "The roots of "Michurinism": transformist biology and acclimatization as currents in the Russian life sciences," *Annals of Science*, 1985, vol. 42, 243–60; Valerii Soyfer, *T. D. Lysenko and the Tragedy of Soviet Science*, New Brunswick: Rutgers University Press, 1994; Nikolai Krementsov, *Stalinist Science*, Princeton: Princeton University Press, 1997.

33 See, for instance, Helen M. Rozwadowski, *The Sea Knows No Boundaries: A Century of Marine Science Under ICES*, Copenhagen: ICES and the University of Washington Press, Seattle, 2002.

34 During the post-World War II period, however, this also would change. See, for example, Jacob D. Hamblin, "Science in isolation: American marine geophysics research, 1950–1968," *Physics in Perspective*, 2000, vol. 2, no. 3, 293–312.

35 This aspect of the history of genetics has partially been explored in Diane B. Paul, *The Politics of Heredity: Essays on Eugenics, Biomedicine, and the Nature–Nurture Debate*, Albany: State University of New York Press, 1998.

36 Otto Mohr to Nikolai Vavilov, July 21, 1937. Vavilov's papers in the Central State Archive of Scientific–Technical Documentation (hereafter—TsGANTD), f. 318, op. 1–1, d. 1436, 11. 70–76.

1 International genetics congresses, 1899–1939

1 See Daniel J. Kevles, "Into hostile political camps: the reorganization of international science in World War I," *Isis*, 1970, vol. 62, 47–60; Elizabeth Crawford, "Internationalism in science as a casualty of the First World War," *Social Science Information*, 1988, vol. 27, 163–201.

2 See Seigfried Grundmann, "Zum Boykott der deutschen Wissenschaft nach dem ersten Weltkrieg," *Wissenschaftliche Zeitschrift der Technischen Universität Dresden*, 1965, vol. 14, 799–906; Brigitte Schroeder-Gudehus, "Challenge to transnational loyalties: international scientific organizations after the First World War," *Science Studies*, 1973, vol. 3, 93–118; Brigitte Schroeder-Gudehus, "Pas de Locarno pour la science," *Relations internationales*, 1986, vol. 46, 173–94.

3 On the role of the Royal Horticultural Society and plant breeding in the early development of genetics in Britain see Robert Olby, "Mendelism: from hybrids and trade to a science," *Comptes Rendus de l'Academie des Sciences*, Ser. III, 2000, vol. 323, 1043–51.

4 See "International conference on hybridization (the cross-breeding of species) and on the cross-breeding of varieties, 1899," *Journal of the Royal Horticultural Society*, 1900, vol. 24.

5 See "Proceedings of the international conference on plant breeding and hybridization, held in the rooms of the American Institute of the City of New York and in the Museum Building of the New York Botanical Garden, September 30 and October 1 and 2, 1902," *Memoirs of the Horticultural Society of New York*, 1904, vol. 1.

6 See William Wilks (ed.) *Report of the Third International Conference on Genetics, London 1906*, London: Royal Horticultural Society, 1907.

7 See a sample letter of invitation to the conference, in William Wilks (ed.) *Report of the Third International Conference on Genetics, London 1906*, London: Royal Horticultural Society, 1907, pp. 6–7.

8 W. Bateson, "The Progress of Genetic Research," in ibid., pp. 90–7, here—p. 91. Bateson had first used the word "genetics" in 1905 in a private letter to his colleague— the Cambridge zoologist Adam Sedgwick. But it was at the 1906 conference that the word was first used publicly and gained acceptance by other students of heredity.

9 See William Bateson, *Mendel's Principles of Heredity: A Defense*, Cambridge: Cambridge University Press; New York: Macmillan Co., 1902.

10 On the biometricians–Mendelians controversy see, for instance, Robert Olby, "The dimensions of scientific controversy: the biometric-Mendelian debate," *British Journal for the History of Science*, 1989, vol. 22, 299–320; Kyung-Man Kim, *Explaining Scientific Consensus: The Case of Mendelian Genetics*, New York: Guilford Press, 1994; Marga Vicedo, "What is that thing called Mendelian genetics?," *Social Studies of Science*, 1995, vol. 25, 370–82.

11 See, for instance, Daniel Kevles, "Genetics in the United States and Britain, 1890–1930: a review with speculations," in Charles Webster (ed.) *Biology, Medicine and Society, 1840–1940*, Cambridge: Cambridge University Press, 1981, pp. 193–215; Diane Paul and Barbara Kimmelman, "Mendel in America: Theory and Practice, 1900–1919," in Keith R. Benson, Ronald Rainger, and Jane Maienschein (eds) *The American Development of Biology*, Philadelphia: University of Pennsylvania Press, 1988, pp. 281–310.

12 See, for instance, Jan Sapp, "The struggle for authority in the field of heredity, 1900–1932: new perspectives on the rise of genetics," *JHB*, 1983, vol. 16, 311–42; and Raphael Falk, "The struggle of genetics for independence," *JHB*, 1995, vol. 28, 219–46.

13 For an impressive application of this thesis to the social history of the medical profession in the United States, see Paul Starr, *The Social Transformation of American Medicine*, New York: Basic Books, 1982, particularly Chapter 3, "The consolidation of authority," pp. 79–144.

14 The question of what constitutes "internal" and "external" spheres for a discipline, of course, requires further clarification. Depending on a specific purpose of analysis, one can distinguish multiple distinct "internal" and "external" spheres in which creators of a discipline need to build up consensus and to establish legitimacy. One can treat, for instance, national scene as an "internal" and international scene as "external" spheres. At the same time, one can treat the emerging disciplinary community as an "internal" sphere and the established or competing community as "external" one. Furthermore, one can treat science as a whole as an "internal" sphere and society at large as an "external" one.

15 As witnessed by Bateson's letters to his wife from the international zoological congress in the United States in 1907, genetics certainly received a much warmer welcome in the United States than in Britain. This correspondence is cited in William Bateson, F. R. S. *His Essays and Addresses with a Memoir by Beatrice Bateson*, New York, London: Garland Publishing, Inc., 1984, pp. 107–11.

16 See Philippe de Vilmorin (ed.) *Comptes rendus et rapports, IV Conférence internationale de génétique, Paris, 1911*, Paris: Masson et cite, 1913. On the Vilmorin family and the role of the Vilmorin company in the early development of genetics in France, see J. Gayon and D. T. Zallen, "The role of the Vilmorin company in the promotion and diffusion of the experimental science of heredity in France, 1840–1920," *JHB*, 1998, vol. 31, 241–62.

17 Philippe de Vilmorin (ed.) *Comptes rendus et rapports, IV Conférence internationale de génétique, Paris, 1911*, Paris: Masson et cite, 1913, pp. 27–8.

18 See Erich Tschermak, "Ueber Bildung neuer Formen durch Kreuzung," in J. P. Lotsy (ed.) *Résultats scientifiques du congrès international botanique, Vienne, 1905*, Jena: G. Fisher, 1906, pp. 323–32.

19 W. Bateson to Beatrice Bateson, August 24, 1907. Cited in William Bateson, F. R. S. *His Essays and Addresses with a Memoir by Beatrice Bateson*, New York, London: Garland Publishing, Inc., 1984, p. 109.

20 See N. M. Stevens, "The chromosomes in *Drosophila ampelophila*," in *Proceedings of the Seventh International Zoological Congress, Boston, 19–24 August, 1907*, Cambridge: The University Press, 1912, pp. 380–81; and F. E. Lutz, "Inheritance of abnormal wing-venation in Drosophila," in ibid., pp. 411–19.

21 On Galton, see Ruth Schwartz Cowan, *Sir Francis Galton and the Study of Heredity in the Nineteenth Century*, New York: Garland Publishing, 1985; and Nicholas W. Gillham, *A Life of Sir Francis Galton: From African Exploration to the Birth of Eugenics*, New York: Oxford University Press, 2001.

22 The literature on the history of eugenics is quite voluminous and continues to grow. On eugenics in Britain and the United States see, Daniel J. Kevles, *In the Name of Eugenics*, New York: Knopf, 1985; Pauline M. H. Mazumdar, *Eugenics, Human Genetics, and Human Failings: The Eugenics Society, its Sources and its Critics in Britain*, London; New York: Routledge, 1992; Elof Axel Carlson, *The Unfit: A History of a Bad Idea*, Cold Spring Harbor: Cold Spring Harbor Laboratory Press, 2001; on eugenics in Germany see Sheila Faith Weiss, *Race Hygiene and National Efficiency: The Eugenics of Wilhelm Schallmayer*, Berkeley: University of California Press, 1987; Robert N. Proctor, *Racial Hygiene*, Cambridge: Harvard University Press, 1988; Peter Weingart, Jürgen Kroll, and Kurt Bayertz, *Rasse, Blut und Gene*, Frankfurt am Main: Suhrkamp, 1988; and Paul Weindling, *Health, Race, and German Politics between National Unification and Nazism, 1870–1945*, Cambridge: Cambridge University Press, 1989; on eugenics in France see William H. Schneider, *Quality and Quantity: The Quest for Biological Regeneration in Twentieth-century France*, Cambridge: Cambridge University Press, 1990.

23 For a comparative history of eugenics in various countries, see Mark B. Adams (ed.) *The Wellborn Science: Eugenics in Germany, France, Brazil, and Russia*, New York: Oxford Univeristy Press, 1990; Alexandra Stern, *Eugenics beyond Borders: Science and Medicalization in Mexico and the U.S. West, 1900–1950*, unpublished PhD thesis, University of Chicago, 1999.

24 Paul Weindling, "The 'Sonderweg' of German eugenics: nationalism and scientific internationalism," *British Journal of the History of Science*, 1989, vol. 22, 321–33.

25 See also Daniel Kevles, "Genetics in the United States and Britain, 1890–1930: a review with speculations," in Webster (ed.) *Biology, Medicine and Society*, pp. 193–215.

26 Raymond Pearl, "The inheritance of fecundity," in *Problems in Eugenics. Papers communicated to the First International Eugenics Congress held at the University of London, July 24th to 30th, 1912*, London: The Eugenics Education Society, 1913, reprinted by New York, London: Garland Publishing, Inc. 1984, pp. 47–57.

27 See *Problems in Eugenics. Report on Proceedings of the First International Eugenics Congress held at the University of London, July 24th to 30th, 1912*, London: The Eugenics Education Society, 1913, p. 15.

28 R. C. Punnett, "Genetics and eugenics," in *Problems in Eugenics. Papers communicated to the First International Eugenics Congress held at the University of London, July 24th to 30th, 1912*, London: The Eugenics Education Society, 1913, pp. 137–38.

29 See *Problems in Eugenics. Report on Proceedings of the First International Eugenics Congress held at the University of London, July 24th to 30th, 1912*, London: The Eugenics Education Society, 1913, p. 19.

30 See T. H. Morgan, A. H. Sturtevant, H. J. Muller, and C. B. Bridges, *The Mechanism of Mendelian Heredity*, New York: Holt, 1915.

31 For details on Morgan and his school see Garland Allen, *Thomas Hunt Morgan: The Man and His Science*, Princeton: Princeton University Press, 1978; and Robert Kohler, *Lords of the Fly*, Chicago: University of Chicago Press, 1994.

32 See T. H. Morgan and C. B. Bridges, *Sex-linked Inheritance in Drosophila*, Washington: Carnegie Institution of Washington, 1916; T. H. Morgan, C. B. Bridges, and A. H. Sturtevant, *Contributions to the Genetics of Drosophila melanogaster*, Washington: Carnegie Institution of Washington, 1919; T. H. Morgan, *The Physical Basis of Heredity*, Philadelphia: J. B. Lippincott, 1919; T. H. Morgan, A. H. Sturtevant, H. J. Muller, and C. B. Bridges, *The Mechanism of Mendelian Heredity*, New York: Holt, 1923, revised edition.

33 See correspondence between Erwin Baur and Albert Blakeslee of December 10, 1921 in APS, William Bateson Correspondence. D: B319 (hereafter—Bateson Papers). This correspondence with a commentary was published in Bentley Glass, "A hidden chapter of German eugenics between the two World Wars," *Proceedings of the American Philosophical Society*, 1981, vol. 125, 357–67.

34 See correspondence between Bateson and Baur in Bateson Papers. For a general analysis of the "normalization" of the international scientific relations in the aftermath of the war see Brigitte Schroder-Gudehus, *Deutsche Wissenschaft und internationale Zusammenarbeit, 1914–1928*, Geneva: Dumaret & Golay, 1966; Brigitte Schroeder-Gudehus, "Internationale wissenschaftsbeziehungen und auswärtige Kulturpolitik 1919–1933," in Rudolf Vierhaus and Bernhard vom Brocke (eds) *Forschung im Spannungsfeld von Politik und Gesellschaft: Geschichte und Struktur der Kaiser-Wilhem-/Max Planck Gesellschaft*, Stuttgart: Deutsche Verlags Anstalt, 1990, pp. 858–85; Paul Forman, "Scientific internationalism and the Weimar physicists: the ideology and its manipulation in Germany after World War I," *Isis*, 1973, vol. 37, 151–80.

35 Although, of course, dominated by the Americans, the congress included participants from Belgium, Britain, Czechoslovakia, France, Italy, Mexico, and Norway—neither Russian, nor German eugenicists were invited. See *Eugenics, Genetics and the Family. Scientific papers of the Second International Congress of Eugenics*, Baltimore: Williams & Wilkins Company, 1923, vol. 1; and *Eugenics in Race and State. Scientific papers of the Second International Congress of Eugenics*, Baltimore: Williams & Wilkins Company, 1923, vol. 2.

36 Morgan to Babkock, June 12, 1920, APS, Collection of the University of California. Genetics department, 378.794:c12gen, (hereafter—UC Papers).

37 Bateson to Morgan, May 19, 1920, UC Papers. On Bateson's general attitude towards eugenics see R. D. Harvey, "Pioneers of genetics: a comparison of the attitudes of William Bateson and Erwin Baur to eugenics," *Notes and Records of the Royal Society of London*, 1995, vol. 49, 105–17.

38 William Bateson, "Common-sense in racial problems," *Eugenics Review*, 1921–22, vol. 13, 325–38, here—p. 325.

39 On Bateson's attitude toward international activities in the aftermath of the war see A. G. Cock, "Chauvinism and internationalism in science: the International Research Council, 1919–1926," *Notes and Records of the Royal Society of London*, 1983, vol. 37, 249–88.

40 See Baur letters to Bateson, of January 6, 1920; March 14, 1920; April 18, 1920; and October 28, 1921; all in Bateson Papers.

41 See "Vorgeschichte des Kongress," in *Verhandlungen des V. Internationalen Kongresses für Vererbungewissenschaft, Berlin 1927*, Leipzig: Verlag von Gebrüder Borntraeger, 1928, Bd. 1, SS. 1–3.

42 On the combined impact of breeding, eugenics, and experimental zoology on the emergence genetics as a discipline in other countries, see Barbara A. Kimmelman, "The American Breeders Association: genetics and eugenics in an agricultural context," *Social Studies of Science*, 1983, vol. 13, 163–204; Paolo Palladino, "Between craft and science: plant breeding, Mendelian genetics, and British universities, 1900–1920," *Technology and Culture*, 1993, vol. 34, 300–23; and Robert Olby, "Mendelism: from hybrids and trade to a science," *Comptes Rendus de l'Académie des Sciences*, Ser. III, 2000, vol. 323, 1043–51.

43 See O. Iu. Elina, "Nauka dlia sel'skogo khoziaistva v Rossiiskoi Imperii: formy patronazha," *Voprosy Istorii Estestvoznaniia i Tekhniki* (hereafter—*VIET*), 1995, no. 1, 40–63; and Olga Elina, "Planting seeds for the revolution: the rise of Russian agricultural science, 1860–1920," *Science in Context*, 2002, vol. 15, 209–237.

44 For a detailed study of the early development of Russian genetics see Abba E. Gaissinovitch [Gaisinovich], "The origin of Soviet genetics and the struggle against Lamarckism, 1922–1929," *JHB*, 1980, vol. 13, 1–51; and A. E. Gaissinovich, *Zarozhdenie i Razvitie Genetiki*, Moscow: Nauka, 1988, pp. 173–98, 244–327.

45 For instance, US breeders were much more enthusiastic about "Mendelism." See, Diane B. Paul and Barbara A. Kimmelman, "Mendel in America: theory and practice, 1900–1919," in Ronald Rainger, Keith R. Benson, and Jane Maienschein (eds) *The American Development of Biology*, Philadelphia: University of Pennsylvania Press, 1988, pp. 281–310.

46 On Timiriazev's attitude towards Mendelism see Abba E. Gaissinovitch [Gaisinovich], "Contradictory appraisal by K. A. Timiriazev of Mendelian principles and its subsequent perception," *History and Philosophy of the Life Sciences*, 1985, vol. 7, 257–86.

47 See, for example, P. N. Kuleshov, "Teoria Mendelia o nasledstvennosti," in *Sel'skokhoziaistvennoe Zhivotnovodstvo*, Moscow, 1907, pp. 1–3.

48 See E. Baur, *Vvedenie v Izuhenie Nasledstvennosti*, translated by R. Regel', St Petersburg: Izdatel'stvo Biuro po Prikladnoi Botanike, 1913.

49 E. A. Bogdanov, *Mendelizm ili Teoriia Skreshchivaniia*, Moscow: Knigoizdatel'stvo Studentov Moskovskogo Sel'sko-xoziaistvennogo Instituta, 1914.

50 Renamed Petrograd in 1914, Leningrad in 1924, and again St Petersburg in 1991.

51 On the history of Russian eugenics, see Loren R. Graham, "Science and values: the eugenics movement in Germany and Russia in the 1920s," *American Historical Review*, 1977, vol. 82, 1133–64; and Mark B. Adams, "Eugenics in Russia," in Mark B. Adams (ed.) *The Wellborn Science: Eugenics in Germany, France, Brazil, and Russia*, New York: Oxford University Press, 1990, pp. 153–216.

52 See, for instance, F. Gal'ton, *Nasledstvennost' Talanta, Eie Zakony i Posledstviia*, Moscow: Izdatel'stvo zhurnala "Znanie," 1875.

53 See, for example, P. I. Kovalevskii, *Vyrozhdenie i Vozrozhdenie*, Moscow: Izdatel'stvo Russkogo Meditsinskogo Vestnika, 1899; V. M. Bekhterev, "Voprosy vyrozhedniia i bor'ba s nim," *Obozrenie Psikhiatrii i Nevropatologii*, 1908, no. 9, 34–45.

54 On the general system of Russian science under the Soviets, see Krementsov, *Stalinist Science*.

55 For a short biography of Iu. Filipchenko, see Mark B. Adams, "Filipchenko, Iurii Aleksandrovich," in Frederic Holmes (ed.) *Dictionary of Scientific Biography*, vol. 17, Suppl. 2, pp. 297–303; also N. N. Medvedev, *Iurii Aleksandrovich Filipchenko*, Moscow: Nauka, 1978.

56 On the genetics work at these stations see N. K. Kol'tsov, "O rabotakh geneticheskogo otdela Instituta Eksperimental'noi Biologii i ego Anikovskoi geneticheskoi stantsii," *Uspekhi Eksperimental'noi Biologii*, 1922, vol. 1, no. 3–4, 2–12; and Nic. Koltzoff [Kol'tsov], "Experimental biology and the work of the Moscow institute," *Science*, 1924, vol. 59, 497–502.

57 Later, in 1930, these two institutes were merged into the All-Union Institute of Plant Breeding (VIR) under Vavilov's directorship.

58 On Gorky's involvement with science and scientists see a special issue of *Soviet and Post-Soviet Review* edited by James Andrews, "Maksim Gor'kii, science and the scholarly community in revolutionary Russia," *Soviet and Post-Soviet Review*, 1995, vol. 22, no. 1, 1–5.

59 On Communist science see Krementsov, *Stalinist Science*; on Communist academy see Michael David-Fox, *Revolution of the Mind: Higher Learning among the Bolsheviks*, New Haven: Yell University Press, 1998.

60 On Kol'tsov and his institute see Mark B. Adams, "Science, ideology, and structure: the Kol'tsov institute, 1900–1970," in Linda L. Lubrano and Susan G. Solomon (eds) *The Social Context of Soviet Science*, Boulder: Westview Press, 1980, pp. 173–204.

61 There are numerous accounts of Vavilov's life and works, see, for example, Mark Popovskii, *The Vavilov Affair*, Humden, Conn., 1984.

62 On Davenport and the Eugenics Record Office see Garland E. Allen, "The eugenics record office at Cold Spring Harbor, 1910–1940: an essay in institutional history," *Osiris*, 1986, 2nd Series, vol. 2, 225–64.

63 Vavilov to Davenport, September 21, 1921, Davenport Papers.

64 See Koltzoff [Kol'tsov] to Davenoport, June 25, 1921, Davenport Papers.

65 See Philiptschenko [Filipchenko] to Davenport, October 28, 1921, Davenport Papers.

66 On Muller, see Elof A. Carlson, *Genes, Radiation, and Society: The Life and Work of H. J. Muller*, Ithaca: Cornell University Press, 1970.

67 On Serebrovskii's life and work, see Mark B. Adams, "Serebrovskii, Aleksandr Sergeevich," in F. Holmes (ed.) *Dictionary of Scientific Biography*, vol. 18, Suppl. 2, pp. 803–11; and N. N. Vorontsov (ed.) *Aleksandr Sergeevich Serebrovskii*, Moscow: Nauka, 1993.

68 See G. G. Meller [H. J. Muller], "Rezul'taty desiatiletnikh geneticheskikh issledovanii s Drosophila," *Uspekhi Eksperimental'noi Biologii*, 1923, vol. 1, 292–321; H. J. Muller, "Observations of biological science in Russia," *Scientific Monthly*, 1923, vol. 16, 539–52.

69 See *Akademiia Nauk SSSR. Personal'nyi Sostav, 1917–1974*, Moscow: Nauka, 1974, vol. 2, pp. 366–83.

70 See, for instance, Iu. A. Filipchenko, "Iz vpechatlenii o zagranichnoi poezdke," *Nauchnyi Rabotnik*, 1925, no. 1, 150–9.

71 See N. K. Kol'tsov, "Evgenicheskie s"ezdy v Milane v sentiabre 1924 g.," *Russkii Evgenicheskii Zhurnal*, 1925, vol. 3, 73–7.

72 V. I. Lenin, "Lozhka degtia v bochke meda," in *Polnoe sobranie sochinenii*, Moscow: Politizdat, 1970, 5th ed., vol. 45, pp. 206–7.

73 See *Organizatsiia Nauki v Pervye Gody Sovetskoi Vlasti (1917–1925)*, Leningrad: Nauka, 1968, pp. 377–9.

74 For path-breaking research on VOKS, see Michael David-Fox, "From illusory 'society' to intellectual 'public': international travel and the party intelligentsia in the interwar period," *Contemporary European History*, 2002, vol. 2, 7–32; and idem., "Showcases, fronts, and boomerangs: the prominence of Germany in the map of VOKS, 1925–1933 and after," forthcoming.

75 For a careful analysis of the jubilee based on the newly available archival materials, see M. Iu. Sorokina, "Pridat' . . . impozantnyi kharakter," *Priroda*, 1999, no. 1, 59–72; and Marina Sorokina, *Trigger or Window of Opportunity*, unpublished manuscript, 1999.

76 The letter is preserved in the Archive of Foreign Policy of the Russian Federation (hereafter—AVPR), f. 04, op. 59, papka 424, d. 56954, 11. 2–9; Rykov's memorandum for the Politburo regarding the letter is preserved in his personal collection in the Russian State Archive for Socio-political History (hereafter—RGASPI), f. 669, op. 1, d. 5, ll. 11–11 reverse. Both documents have been recently published by M. Sorokina, "Iz arkhivnogo dos'e," *Priroda*, 1999, no. 1, pp. 68–73. All the following citations are from this source.

77 The Central Committee's governing apparatus also included the Secretariat and the Political Bureau (Politburo), which oversaw its numerous specialized departments. On the detailed structure (and its changes) of the party organs involved with science policy issues see Krementsov, *Stalinist Science*.

78 See correspondence between Bateson and Vavilov during 1924–25, in N. I. Vavilov, *Nauchnoe Nasledie v Pis'makh*, Moscow: Nauka, 1994–2002, vol. 1–5.

79 See Bateson's Russian impressions in his article W. Bateson, "Science in Russia," *Nature*, 1925, vol. 116, 681–2; and letters to his wife Beatrice.

80 Bateson died shortly before Karpechenko's arrival.

81 See, for instance, C. Leonard Huskins, "Some Russian impressions," *Scientific Agriculture*, 1927, vol. 7, no. 8, 300–5.

82 On Vavilov's expeditions see N. I. Vavilov, *Piat' Kontinentov*, Leningrad: Nauka, 1987.

83 See, for instance, Jean-Jacques Solomon, "The 'internationale' of science," *Science Studies*, 1971, vol. 1, 23–42; A. J. Cock, "Chauvinism and internationalism in science: the International Research Council, 1919–1926," *Notes and Records of the Royal Society of London*, 1983, vol. 37, 249–88.

84 A. E. Ivanov, "Rossiiskoe 'uchenoe soslovie' v gody 'vtoroi otechestvennoi voiny'," *VIET*, 1999, no. 2, 108–28.

85 For a detailed description of German–Soviet scientific relations in the 1920s see D. A. Aleksandrov, A. N. Dmitriev, Iu. Kh. Kopelevich, B. Lange, T. A. Lukina, A. V. Patralov, I. Rikhter, *Sovetsko-germanskie Nauhnye Sviazi Vremeni Veimarskoi Respubliki*, St Petersburg: Nauka, 2001.

86 See the State Archive of the Russian Federation (hereafter—GARF), f. A2307, op. 2, dd. 543–96.

87 RGASPI, f. 17, op. 85, dd. 649–659.

88 See RGASPI, f. 17, op. 13, d. 329, l. 145.

89 RGASPI, f. 17, op. 85, d. 652, l. 105.

90 Kol'tsov to Semashko, June 26, 1927, the Archive of the Russian Academy of Sciences (hereafter—ARAN), St Petersburg Branch, f. 160, op. 1, d. 107, l. 1. Published in *Mezhdunarodnye Nauchnye Sviazi Akademii Nauk SSSR, 1917–1941*, Moscow: Nauka, 1992, p. 127.

91 RGASPI, f. 17, op. 85, d. 652, l. 145.

92 The Fifth international genetics congress was in this sense absolutely unique. I know of no other international congress that was attended by such a large delegation of Soviet scientists. See, for instance, *Mezhdunarodnye Nauchnye Kongressy*, Leningrad: BAN, 1964; *Mezhdunarodnye Nauchnye Sviazi Akademii Nauk SSSR: 1917–1941*, Moscow: Nauka, 1992.

93 E. W. Lindstrom, "Report on Fifth international genetics congress. Berlin, Sept. 11–17, 1927," in Rockefeller Archive Center (hereafter—RAC), IEB, 1.1.25.350

E. W. Lindstrom, 1926–28. I am particularly grateful to Tom Rosenbaum for pointing me to this source.

94 Ibid.
95 See Lunacharskii to Agitprop, September 3, 1927, RGASPI, f. 17, op. 113, d. 329, l. 124.
96 See Gorbunov and Vavilov to SNK, August 31, 1927, RGASPI, f. 17, op. 113, d. 329, l. 148. At that time Gorbunov also headed the VSNKh Science Department.
97 See RGASPI, f. 17, op. 113, d. 329, l. 146.
98 See S. Krylov to Secretariat, September [not earlier than 13], 1927, RGASPI, f. 17, op. 113, d. 329, l. 145.
99 RGASPI, f. 17, op. 113, d. 329, ll. 7–8.
100 On relationship between the Rockefeller philanthropies and the Soviet Union, see Susan G. Solomon and Nikolai Krementsov, "Giving and taking across borders: the Rockefeller Foundation and Russia, 1919–1928," *Minerva*, 2001, no. 3, 265–98.
101 See W. Rose Diary. 53, (1922–23), in RAC, RF 12.1.
102 On the Rockefeller activities in supporting science see Robert Kohler, *Partners in Science: Foundations and Natural Scientists, 1900–1945*, Chicago: University of Chicago Press, 1991.
103 RAC, IEB minutes and dockets, April 30, 1923.
104 RAC, IEB dockets, 1923–24, meeting of May 26, 1924.
105 For Gabrichevskii's fellowship see his file in RAC, IEB collection, Gabrichevskii.
106 Gabrichevskii chose not to return to Russia, despite the urgings of Morgan and Rockefeller foundation officers who were afraid that other Russians would not be allowed to accept fellowships, if Gabrichevskii failed to come back to his homeland.
107 See Dobzhansky's file in RAC, IEB, 1. 3. 47. 699.
108 On Dobzhansky see Mark B. Adams (ed.) *The Evolution of Theodosius Dobzhansky*, Princeton: Princeton University Press, 1994. See also Dobzhansky's recently published correspondence with his teacher Filipchenko in Mikhail Konashev (ed.) *U Istokov Akademicheskoi Genetiki v St. Peterburge*, St Petersburg: Nauka, 2002.
109 It seems likely that Navashin's visa troubles were provoked by the fact that his brother Dmitrii occupied important posts in the Bolshevik government.
110 See Agol's report on his fellowship in GARF, f. A2307, op. 19, d. 232, ll. 4–7; Levit's in GARF, f. A2307, op. 19, d. 241, ll. 2–5. For a short biography of Levit, see Mark B. Adams, "Levit, Solomon Grigori'evich," in F. Holmes (ed.) *Dictionary of Scientific Biography*, vol. 18, Suppl. 2, pp. 812–9.
111 O'Brien to Serebrovskii, February 11, 1931, ARAN, f. 1595, op. 1, d. 377, l. 101.
112 See correspondence regarding Zhebrak's stay at Columbia in Dunn Papers.
113 See Dunn's report on his travels to Moscow recently published in Joe Cain and Iona Layland, "The situation in genetics: Dunn's 1927 Russian tour," *The Mendel Newsletter*, 2003, New Series, no. 12, 10–15.

2 The road to Moscow

1 On the "revolution from above" see Sheila Fitzpatric, *The Russian Revolution*, New York: Oxford University Press, 1982; Graeme Gill, *The Origins of the Stalinist Political System*, New York: Cambridge University Press, 1990; and Moshe Lewin, *The Making of the Soviet System*, New York: Pantheon Books, 1985.
2 On the effects of the "Great Break" in Soviet science system see Nikolai Krementsov, *Stalinist Science*, Princeton: Princeton University Press, 1997.
3 On the Shakhty trial and its effect on science see Kendall Bailes, *Technology and Society under Lenin and Stalin*, Princeton: Princeton University Press, 1978; Loren Graham, *The Ghost of Executed Engineer*, Cambridge: Harvard University Press, 1993.
4 On his life and work, see Mark B. Adams, "Chetverikov, Sergei Sergeevich," in F. Holmes (ed.) *Dictionary of Scientific Biography*, vol. 17, Suppl. 2, pp. 155–65; also N. M. Artemov and T. E. Kalinina, *Sergei Sergeevich Chetverikov*, Moscow: Nauka, 1994.

New documents illuminating his arrest and exile have been recently published in T. E. Kalinina (ed.) *Sergei Sergeevich Chetverikov. Dokumenty k Biografii, Neizdannye Raboty, Perepiska i Vospominaniia*, Moscow: Nauka, 2002, particularly, pp. 117–25.

5 On Chetverikov's school see Mark B. Adams, "The founding of population genetics: contributions of the Chetverikov school, 1924–1934," *JHB*, 1968, vol. 1, 23–39; idem., "Sergei Chetverikov, the Kol'tsov institute, and the evolutionary synthesis," in Ernst Mayr and William Provine (eds) *The Evolutionary Synthesis: Perspectives on the Unification of Biology*, Cambridge: Harvard University Press, 1980, pp. 242–78; V. V. Babkov, *Moskovskaia Shkola Evoliutsionnoi Genetiki*, Moscow: Nauka, 1985.

6 So far, the assumption that the Russian Eugenics Society was liquidated by a direct governmental decree has not been supported by documentary evidence. It seems more likely that eugenicists themselves decided to abandon the society. During the Great Break, the government issued new rules for the registration of all scientific societies, moving them from the auspices of Narkompros to those of the secret police— NKVD. All societies were required to present their statutes and membership to the secret police for approval in three months. A number of societies did so, but the Russian Eugenics Society did not.

7 See "Evgenika," in *Bol'shaia Sovetskaia Entsiklopediia*, Moscow: Politizdat, 1931, vol. 23, pp. 812–19.

8 On transition from eugenics to medical genetics see Mark B. Adams, "The politics of human heredity in the USSR," *Genome*, 1989, vol. 31, 879–84.

9 For an account of the institute's activities and its director, see Mark B. Adams, "Eugenics in Russia," in Mark B. Adams (ed.) *The Wellborn Science: Eugenics in Germany, France, Brazil, and Russia*, New York: Oxford University Press, 1990, pp. 153–216.

10 See *Materialy k Vsesoiuznoi Konferentsii po Planirovaniiu Genetiko-Selektsionnykh Issledovanii*, Leningrad: VASKhNIL, 1932.

11 See correspondence between Davenport and Vavilov regarding this visit in Davenport Papers.

12 TsIK created the Temporary Committee to supervise research and educational institutions (*Vremennyi Komitet po Zavedyvaniiu Uchenymi i Uchebnymi Zavedeniiami*) in August 1925. The committee became "permanent" and gained much power during the Great Break.

13 Serebrovskii to Scientific Committee, July 15, 1930, GARF, f. 7668, op. 1, d. 317, l.1.

14 See GARF, f. 7668, op. 1, d. 317, ll. 3–6.

15 GARF, f. 7668, op. 1, d. 317, l. 8.

16 GARF, f. 7668, op. 1, d. 317, l. 11.

17 GARF, f. 7668, op. 1, d. 317, l. 12.

18 GARF, f. 7668, op. 1, d. 317, ll. 13–14.

19 GARF, f. 7668, op. 1, d. 317, l. 14.

20 GARF, f. 7668, op. 1, d. 317, ll. 15–25.

21 GARF, f. 7668, op. 1, d. 317, l. 15.

22 GARF, f. 7668, op. 1, d. 317, l. 26.

23 GARF, f. 7668, op. 1, d. 317, ll. 28–9.

24 GARF, f. 7668, op. 1, d. 317, ll. 30–31.

25 GARF, f. 7668, op. 1, d. 317, ll. 27, 35, 42.

26 GARF, f. 7668, op. 1, d. 317, ll. 32–4, 39.

27 GARF, f. 7668, op. 1, d. 317, ll. 38–38 reverse.

28 GARF, f. 7668, op. 1, d. 317, l. 40.

29 See the report of Ezhov's commission to the Politburo on December 15, 1931 in RGASPI, f. 17, op. 114, d. 271, ll. 2–3, 33–5.

30 RGASPI, f. 17, op. 114, d. 307, l. 33.

31 RGASPI, f. 17, op. 114, d. 307, l. 3.

32 RGASPI, f. 17, op. 114, d. 307, ll. 34–5.

33 RGASPI, f. 17, op. 114, d. 311, l. 93.

34 RGASPI, f. 17, op. 114, d. 310, l. 14.

35 Another Soviet representative, Vladimir Saenko, the head of the agricultural section of Amtorg—the Soviet trade agency in the United States—also attended the congress.

36 See, for instance, William L. Laurence, "Finds way to create more food plants," *NYT*, August 31, 1932; p. 8; "Orange production in north succeeds," *Washington Post*, August 31, 1932; p. 4; and "Russian 'Burbank' shuffles seasons," *NYT*, November 21, 1932, p. 19.

37 See, for instance, a correspondence between Mililslav Demerec and the director of the Odessa Institute of Genetics Andrei Sapegin in Demerec Papers.

38 See GARF, f. 7668, op. 1, d. 317, ll. 30–4.

39 See *Akademiia Nauk SSSR. Personal'nyi Sostav, 1917–1974*, Moscow: Nauka, 1974, vol. 2, pp. 406–08. This edition does not mention that Hermann J. Muller was elected a corresponding member of the academy in February 1933.

40 See RGASPI, f. 17, op. 114, d. 348, l. 71. For a detailed analysis of the relationship between the USSR and the Rockefeller philanthropies in the 1930s see Nikolai Krementsov and Susan Gross Solomon, "The structure of giving and the structure of taking: the Rockefeller foundation in Russia, 1928–1935," forthcoming.

41 See, for instance, the Archive of Moscow State University, f. 43, op. 1, d. 121, 1. 46.

42 Vavilov to Harland, August 13, 1936, the Central State Archive of Scientific–Technical Documentation (hereafter—TsGANTD), f. 318, op. 1–1, d. 1185, 1. 34.

43 For instance, in 1935, Vavilov was not permitted to attend the international botanical congress, though a small delegation of Soviet botanists, headed by a "nonparty Bolshevik," director of the Institute of Botany Boris Keller, did come to Amsterdam. The next year, no Soviet scientist took part in a single international congress. Furthermore, basically all foreign travel of Soviet scientists was curtailed. For instance, despite the fact that the Academy of Sciences paid the rent for a working place at the Naples marine station both in 1935 and in 1936, no Soviet scientist used it. At the end of 1937, the academy cancelled its agreement with the station. See ARAN, f. 2 op. 1–1937. d. 667, l. 83.

44 Mohr to Vavilov, April 16, 1935, a copy of this letter is preserved among L. C. Dunn Collection in the American Philosophical Society Library (hereafter—Dunn Papers).

45 The Russian State Archive of Economics (hereafter—RGAE), f. 8390, op. 1, d. 656, ll. 2–2 reverse.

46 ARAN, f. 2, op. 1–1935, d. 83, l. 186.

47 Vavilov to Mohr, July 3, 1935, a copy of this letter is preserved in Dunn Papers and among Otto Mohr Papers at the Anatomical Institute of Oslo University (hereafter—Mohr Papers) found by Guil Winchester.

48 RGASPI, f. 17, op. 114, d. 590, l. 49.

49 RGASPI, f. 17 op. 3, d. 970. l. 9.

50 Vavilov to Mohr, August 29, 1935, Dunn Papers.

51 ARAN, f. 2, op. 1–1935, d. 83, ll. 171–2.

52 ARAN, f. 2, op. 1–1935, d. 83, ll.165–165 reverse; published in *Mezhdunarodnye Nauchnye Sviazi Akademii Nauk SSSR, 1917–1941*, Moscow: Nauka, 1992, pp. 183–4.

53 Vavilov to Mohr, December 7, 1935, Dunn Papers.

54 RGASPI, f. 17, op. 114, d. 601, l. 42.

55 RGASPI, f. 17, op. 3, d. 974, l. 73.

56 ARAN, f. 201, op. 1, d. 42, l. 22.

57 ARAN, f. 201, op. 3, d. 3, ll. 41–4.

58 GARF, f. 5446, op. 18, d. 788, l. 15.

59 ARAN, f. 201, op. 3, d. 3, ll. 25–7.

60 American geneticists to Levit, April 2, 1936, ARAN, f. 201, op. 5, d. 2, ll. 35–7. The signatories of the letter were Edgar Altenberg, T. H. Bissonnette, C. B. Bridges, George Child, L. J. Cole, R. C. Cook, L. T. David, P. R. David, W. F. Dove, L. C. Dunn, W. H. Gates, A. J. Coldforb, Myron Gordon, G. W. Gowen, Mark Graubard,

H. R. Hunt, F. B. Hutt, Viktor Jollos, Walter Landauer, E. W. Lindstrom, C. C. Little, E. C. MacDowell, O. S. Margolis, J. T. Patterson, Raymond Pearl, H. H. Plough, Oscar Riddle, L. H. Snyder, L. J. Stadler, Alexander Weinstein, and P. H. Whiting. A few days later Levit also received letters from Julian Huxley and Herbert Jennings who added their support to the proposal of his American colleagues. See Huxley to Levit, April 15, 1936, ibid., l. 34, Jennings to Levit, April 9, 1936, ibid., l. 38.

61 On Schaxel's life and work see Dieter Fricke, *Julius Schaxel, 1887–1943: Leben und Kampf eines marxistischen deutschen Naturwissenschaftlers und Hochschullehrers*, Leipzig: Urania-Verlag, 1964; and Heinz Penzlin (ed.) *Theoretische Grundlagen und Probleme der Biologie: Festveranstaltung und wissenschaftliche Vortragstagung am 20 und 21 März 1987 an der Friedrich-Schiller-Universität Jena, aus Anlass des 100 Geburtstages von Julius Schaxel*, Jena: Universität Jena, Abteilung Wissenschaftliche Publikationen, 1988.

62 Schaxel to Landauer, November 28, 1935; and May 3, 1936, Dunn Papers.

63 Not all American geneticists supported Landauer's proposal. See, for instance, correspondence between Landauer and Ch. Davenport in Davenport Papers.

64 Landauer to Levit, April 2, 1936, ARAN, f. 210, op. 5, d. 2, ll. 40–1.

65 ARAN, f. 201, op. 3, d. 3, ll. 19–21.

66 GARF, f. 5446, op. 18, d. 788, l. 12.

67 Muralov to Stalin and Molotov, May 4, 1936, GARF, f. 5446, op. 18a, d.192, ll. 4–17.

68 See, for instance, Vavilov to Morgan, June 15, 1936, TsGANTD, f. 318, op. 1–1, d. 1186, l. 35.

69 ARAN, f. 201, op. 3, d. 16, l. 17.

70 Muralov and Levit to the Central Committee's Science Department, September 28, 1936, ARAN, f. 201, op. 3, d. 2, ll. 1–5.

71 GARF, f. 5446, op. 18, d. 788, l. 1.

72 See GARF, f. 5446, op. 18a, d. 192, l. 46.

73 A copy-edited text of the bulletin is preserved in ARAN, f. 201, op. 3, d. 49.

74 RGASPI, f. 17, op. 3, d. 982, l. 40.

75 Muller to Gorbunov, November 25, 1936, ARAN, f. 2, op. 1–1935, d. 83, l. 105.

76 See, for instance, Muller to Dunn, December 9, 1936, Dunn Papers; Muller to Darlington, December 4, 1936, Darlington Papers. C. 98. H. 57.

77 Vavilov to Mohr, December 9, 1936, ARAN, f. 201, op. 5, d. 1, l. 23.

78 See GARF, f. 5446, op. 20a, d. 524, ll. 7–5. A copy was also sent to Bauman.

79 GARF, f. 5446, op. 20a, d. 524, l. 4.

80 Krzhizhanovskii and Gorbunov to Molotov, November [?], 1936, ARAN, f. 2, op. 1–1935, d. 83, l. 104. Vavilov prepared a draft of the letter and discussed it with Krzhizhanovskii. See ibid., ll. 102–3.

81 East to Demerec, December 9, 1936, Manuscript collections of the American Philosophical Society Library, Milislav Demerec's Collection (hereafter—Demerec Papers).

82 Demerec to East, December 10, 1936, Demerec Papers.

83 Rose Kuler to Demerec, December 12, 1936, Demerec Papers.

84 "Moscow Cancels Genetics Parley," *NYT*, December 14, 1936, p. 18.

85 For a detailed analysis of the first stage of the so-called Lysenko controversy see David Joravsky, *The Lysenko Affair*, Chicago: University of Chicago Press, 1986; Krementsov, *Stalinist Science*, and particularly, Nikolai Krementsov, "Printsip 'konkurentnogo iskliucheniia'," in E. Kolchinskii (ed.) *Na Perelome*, St Petersburg, 1999, pp. 107–64.

86 See Arne Muntzing to Demerec, January 30, 1937, APS, Papers of the Genetics Society of America. 575.06. G28p. (hereafter—GSA). box 1. 1937. Folder "Mendelian Society of Lund."

87 Dunn to Demerec, December 15, 1936, Dunn Papers.

88 Emerson to Dunn, December 17, 1936, Dunn Papers.

89 Davenport to the Secretary of State, December 17, 1936, Davenport Papers.

90 On Darlington's general attitude towards events in Russian genetics, see Oren Solomon Harman, "C. D. Darlington and the British and American reaction to Lysenko and the Soviet conception of Science," *JHB*, 2003, vol. 36, 309–52. Unfortunately, this work deals mostly with the post-World War II period.

91 C. J. Nicoll to Darlington, February 1, 1937, Darlington Papers, C. 91. G. 10.

92 See Robert F. Kelley to Davenport, December 29, 1936, Davenport Papers.

93 I was unable to find any documents related to this episode either in the Soviet Embassy's files in AVPR or in Wallace's personal papers in the US National Archives. There is also no mention of Wallace's response in further correspondence between Emerson and Dunn.

94 AVPR, f. 192, op. 3, papka 24, d. 53, ll. 52–3, 57–9, 68; f. 192, op. 4, papka 36, d. 76, l. 1.

95 "Science and Dictators," *NYT*, December 17, 1936, p. 26.

96 "Abandonment of the Moscow meeting of the international congress of genetics," *Science*, 1936, vol. 84, 553–4.

97 Demerec to East, December 16, 1936, Demerec Papers.

98 "Otvet klevetnikam iz 'Sains Servis' i 'N'iu-Iork Taims'," *Izvestiia*, December 21, 1936, p. 1; see also "Moscow defends delay on genetics," *NYT*, December 22, 1936, p. 19.

99 This quotation is from a follow-up story, entitled "Genetics in the USSR," distributed by the Science Service on December 21, 1936. After the *Izvestiia* publication, the Soviet Embassy in Washington began to carefully monitor the Science Service dispatches. A copy of this story is preserved in the Embassy's files in AVPR, f. 192, op. 3, papka 24, d. 53, l. 67.

100 See RGASPI, f. 588, op. 11, d. 199, ll. 6–12.

101 An English translation of the editorial was sent to the Soviet Embassy in Washington, apparently for distribution in the American press. AVPR, f. 192, op. 4, papka 36, d. 76, ll. 17–18, here l. 17.

102 "Telegramma akademika N. I. Vavilova v amerikanskuiu gazetu 'N'iu Iork Taims'," *Izvestiia*, December 22, 1936, p. 4.

103 "Vaviloff defends science in Soviet," *NYT*, December 23, 1936, p. 8.

104 The next day, several Moscow newspapers published notes with a telling title, "New York Times and Science Service attempt to vindicate themselves." See " 'N'iu Iork Taims' i 'Saiens Servis' opravdyvaiutsia," *Vecherniaia Moskva*, December 23, 1936, p. 1; and *Izvestiia*, December 24, 1936, p. 3.

105 Troyanovskii's cables preserved in papers of many American geneticists. See, for instance, Dunn Papers.

106 Dobzhansky to Dunn, December 21, 1936, Dunn Papers.

3 The road to Edinburgh

1 This quotation is from a resolution adopted at the meeting of the American Genetics Society on December 30, 1936, which was cited in an information letter that Demerec distributed to his mailing list two weeks later. See Demerec Papers or the GSA Papers in APS.

2 Emerson to Mohr, December 19, 1936, Mohr Papers.

3 Mohr to Muralov, January 7, 1937, ARAN, f. 201, op. 5, d. 1, ll. 4–5; a copy of this letter is also in Dunn Papers.

4 Mohr to Emerson, January 5, 1937, Demerec Papers.

5 Muralov to Mohr, December 26, 1936, Mohr Papers.

6 Vavilov to Mohr, December 28, 1936 (cable); original is in Mohr Papers, a draft is in ARAN, f. 201, op. 3, d. 16, l. 13.

7 Mohr to Emerson, January 5, 1937, copies of this letter were also sent to Demerec and Dunn.

8 Mohr to Muralov, January 7, 1937, ARAN, f. 201, op. 5, d. 1, ll. 4–5; a copy of this letter is also in Dunn Papers.

9 Vavilov to Mohr, December 9, 1936, ARAN, f. 201, op. 5, d. 1, l. 23.

10 The resolution was included in an information letter that Demerec distributed to his mailing list two weeks later. See Demerec Papers or the GSA Papers.

11 Dunn to Little, January 12, 1937, Dunn Papers.

12 Cook to Dunn, January 18, 1937, Dunn Papers.

13 See R. C. [Robert Cook], "The genetics congress," *Journal of Heredity*, 1937, vol. 28, 24–6.

14 Demerec to Cook, January 22, 1937, Dunn Papers.

15 Dunn to Mohr, January 13, 1937, Dunn Papers.

16 Mohr to the Organizing Committee, February 3, 1937, Russian translation in ARAN, f. 201, op. 5, d. 2, l. 17.

17 Gorbunov and Vavilov to Mohr, February 13, 1937, Mohr Papers.

18 TsGANTD, f. 318, op. 1–1, d. 1436, ll. 58–58 reverse.

19 Mohr to Cook, March 16, 1937, Dunn Papers.

20 Haldane to Mohr, February 2, 1937, Mohr Papers.

21 On Haldane, see Ronald W. Clark, *JBS: The Life and Work of J. B. S. Haldane*, New York: Coward-McCann, Inc., 1968.

22 Crew to Mohr, February 20, 1937, Mohr Papers. Unfortunately, I was unable to locate F. Crew's personal papers. Reportedly, he burned all his correspondence shortly before he died. Most of his letters cited are preserved in the archives of other geneticists, while many letters to Crew from other people did not survive, which makes any assessment of his role in our story somewhat one-sided. On Crew's life and work see Lancelot Hogben, "Francis Albert Eley Crew, 1886–1973," *Biographical Memoirs of Fellows of the Royal Society*, 1974, vol. 20, 135–53.

23 Muller to Huxley, December 31, 1936, a copy of this letter is preserved in Darlington Papers. C. 109. J. 107.

24 ARAN, f. 201, op. 3, d. 16, l. 11.

25 See ARAN, f. 201, op. 3, d. 16, l. 11.

26 Cited in V. D. Esakov (ed.) *Akademiia Nauk v Resheniiakh Politbiuro*, Moscow: ROSSPAN, 2000, p. 246. Emphasis is in the document.

27 See Bauman to Stalin and Molotov, February 5, 1937, GARF, f. 5446, op. 20a, d. 524, ll. 26–21. All following citations are from this source. These documents have been recently published by Esakov (see Esakov, *Akademiia Nauk v Resheniiakh Politbiuro*, pp. 246–7), from the copies he found in the Presidential Archive. However, the copy of Bauman's letter from this archive is not dated, which led Esakov to assume that Bauman's letter prompted the Politburo decision on holding the congress in August 1938 adopted in March 1937 (see following notes).

28 On Molotov's copy the last sentence is underlined in red pencil.

29 Unfortunately, Landauer's letter was given in Russian translation, and I was unable to find the English original in the archives either in the United States or in Russia. The following citations are my translations from the Russian text.

30 Schaxel's letter was also given in Russian translation and I was unable to find the German original in the archives either in the United States or in Russia, though there are indications that it had been sent and received by the addressee. See, for instance, Dunn to Landauer, February 23, 1937, Dunn Papers. The following citations are my translation from the Russian text.

31 See GARF, f. 5446, op. 20a, d. 524, ll. 27–26.

32 For the complete text of the memorandum see, Komarov and Gorbunov to Molotov, February 7, 1937, GARF, f. 5446, op. 20a, d. 524, ll. 39–32. All following citations are from this source.

33 Of course, in the memorandum Mohr's letter was quoted in translation. Here I am citing the English original.

34 See GARF, f. 5446, op. 20a, d. 524, ll. 19–17. All the following quotations are from this source.

35 See GARF, f. 5446, op. 20a, d. 524, ll. 17–15.

36 Of course, Demerec's letter was quoted in Russian. Here I used the English original: Demerec to Troyanovskii, December 20, 1936, Dunn Papers.

37 Muralov and Vavilov to Mohr, February 17, 1937, Dunn Papers; the Russian draft is in ARAN, f. 201, op. 5, d. 1, ll. 6–8.

38 Mohr to Muralov and Vavilov, March 13, 1937, an English copy in Dunn Papers; a Russian translation in ARAN, f. 201, op. 5, d. 1, l. 9.

39 Mohr to Cook, March 16, 1937, a copy in Dunn Papers.

40 I was unable to determine how long Lund had stayed in Moscow, but he had certainly won Muller's confidence. Muller had even entrusted him to smuggle to Mohr the proofs of his book *Bibliography of Drosophila Genetics*, which had been planned for publication by the Academy of Sciences, but encountered difficulties (Muller was asked to remove references to the works of arrested Soviet geneticists, like Agol, and works of some Western geneticists considered to be "Fascist," like Paula Hertwig). Perhaps Lund had also brought Mohr a personal letter from Muller, though Guil Winchester found no trace of such a letter in Mohr Papers. See Muller to Mohr, November 22, 1937, Mohr Papers. A copy of this letter is also preserved among the documents of H. J. Muller's collection held at the Lilly Library of the University of Indiana in Bloomington (hereafter—Muller Papers).

41 Lund also shared his impressions with L. C. Dunn, whose name and phone number Mohr had given him during their meeting in Oslo. After a short phone conversation, Lund sent Dunn a long letter, from which the following lines are cited. Lund to Dunn, March 19, [1937], Dunn Papers.

42 RGASPI, f. 17, op. 3, d. 985, l. 5.

43 See GARF, f. 5446, op. 1, d. 128, l. 95, and op. 20a, d. 524, l. 51.

44 Gubkin and Gorbunov to Molotov, Iakovlev, and Bauman, March 23, 1937, GARF, f. 5446, op. 20a, d. 524, ll. 11–10. The letter was co-signed by a vice-president of the Academy of Sciences, president of the forthcoming International Geological Congress Ivan Gubkin.

45 See ARAN, f. 201, op. 3, d. 16, l. 8.

46 Gorbunov to Molotov, March 27, 1937, GARF, f. 5446, op. 20a, d. 524, ll. 14–12.

47 In this, as in many other cases, Gorbunov certainly relied on Vavilov's information.

48 The original of the memorandum is in TsGANTD, f. 318, op. 1–1, d. 1436, ll. 61–7.

49 See Vavilov to Federley, April 5, 1937, TsGANTD, f. 318, op. 1–1, d. 1437, ll. 49–50; Vavilov to Tschermak, April 5, 1937, TsGANTD, f. 318, op. 1–1, d. 1438, ll. 106–7; Vavilov to Haldane, April 5, 1937, TsGANTD, f. 318, op. 1–1, d. 1437, l. 67; Vavilov to Demerec, April 5, 1937, TsGANTDf. 318, op. 1–1, d. 1437, l. 35.

50 See Vavilov to Mohr, April 8, 1937, Dunn Papers and TsGANTD, f. 318, op. 1–1, d. 1436, ll. 59–60. All the following quotations are from this source.

51 Vavilov to Muller, April 8, [1937], TsGANTD, f. 318, op. 1–1, d. 1436, l. 102–3.

52 Serebrovskii to Dunn, April 14, 1937, Dunn Papers.

53 The letter was cited in E. B. Babcock, May 18, 1937. "Memo 2. Bearing on the International Genetics congress," Mohr Papers.

54 Darlington to Mohr, May 14, 1937, Mohr Papers.

55 Ibid.

56 Demerec to Dunn, Emerson, and Mohr, May 20, 1937, Dunn Papers.

57 Mohr to Muralov and Vavilov, May 20, 1937, ARAN, f. 201, op. 5, d. 4, ll. 28–9.

58 See Koller to Mohr, June 10, 1937, Mohr Papers.

59 Vavilov to Mohr, May 28, 1937, ARAN, f. 201, op. 5, d. 4, l. 25; also Mohr Papers.

60 Serebrovskii to Mohr, June 10, 1937, Mohr Papers. The letter was written in German.

61 For the stenographic record of this meeting see ARAN, f. 201, op. 3, d. 3, ll. 19–21.

62 Komarov, Muralov, Vavilov, Meister to Mohr, June 17, 1937, TsGANTD, f. 318, op. 1–1, d. 1436, ll. 71–2; also Mohr Papers.

63 Mohr to the Organizing Committee, June 29, 1937, ARAN, f. 201, op. 5, d. 4, l. 53; also TsGANTD, f. 318, op. 1–1, d. 1436, ll. 72–3.

64 Haldane to Mohr, June 27, 1937, Mohr Papers.

65 See, for instance, Muller to Dunn, June 17, 1937, Dunn Papers.

66 See, for instance, a letter from Leon J. Cole, head of the genetics department at the University of Wisconsin, Madison, to Muller, of July 9, 1937 in Muller Papers, Box 1, Folder 1937, January–October.

67 There are numerous copies of this memorandum in various collections. See, for instance, Dunn Papers.

68 Muller to Mohr, November 22, 1937, Mohr Papers and Muller Papers.

69 Emerson to Mohr, April 19, 1937, Mohr Papers.

70 See Crew to Vavilov, February 12, 1938, ARAN, f. 2, op. 1–1935, d. 83, l. 30.

71 Vavilov to the Presidium, March 3, 1938, ARAN, f. 2, op. 1–1935, d. 83, l. 28.

72 Vavilov to Molotov, February 20, 1938, ARAN, f. 2, op. 1/735 (1939), d. 157, ll. 1–3. All the following citations are from this source.

73 See Muller to Vavilov, February 21, 1938, ARAN, f. 2, op. 1–1935, d. 83, l. 32; and Muller to Vavilov, December 8, 1937, ARAN, f. 450, op. 3, d. 194, ll. 2–5.

74 Vavilov to Crew, October 1, 1938, a copy of this letter is preserved among the documents of J. B. S. Haldane held at the Library and Archives of the London University College (hereafter—Haldane Papers), Box 35.

75 Crew to Lindstrom, September 16, 1938, GSA Papers, Box 2, Folder 1939. Seventh international genetics congress.

76 See copies of these presentations in ARAN, f. 2, op. 1/735 (1939), d. 157, ll. 4–7.

77 See Muller to Darlington, July 12, 1939, Darlington Papers, C. 100. J. 130.

78 See copies of British geneticists' correspondence with the Soviet Ambassador in Darlington Papers. C. 110. J. 130. A copy of the letter signed among others by Crew, Haldane, Darlington, Muller, and Huxley to the Soviet Ambassador of July 14, 1939, is also in ARAN, f. 2, op. 1/735 (1939), d. 157, ll. 51–3.

79 [Hall] to Lord Halifax, July 14, 1939, Darlington Papers, C. 110. J. 130.

80 W. Maller to Hall, July 15, 1939, Darlington Papers, C. 110. J. 130.

81 Crew immediately circulated copies of the letter through his mailing list. It was later published in its entirety in the proceedings of the congress. See R. C. Punnet (ed.) *Proceedings of the Seventh International Genetical Congress, Edinburgh, Scotland, 23–30 August 1939*, Cambridge: Cambridge University Press, 1941, pp. 2–3.

82 See Ritchie Calder, "Russians abandon genetics meeting," *NYT*, August 23, 1939, p. 20; and "The international congress of genetics," *Science*, 1939, vol. 90, 228.

83 Mohr's speech was printed in the congress's proceedings. See Punnet (ed.) *Proceedings of the Seventh International Genetical Congress*, p. 3–4, here—p. 4.

84 Crew's speech was also included in the proceedings. See ibid., pp. 4–5, here—p. 5.

85 Punnet (ed.) *Proceedings of the Seventh International Genetical Congress*, p. 6.

4 Soviet geneticists and their patrons

1 On this expedition see J. J. R., "The Harvard-M. I. T. Russian eclipse expedition," *Scientific Monthly*, 1936, vol. 42, 565–7.

2 See Hans Harmsen and Franz Lohse (eds) *Bevölkerungsfragen: Bericht des Internationalen Kongresses für bevölkerungswissenschaft, Berlin, 26 August–1 September, 1935*, Munich: J. F. Lehmann, 1936. Nor did students of industrial medicine attempt to withdraw their congress from Frankfurt in 1938, despite the worldwide reaction against Nazi policies toward scientists and physicians at the time.

3 See *Science*, 1937 (June 26), vol. 83, p. 619. Ironically, the announcement of the forthcoming genetics congress in Moscow and the membership of its organizing committee were published on the same page. Perhaps, it was the phrasing of the

postponement of the fever therapy conference that provided a suitable model for the Soviet official statement regarding the postponement of the genetics congress. On the same page was also published the announcement of the postponement of the Madrid psychology congress.

4 See Kuzhnik, *Beyond the Laboratory*, p. 153.

5 See ARAN, f. 2, op. 1–1935, d. 83, ll. 165–165 reverse. The congress's cancellation put a stop on this project.

6 See GARF, f. 5446, op. 18, d. 3151.

7 See ARAN, St Peteresburg Branch, f. 2, op. 1–1932, d. 37, ll. 109–109 reverse, cited in *Mezhdunarodnye Nauchnye Sviazi Akademii Nauk SSSR, 1917–1941*, Moscow: Nauka, 1992, p. 141.

8 GARF, f. 7668, op. 1, d. 317, l. 38 reverse.

9 RGASPI, f. 17, op. 3, d. 1056, l. 188.

10 RGASPI, f. 17, op. 3, d. 970, l. 5.

11 See "Vstupitel'naia rech' prezidenta kongressa akad. Pavlova," in B. I. Zbarskii and V. M. Kaganov, *XV Mezhdunarodnyi Fiziologicheskii Congress*, Moscow-Leningrad: Biomedgiz, 1936, pp. 15–16; "Rech' Sekretaria TsIK SSSR tov. I. A. Akulova," in ibid., pp. 19–21.

12 RGASPI, f. 17, op. 162, d. 18, l. 113. Cited in V. D. Esakov (ed.) *Akademiia Nauk v Resheniiakh Politbiuro*, Moscow: ROSSPAN, 2000, p. 188.

13 See Zbarskii and Kaganov, *XV Mezhdunarodnyi Fiziologicheskii Congress*, pp. 142–51.

14 See, Walter Duranty, "Tests on animals aid insanity study," *NYT*, August 10, 1935, p. 5; Walter Duranty, "Physiologists see great new field," *NYT*, August 11, 1935, p. N1; "Pravda lauds talk," *Washington Post*, August 12, 1935, p. 5; Walter Duranty, "Scientists' group hails Soviet's aid," *NYT*, August 12, 1935, p. 17; Walter Duranty, "Hormones shown to modify organs," *NYT*, August 13, 1935, p. 7; Walter Duranty, "Soviet bountiful honoring science," *NYT*, August 18, 1935, p. E4; Walter Duranty, "Molotoff greets world scientists," *NYT*, August 18, 1935, p. 5; and Waldemar Kaempffert, "The week in science," *NYT*, August 18, 1935, p. XX8.

15 See, for instance, Walter Duranty, "Soviet bountiful honoring science; admiration shown for the world physiologists is 'startling' to Cannon," *NYT*, August 18, 1935, p. E4; and Dean Burk, "A scientist in Moscow," *Scientific Monthly*, 1938, vol. 47, 227–41.

16 Percy M. Dawson, *Soviet Samples. Diary of an American Physiologist*, Ann Arbor: Edwards Brothers, Inc., 1938, pp. 47–8. This book was published in a "simplified" English and I preserved the original spellings and grammar in the quotation.

17 Cited in Zbarskii and Kaganov, *XV Mezhdunarodnyi Fiziologicheskii Congress*, p. 147.

18 On the "Luzin affair" see Alex E. Levin, "Anatomy of a public campaign: 'Academician Luzin's case' in Soviet political history," *Slavic Review*, 1990, vol. 49, 90–108; A. P. Iushkevich, " 'Delo' akademika N. N. Luzina," in *Repressirovannaia Nauka*, Leningrad: Nauka, 1991, pp. 377–94.

19 See S. S. Demidov and B. V. Levshin (eds) *Delo Akademika Nikolaia Nikolaevicha Luzina*, St Peteresburg: RKhGI, 1999, pp. 22–3, 257–8.

20 A few days after the "Lusin affair" had begun, another prominent Soviet scientist, astronomer Gerasimovich was accused of the same sins. See Harold Denny, "Russian astronomer is accused of 'servility' to foreign science," *NYT*, July 20, 1936, pp. 1–2.

21 See V. Komarov, "Akademiki nevozvrashchentsy," *Pravda*, December 21, 1936, p. 3.

22 See "Nedostoinye grazhdanstva SSSR," *Pravda*, January 6, 1937, p. 2.

23 Vavilov to Mohr, January 4, 1937, TsGANTD, f. 318, op. 1–1, d. 1436, ll. 58–58 reverse. I was unable to find any publication of the letter in Soviet newspapers. The only publication that mentioned the letter was an article by J. Shaxel published in *Izvestiia* in June 1936. See Iu. Shaksel', "Rassovoe uchenie, nauka i proletarskii internatsionalizm," *Izvestiia*, June 18, 1936, pp. 2–3.

24 See E. Kol'man, "Chernosotennyi bred fashizma i nasha mediko-biologicheskaia nauka," *Pod Znamenem Marksizma*, 1936, no. 11, 64–72.

25 See L. Karlik, "Trudy Mediko-geneticheskogo instituta im. M. Gor'kogo," *Pod Znamenem Marksizma*, 1936, no. 12, 169–86.
26 See "Po lozhnomu puti," *Pravda*, December 26, 1936, p. 4.
27 See A. S. Serebrovskii, "Antropogenetika i evgenika v sotsialisticheskom obshchestve," *Trudy Kabineta Nasledstvennosti i Konstitutsii Cheloveka pri Mediko-Biologicheskom Institute*, 1929, no. 1, 1–19.
28 See, *Biulleten' IV Sessii* [VASKhNIL], no. 8, December 30, 1936, p. 21.
29 Bauman to Stalin and Molotov, June 26, 1936, GARF, f. 5446, op. 18a, d. 192, ll. 37–40. A copy of this document was found by V. D. Esakov in the Archive of the President of the Russian Federation (hereafter—APRF), f. 3, op. 33, d. 210, ll. 34–7 and recently published in Esakov (ed.) *Akademiia Nauk v Resheniiakh Politbiuro*, pp. 214–16. In the publication, the document is undated, but the original found in GARF is dated June 26, 1936.
30 See Shaksel', "Rassovoe uchenie, nauka i proletarskii internatsionalizm," p. 2.
31 See GARF, f. 5446, op. 18a, d. 192, ll. 46–52.
32 See GARF, f. 501, op. 3, d. 341, ll. 1–39. I am particularly grateful to Carola Sachse for directing my attention to these documents and providing copies.
33 The literature on the "Lysenko controversy" is quite extensive. For details see Zhores Medvedev, *The Rise and Fall of T. D. Lysenko*, New York: Columbia University Press, 1969; David Joravsky, *The Lysenko Affair*, Chicago: University of Chicago Press, 1986; Loren R. Graham, *Science and Philosophy in the Soviet Union*, New York: Vintage Books, 1974; Dominique Lecourt, *Proletarian Science? The Case of Lysenko*, London: NLB, 1977; V. A. Soyfer, *T. D. Lysenko and the Tragedy of Soviet Science*, New Brunswick: Rutgers University Press, 1994; and Nikolai Krementsov, *Stalinist Science*, Princeton: Princeton University Press, 1997.
34 See Niels Roll-Hansen, "A new perspective on Lysenko?" *Annals of Science*, 1985, vol. 42, 261–78.
35 On the phenomenon of "founding fathers" see Krementsov, *Stalinist Science*.
36 See RGAE, f. 7486, op. 1, d. 1107, p. 64; f. 8390, op. 1, dd. 757–67, 789.
37 Zavadovskii, one of the pupils of Nikolai Kol'tsov, at that time worked mostly on embryology and "developmental mechanics." See his memoirs M. M. Zavadovskii, *Stranitsy Zhizni*, Moscow: MGU, 1991.
38 For analysis of "public discussion" as a special feature of Soviet scientific culture, see Krementsov, *Stalinist Science*.
39 Chernov and Muralov to Stalin and Molotov, July 8, 1936. GARF, f. 5446, op. 18a, d. 828, l. 3. Characteristically, when the idea of the congress's postponement began to circulate in the SNK apparatus in late July, one of SNK officials also raised the issue of rescheduling the VASKhNIL discussion. See ibid., l. 5.
40 GARF, f. 5446, op. 18a, d. 828, l. 1.
41 See *Sbornik Pabot po Diskussionym Problemam Genetiki i Selektsii*, Moscow: VASKhNIL, 1936.
42 GARF, f. 5446, op. 18a, d. 192, ll. 37–40. Also cited in Esakov, *Akademiia Nauk v Resheniiakh Politbiuro*, p. 215.
43 RGAE, f. 8390, op. 1, d. 781, l. 1.
44 See *Spornye Voprosy Genetiki i Selektsii*, Moscow: Sel'khozgiz, 1937.
45 RGASPI, f. 17, op. 3, d. 982, l. 40.
46 See GARF, f. 6824, op.1, d. 16, l. 79.
47 See GARF, f. 5446, op. 29, d. 30, ll. 17–21.
48 ARAN, f. 201, op. 3, d. 2, ll. 10–12, here l. 10.
49 ARAN, f. 201, op. 3, d. 2, ll. 6–9, here l. 6.
50 See Esakov, *Akademiia Nauk v Resheniiakh Politbiuro*, pp. 212–14.
51 RGASPI, f. 17, op. 163, d. 1128, l. 21.
52 It is possible, however, that Molotov had discussed the situation with Stalin, while visiting him at his dacha on the night of November 13.

53 See GARF, f. 5446, op. 18a, d. 192, ll. 42–4.

54 See, for example, GARF, f. 5446, op. 18a, d. 192, ll. 68–70.

55 See GARF, f. 5446, op. 18, d. 788, l. 1.

56 See GARF, f. 6824, op. 1, d. 17, l. 14.

57 See GARF, f. A-2206, op. 69, d. 2215, ll. 90–2.

58 Prokhorov to Gorbunov, November 16, 1936, ARAN, f. 2, op. 1–1935, d. 83, l. 101.

59 See, for instance, Otto Mohr, "The next international genetics congress," *Science*, December 13, 1935, vol. 82, 565–6.

60 RGASPI, f. 17, op. 163, d. 1141, l. 8.

61 On the Great Terror see, for instance, Robert Conquest, *The Great Terror: A Reassessment*, New York: Oxford University Press, 1990; J. Arch Getty and Oleg V. Naumov, *The Road to Terror: Stalin and the Self-Destruction of the Bolsheviks, 1932–1939*, New Haven: Yale University Press, 1999.

62 Muller to Huxley, March 9, 1937, Darlington Papers.

63 One of the new regime's first show trials of the Mensheviks was held in 1922 and the Mensheviks were the first of the many "deviations" and "oppositions" excommunicated from the new, Soviet Russia.

64 Unfortunately, the documents related to Levit's expulsion from the Communist Party, subsequent arrest, and execution are still unavailable.

65 See Brat'ia Tur, "V pylu uvlecheniia," *Izvestiia*, December 10, 1936, p. 3.

66 Kol'man to Molotov, November 5, 1936, GARF, f. 5446, op. 29, d. 30, ll. 185–90.

67 Brat'ia Tur, "Kontramarka v Panteon," *Izvestiia*, November 16, 1936, p. 4; also Brat'ia Tur, "V pylu uvlecheniia," *Izvestiia*, December 10, 1936, p. 3.

68 See ARAN, f. 2, op. 1–1935, d. 83, l. 100.

69 GARF, f. 8009, op. 1, d. 113, l. 27.

70 They were also discussing the Soviet participation at the Fifteenth International Aeronautic Exhibition that was to open in Paris in December 1936. See RGASPI, f. 17, op. 3, d. 980.

71 See GARF, f. 5446, op. 26, d. 61, ll. 138–130.

72 For the extensive press coverage of the geological congress, see *Pravda* and *Izvestiia* for July 21–24, 27, 29–30, 1937; and the *New York Times* for July 11, 22, 23, 1937.

73 RGASPI, f. 17, op. 3, d. 985, l. 5.

74 During 1936, Soviet policies run contrary to certain principles and findings of human genetics. Two governmental decrees announced in July 1936 are particularly noteworthy in this respect: a new anti-abortion law and the Central Committee's resolution on the so-called "pedological perversions in the system of Narkomproses."

75 GARF, f. 8009, op. 1, d. 113, l. 24.

76 Muller to Huxley, March 9 and 13, 1937, Muller Papers and Darlington Papers.

77 See H. J. Muller, *Out of the Night. A Biologist's View of the Future*, New York: Vanguard, 1935.

78 Among Muller's papers in the Lilly Library, I found two copies of a text that had been identified as Muller's letter to Stalin. The first, undated and untitled typed text that begins with words "As a scientist . . . " is located among Muller's writings, see Muller MSS, Writings, Box 3, Folder 1936. The second, entitled "The social dimensions of human biological evolution," represents a slightly abridged version of the first and is dated May 4, 1936, see Muller MSS, General papers. Recently, a Russian translation of the letter has been found in Stalin's personal archive. See, "Pis'mo Germana Miollera— I. V. Stalinu," *VIET*, 1997, no. 1, pp. 65–78. A comparison of all three texts demonstrates that the first copy found in the Lilly Library is the complete English text of the letter. Following citations from Muller's letter to Stalin are given from this source.

79 See, for instance, *Rassovaia teoriia na sluzhbe fashizma*, Kiev: Gosmedgiz, 1935.

80 See G. Frizen, "Genetika i fashizm," *Pod Znamenem Marksizma*, 1935, no. 3, 86–95.

81 Cited in Esakov, *Akademiia Nauk v Resheniiakh Politbiuro*, p. 246. Emphasis is in the document.

82 See Komarov and Gorbunov to Molotov, February 7, 1937, GARF, f. 5446, op. 20a, d. 524, ll. 39–32, here—l. 34.

83 See Joravsky, *Lysenko Affair*.

84 A few months later, Iakovlev published in *Pravda* a long diatribe against genetics as "anti-Darwinist" doctrine. See Ia. Iakovlev, "O darvinizme i nekotorykh anti-darvinistakh," *Pravda*, April 12, 1937, pp. 2–3.

85 See Krementsov, *Stalinist Science*, and idem., "Printsip konkurentnogo iskliucheniia."

86 In the 1930s all appointments to various administrative positions followed the system of *nomenklatura*, which was, literally, a list of posts that could not be occupied or vacated without permission from the appropriate party committee. On the role of *nomenklatura* in the Soviet science system see Krementsov, *Stalinist Science*.

87 For Prokhorov's biographical data see ARAN, f. 411, op. 6, d. 2756.

88 Prokhorov to Gorbunov, November 16, 1936, ARAN, f. 2, op. 1–1935, d. 83, l. 101. Underlined by Prokhorov.

89 See Bankin and Gershenzon to Gorbunov, June 7, 1937, ARAN, f. 201, op. 5, d. 2, ll. 90–2. The memo was co-signed by one of the workers of the technical apparatus—a young geneticist, Mikhail Gershenzon, who was employed as an interpreter and translated official correspondence between the organizing committee and Mohr. All the following quotations are from this source.

90 See The presidium to Molotov, November 20, 1937, ARAN, f. 2, op. 1 (1935), d. 83, ll. 1–2.

91 See the stenographic record of a meeting in the Academy of Science on June 16, 1937, ARAN, f. 201, op. 6, d. 4, l. 3.

92 See ARAN, f. 2, op. 1 (1937), d. 20, ll. 1–12.

93 Vavilov to Molotov, February 20, 1938, ARAN, f. 2, op. 1 (1939), d. 159, ll. 1–3. All the following citations are from this source.

94 See Komarov to Molotov, February 21, 1938, ARAN, f. 2, op. 1 (1939), d. 157, l. 2.

95 See "V Sovnarkome SSSR," *Pravda*, 11 May 1938, p. 2.

96 See V. Soifer, *Vlast' i Nauka*, Ann Arbor: Hermitage, 1989, pp. 299–302. In 1935 Lysenko began his career as a state official, becoming a member of the Central Executive Committee (TsIK) of the Ukraine; in 1936 he became a member of TsIK of the USSR and was a delegate to the Eighth Congress of Soviets, which adopted a new "Stalin" constitution; in 1938 he became a member of the USSR Supreme Soviet. He was a deputy-head of the Soviet of the Union—the highest legislative agency of the USSR.

97 Although Lysenko was not yet a member of the academy, he nevertheless participated in the meeting.

98 Vavilov to Crew, October 1, 1938, a copy of this letter is in Haldane Papers, Box 35.

99 For details of the second stage in the Vavilov–Lysenko debate during 1939 see Krementsov, *Stalinist Science*, and "Printsip 'konkurentnogo iskliucheniia."

100 Before 1938, the institute was subordinate to Narkomzdrav. In October 1938, it was transferred to the authority of the Academy of Sciences and renamed the Institute of Cytology, Histology, and Embryology.

101 See ARAN, f. 2, op. 1 a, dd. 68, 160 a.

102 See *Vestnik Akademii Nauk SSSR*, 1939, no. 4–5, p. 82.

103 ARAN, f. 2, op. 1–1939, d. 172, ll. 27–30.

104 ARAN, f. 1595, op. 1, d. 411, l. 26.

105 Nikolai Vavilov, "Speech from the 1939 conference on genetics and selection," *Science and Society*, 1940, no. 4, 184–96, here—p. 187.

106 The struggle was reflected in the press. For example, on February 1, 1939, Narkomzem's newspaper, *Sotsialisticheskoe Zemledelie*, carried two articles devoted to genetics education—one written by Vavilov, the other by Lysenko.

107 Vavilov to Andreev, July 15, 1939, ARAN, f. 2, op. 1 (1939), d. 157, ll. 19–23.

108 Komarov to SNK, June 8, 1939, ARAN, f. 2, op. 1 (1939), d. 157, ll. 12–14.

109 See Vyshinskii to Molotov, July 23, 1939, AVPR, f. 062, op. 1, papka 4, d. 28, l. 42.

110 Vavilov's draft is preserved in the same file in AVPR, f. 062, op. 1, papka 4, d. 28, l. 45.
111 See correspondence between Vavilov and the academy's scientific secretary P. Svetlov in ARAN, f. 2, op. 1 (1939), d. 157, ll. 18, 26–7, 31–2.

5 Soviet geneticists and their peers

1 See Robert Kohler, *Lords of the Fly*, Chicago: University of Chicago Press, 1994, pp. 296–7.
2 Davenport to the Secretary of State, December 17, 1936. Davenport Papers.
3 His recently published international correspondence from 1921 through 1937, though definitely not complete, constitutes five large volumes. See N. I. Vavilov, *Nauchnoe Nasledie v Pis'makh. Mezhdunarodnaia Perepiska*, Moscow: Nauka, 1994–2002, vol. 1–5.
4 On Dobzhansky see Mark B. Adams (ed.) *The Evolution of Theodosius Dobzhansky: His Life and Thought in Russia and America*, Princeton: Princeton University Press, 1994; also see a recently published volume of Dobzhansky's correspondence with his mentor Filipchenko and other Soviet scientists in M. B. Konashev (ed.) *U Iistokov Akademicheskoi Genetiki v Sankt-Peterburge*, St Petersburg: Nauka, 2002.
5 I was unable to find any evidence, either in his personal papers or in the Soviet Embassy's documents, that Henry Wallace took any part in the affair. It is safe to assume that the US Secretary of Agriculture abstained from any intervention, as did other Western state officials (see Chapter 6).
6 John C. Merriam was president of the American paleontological and geological societies and president of the Carnegie Institution of Washington. It is unclear to which presidency Dunn is referring to in the letter.
7 Dunn to Demerec, December 15, 1936; see also Dunn to Jennings, December 19, 1936, both in Dunn Papers.
8 Jennings to Dunn, December 22, 1936, Dunn Papers.
9 Dunn to Jennings, December 19, 1936, Dunn Papers.
10 Demerec to Troyanovskii, December 20, 1936, Dunn Papers.
11 Davenport to the Secretary of State, December 17, 1939, Davenport Papers.
12 Hagedoorn to Mohr, April 27, 1937, Mohr Papers.
13 Tammes to Mohr, June 19, 1937, Mohr Papers.
14 Haldane to Mohr, January 30, 1937, Mohr Papers.
15 See J. R. C. Fincham, "Genetics in the United Kingdom: the last half-century," *Heredity*, 1993, vol. 71, 111–18.
16 Haldane to Mohr, June [not later than 23], 1937, Mohr Papers.
17 Crew to Mohr, February 20, 1937, Mohr Papers.
18 Another representative was Crew.
19 Gates to Mohr, March 3, 1937, Mohr Papers.
20 See Mohr to Crew, March 11, 1937, Darlington Papers, C. 98. H. 58.
21 Crew to Mohr, April 9, 1937, Mohr Papers.
22 For the best account of the early history of the Institute, see Margaret Deacon, *The Institute of Animal Genetics at Edinburgh—the First Twenty Years*. Unpublished manuscript. 1973. I am grateful to Margaret for providing me with a copy of her work.
23 On Crew's life and work see Lancelot Hogben, "Francis Albert Eley Crew, 1886–1973," *Biographical Memoirs of Fellows of the Royal Society*, 1974, vol. 20, 135–53.
24 For a detailed account of the early history of the institute since the establishment of the Experimental Station for Animal Breeding in 1920 through its conversion into the Institute of Animal Genetics in 1930 and up to the beginning of World War II, see Francis A. Crew's unpublished autobiography preserved at the Genetics Department of the University of Edinburgh.
25 Crew to Mohr, June 29, 1937, Mohr Papers.
26 See Haldane to Mohr, July 23, 1937, Mohr Papers.
27 Crew to Mohr, June 29, 1937, Mohr Papers.

28 Muller hoped to succeed Haldane at the John Innes Institution, but despite much lobbying on his behalf by Huxley and Darlington, the Committee of Management vetoed his appointment.

29 See Ghigi to Mohr, April 22, 1937; and Babcock to Mohr, May 18, 1937, both in Mohr Papers.

30 See, for instance, copies of his "circulars" of December 16 and 22, 1936, Dunn Papers.

31 See Kohler, *Lords of the Fly*, pp. 296–7.

32 See Emerson to Mohr, May 31, 1937, Mohr Papers.

33 Mohr to Dunn, December 6, 1936, Dunn Papers. It is possible that during their meeting in Copenhagen in mid-November, J. H. Muller provided Mohr with many details of the Kamenev–Zinov'ev trial, which where unavailable in the Western press. Although there is no documentary evidence on Muller's personal attitude towards the unfolding Great Terror, one can assume that Mohr's statement at least in part also reflected Muller's views.

34 Mohr to Dunn, January 25, 1937, Dunn Papers.

35 Haldane to Mohr, February 10, 1937, Mohr Papers.

36 He told this to Mohr during their meeting in Copenhagen, and Mohr duly reported it to Dunn. See Mohr to Dunn, December 6, 1936, Dunn Papers.

37 Dobzhansky to Darlington, January 1, 1937, Darlington Papers, C. 106. J. 37.

38 See *Science*, 1937 (April 9), vol. 85, 355.

39 Babkock to Mohr, March 13, 1937, and April 22, 1937, both in Mohr Papers.

40 Dobzhansky to Darlington, January 1, 1937, Darlington Papers, C. 106. J. 37.

41 In the section entitled "Topics of the Times," there appeared a barbed commentary on the portrayal of Agol's arrest in the *Izvestiia* editorial. See "Crime and Punishment," *NYT*, December 23, 1936, p. 20.

42 Harold Denny, "Row over science renewed in Soviet," *NYT*, December 27, 1936, p. 2. This information also appeared in the *Washington Post*: "Superior race theory quarrel stirs Moscow," *Washington Post*, December 27, 1936, p. M8.

43 Harold Denny, "Geneticists argue work in Moscow," *NYT*, December 28, 1936, p. 2.

44 I was unable to find anything on the subject in major newspapers in Britain, France, and Germany.

45 Ghigi to Mohr, April 22, 1937, Mohr Papers.

46 The *New York Times* second correspondent in Moscow Walter Duranty was covering mostly Soviet economics and politics, particularly the show-trials.

47 Harold Denny, "Soviet twins give science new study," *NYT*, June 16, 1935, p. N1.

48 See "Scientist creates new forms of life," *NYT*, March 29, 1936, p. 29.

49 See, for example, the letter of the Secretary of the British Genetical Society to Levit: A. E. Watkins to Levit, January 5, 1937, ARAN, f. 201, op. 5, d. 2, l. 12.

50 Hagedoorn to Vavilov, April 27, 1937, ARAN, f. 201, op. 5, d. 2, l. 7.

51 Crew to Mohr, February 20, 1937, Mohr Papers.

52 This is from Demerec to Cook, January 22, 1937; see also Dunn to Little, January 25, 1937, both in Dunn Papers.

53 Dobzhansky to Dunn, March 10, 1937, Dunn Papers.

54 Perhaps some of these "confidential" letters were entrusted to visiting foreigners to be mailed abroad, but apparently most of them were sent through regular mail.

55 Haldane to Mohr, July 23, 1937, Mohr Papers.

56 On the peculiar culture of Soviet science in the 1930s see Krementsov, *Stalinist Science*.

57 See Babkock, "Memo 2. Bearing on the international genetics congress," May 18, 1937, Mohr Papers.

58 Mohr to Muller, November 26, 1937, Muller Papers.

59 The Ambassador's worry was perhaps a result of certain tensions between the USSR and Norway at the time, tensions provoked by the decision of the Norwegian government to grant asylum to Leon Trotsky.

60 Dobzhansky to Dunn, March 10, 1937, Dunn Papers.
61 Dunn to Jennings, December 19, 1936, Dunn Papers.
62 Mohr to Dunn, August 4, 1937, Dunn Papers.
63 F. A. E. Crew, "Seventh international genetical congress," *Nature*, September 16, 1939, vol. 144, 496–8, here—p. 496.
64 Cook to Troyanovskii, December 19, 1936, AVPR, f. 192, op. 3, papka 24, d. 53, l. 57.
65 Jennings to Dunn, December 24, 1936, Dunn Papers.
66 On the general efforts of American colleagues to help refugee scholars see Stephen Duggan and Betty Drury, *The Rescue of Science and Learning: The Story of the Emergency Committee in Aid of Displaced Foreign Scholars*, New York: Macmillan, 1948; for a historical analysis of this theme, see G. Gemelli (ed.) *The "Unacceptables": American Foundations and Refugee Scholars between the Two Wars and after*, Brussels: Peter Lang, 2000.
67 See, for instance, Landauer to Davenport, October 19, 1935, Davenport Papers.
68 Davenport to Landauer, October 23, 1935, Davenport Papers.
69 Mohr to Dunn, September 9, 1937, Dunn Papers.
70 Jennings to Dunn, December 22, 1936, Dunn Papers.
71 Davenport to Landauer, March 13, 1936, Davenport Papers.
72 This and following citations are from a copy of a letter by one of Landauer's correspondents, which was sent to Demerec. Unfortunately, the copy is unsigned and I was not able to find the original. It seems possible that the author of the letter was C. C. Little. See [unidentified] to Landauer, March 6, 1936, Demerec Papers.
73 Emphasis is in the original.
74 Demerec to Landauer, March 16, 1936, Demerec Papers.
75 See [unidentifed] to Landauer, March 6, 1936, Demerec Papers.
76 Vavilov to Mohr, December 9, 1936, ARAN, f. 201, op. 5, d. 1, l. 23.
77 Dobzhansky to Dunn, December 21, 1936, Dunn Papers.
78 Jennings to Dunn, December 22, 1936, Dunn Papers.
79 See Harold Denny, "Geneticists argue work in Moscow," *NYT*, December 28, 1936, p. 2; and "Genetic theory and practice in the USSR," *Nature*, January 30, 1937, vol. 139, p. 185.
80 Cook to Dunn, January 18, 1937, Dunn Papers. Cook made up the verb "yarovize" from the name of Lysenko's notorious technique "yarovization" (commonly known in the West as "vernalization").
81 Mohr to Muller, November 26, 1937, Muller Papers.
82 Emerson to Mohr, April 19, 1937, Mohr Papers.
83 Roll-Hansen, "A new perspective on Lysenko?," *Annals of Science*, 1985, vol. 42, pp. 261–78.
84 See, for instance, H. H. McKinney and W. J. Sando, "Russian methods for accelerating sexual reproduction in wheat," *Journal of Heredity*, 1933, vol. 24, 165–6; idem., "Earliness and seasonal growth habit in wheat," ibid., 168–79; R. O. White and P. S. Hudson, *Vernalization or Lyssenko's Method for the Pre-treatment of Seed*, Aberystwyth and Cambridge: Imperial Bureaux of Plant Genetics, 1933; *Vernalization and Phasic Development of Plants*, Aberystwyth and Cambridge: Imperial Bureaux of Plant Genetics, 1935; Roland McKee, *Vernalization Experiments with Forage Crops*, Washington, DC: US Government Printing Office, 1935.
85 P. S. Hudson, "Vernalization in agricultural practice," *Journal of the Ministry of Agriculture*, 1936, 536–43, here—p. 539.
86 Jennings to Dunn, December 22, 1936, Dunn Papers.
87 "Scientific Freedom," *Nature*, January 30, 1937, vol. 139, 185.
88 Muller to Dunn, June 17, 1937, Dunn Papers.
89 Mohr to Dunn, August 4, 1937, Dunn Papers.
90 Fritz von Wettstein replaced Richard Goldschmidt as the German representative on the IOC in April 1937.

91 See Gorbunov to Molotov, March 27, 1937, GARF, f. 5446, op. 20a, d. 524, ll. 14–12. In this, as in many other cases, Gorbunov certainly relied on Vavilov's information.

92 At that time, Switzerland did not have diplomatic relations with the Soviet Union. The Swiss representative was the only member of the IOC who in 1935 had expressed certain doubts about holding the congress in Moscow, afraid that the absence of diplomatic relations between the two countries could complicate the attendance of Swiss geneticists of the congress in Moscow. Relating the result of the 1935 vote, Mohr duly informed Vavilov about the concerns of the Swiss delegate. See ARAN, f. 2, op. 1–1935, d. 83, ll. 171–2.

93 See Vavilov's correspondence over the years with all these geneticists in Nikolai Vavilov, *Nauchnoe Nasledie v Pis'makh*, Moscow: Nauka, 1994–2002, vol. 1–5.

94 See Tschermak to Mohr, May 5, 1937, Mohr Papers. Emphasis is mine—N. K.

95 Crew to Dunn, February 3, 1939, Dunn papers.

96 Dunn to Crew, February 16, 1938, Dunn Papers.

97 See "Genetics Congress. Notice No. 1. April 1938." A copy of this notice is in Dunn Papers.

98 See for instance, Crew to Dunn, February 3 and 8, 1939, Dunn Papers.

99 Here Lindstrom referred to Goldschmidt's rejection of the concept of the "corpuscular" gene in several works, which had just been published (see Richard Goldschmidt, *Physiological Genetics*, New York: McGraw-Hill, 1938, and Richard Goldschmidt, "The theory of the gene," *Scientific Monthly*, 1938, vol. 46, 268–73) and elicited critical response from a number of American geneticists. For details, see Garland Allen, "Opposition to the Mendelian-chromosome theory: the physiological and developmental genetics of Richard Goldschmidt," *JHB*, 1974, vol. 7, 49–92; and Michael R. Dietrich, "Richard Goldschmidt's 'heresies' and the evolutionary synthesis," *JHB*, 1995, vol. 28, 431–61.

100 Lindstrom to Crew, June 9, 1938, GSA Papers, Box 1, Folder: 1938. Seventh international genetics congress.

101 See [Crew?] to Lysenko, January 12, 1939. The invitation was apparently drafted by Muller, for its unsigned copy is preserved in Muller Papers.

102 Muller to H. H. McKinney, April 15, 1939, Muller Papers.

103 Mohr to Muller, November 16, 1937, Muller Papers. Mohr's concern was spurred by a letter of September 25, 1937, from Mrs C. B. S. Hodson of the Bureau of Human Heredity (an arm of the Eugenics Education Society) suggesting that an international eugenics congress be held in coordination with the genetics congress. I am grateful to Guil Winchester for calling my attention to this fact.

104 Mohr's general attitude towards eugenics is partially illuminated in Nils Roll-Hansen, "Eugenic sterilization: a preliminary comparison of the Scandinavian experience to that of Germany," *Genome*, 1989, vol. 31, 890–95.

105 The cable was reproduced in Muller's letter to Darlington, August 4, 1939, Darlington Papers, C. 110. J. 131.

106 The manifesto was published in the *Journal of Heredity* after the congress had ended. See "Men and mice at Edinburgh," *Journal of Heredity*, 1939, vol. 30, 371–4.

107 The original signatories were Crew, Haldane, Harland, Hogben, Huxley, Muller, and Needham. Additional signatures were those of G. P. Child, P. R. David, G. Dahlberg, Th. Dobzhansky, R. A. Emerson, John Hammond, C. L. Huskins, W. Landauer, H. H. Plough, E. Price, J. Schultz, A. G. Steinberg, and C. H. Waddington.

108 Crew to Haldane, August 4, 1939, Haldane Papers, Box 35.

109 Vavilov to Muller, July 26, 1939, a copy in Haldane Papers, Box 35.

110 See AVPR, f. 061, op. 1, papka 4, d. 28, ll. 42–45.

111 Crew to Darlington, August 4, 1939, Darlington Papers, C. 98. H. 60; Crew to Haldane, August 4, 1939, Haldane Papers, Box 35.

112 That was how a *New York Times* correspondent saw it. See Ritchie Calder, "Russians abandon genetics meeting," *NYT*, August 23, 1939, p. 20.

113 See Harold Denny, "Mendel law faces 'repeal' in Soviet," *NYT*, June 15, 1939, p. 1; "Soviet rejection of Mendelian law of genetics called 'absurd' by editor of science journal," *Washington Post*, June 16, 1939, p. 3; and "Class science to the fore," *NYT*, June 16, 1939, p. 20.

114 See Crew to Haldane, August 4, 1939, Haldane Papers, Box 35.

115 Wright to Muller, November 24, 1947. A copy of this letter is preserved among Sewall Wright's papers in APS.

116 See Muller to Huxley, June 7, July 26, and August 2, 1939, all in Muller Papers. Although a few of Soviet reports prepared for the congress were later published in the *Drosophila Information Service*.

117 See Nikolai Krementsov, "A 'second front' in Soviet genetics: the international dimension of the Lysenko controversy," *JHB*, 1996, vol. 29, 229–50.

6 International science

1 See, for instance, Brigitte Schroeder-Gudehus, "Nationalism and internationalism," in R. Olby *et al.* (eds) *Companion to the History of Modern Science*, London-New York: Routledge, 1989, p. 909; Jean-Jacques Solomon, "The 'internationale' of science," *Science Studies*, 1971, vol. 1, p. 24.

2 See, for instance, Elisabeth Crawford, *Nationalism and Internationalism in Science, 1880–1939: Four Studies of the Nobel Population*, Cambridge: Cambridge University Press, 1992; Elisabeth Crawford, Terry Shinn, and Sverker Sorlin (eds) *Denationalizing Science: The Contexts of International Scientific Practice*, Dodrecht: Kluwer Academic Publishers, 1993: and David N. Livingstone, *Putting Science in its Place: Geographies of Scientific Knowledge*, Chicago: University of Chicago Press, 2003.

3 Davenport to the Secretary of State, December 17, 1936, Davenport Papers.

4 Similarly, one can argue, in the late 1920s, the geneticists Evgenii Gabrichevskii, Theodosius Dobzhansky, and Nikolai Timofeeff-Ressovsky chose loyalty to their science and stayed abroad, instead of returning to the Soviet Union.

5 See "Vaviloff defends science in Soviet," *NYT*, December 23, 1936, p. 8.

6 See Paul Forman, "Scientific internationalism and the Weimar physicists: the ideology and its manipulation in Germany after World War I," *Isis*, 1973, vol. 37, 156.

7 Vavilov's patriotism is readily evident, for instance, in a number of letters to Theodosius Dobzhansky, in which Vavilov tried to convince him to return to the Soviet Union. See Dobzhansky Papers in APS, B: D65.

8 Paul Forman, "Scientific internationalism and the Weimar physicists: the ideology and its manipulation in Germany after World War I," *Isis*, 1973, vol. 37, 156.

9 See Gary Werskey, *Visible College: The Collective Biography of British Scientific Socialists of the 1930s*, New York: Holt, Rinehart, and Wiston, 1979, and Peter Kuzhnik, *Beyond the Laboratory: Scientists as Political Activists in 1930s America*, Chicago: University of Chicago Press, 1987.

10 Alessandro Ghigi to Mohr, April 22, 1937, Mohr Papers.

11 Haldane to Mohr, July 23, 1937, Mohr Papers.

12 Jennings to Dunn, December 24, 1936, Dunn Papers.

13 Dunn to Landauer, July 8, 1937, Dunn Papers.

14 Mohr to the IOC members, July 21, 1937. There are numerous copies of this memo in the files of individual geneticists. I quote from a copy preserved in ARAN, f. 201, op. 5, d. 4, ll. 1–8.

15 Of course, in the 1920s and 1930s, many Western governments were uneasy about Soviet (and later German) scientists' visits to their countries, suspecting them of spying or spreading the "germs" of Bolshevism. See, for instance, Jeff Hughes, "Thinker, Toiler, Scientist, Spy? Peter Kapitza and the British Security State," (manuscript, 2003).

16 For instance, some governments appointed "official delegates" to the Sixth and Seventh international genetics congresses, but neither the US, nor British government provided funding or any other organizational support of the congresses.

17 According to Ron Doel's explorations in F. D. Roosevelt's Presidential Library, among its holdings there is a special file, entitled "international genetics congress." The file contains L. C. Dunn's correspondence with the president regarding Dunn's proposal that vice-president Henry Wallace be appointed an "US representative" to the Seventh international genetics congress in Edinburgh. The proposal was politely declined. There is not a word on the cancelled Moscow congress in the correspondence. See "Official File 3565, International Congress of Genetics," FDR Presidential Library, Hyde Park, NY. I am very grateful to Ron Doel for this information.

18 See, for instance, Haldane to Mohr, June [not later than 27] and October 13, 1937, both in Mohr Papers. See also J. G. Crowther, *Soviet Science*, London: Kegan Paul and Co., 1936. Many examples of Western scientists' admiration for the Soviet development of science are given in Kuznik, *Beyond the Laboratory*, pp. 107–70.

19 The dangerous link between the state's funding for and control over scientific endeavors became the subject of a wide debate among Western scientists in the aftermath of World War II, and Soviet genetics figured prominently in the arguments both pro and contra such state involvement with science. See, for instance, S. F. Morse, "On science and government subsidies," *Science*, 1946, vol. 104, 761; and H. C. Urey, "I greatly fear . . . ," *Journal of Heredity*, 1948, vol. 39, 150–2.

20 Similarly, though in early 1933, the Politburo had prohibited Soviet scientists to accept Rockefeller fellowships, this fact was never disclosed to Rockefeller officers, who as late as 1935 traveled to Moscow to find out why Soviet fellows did not use their awards.

21 "Scientific Freedom," *Nature*, January 30, 1937, vol. 139, p. 185.

22 "Science in the USSR," *Nature*, February 6, 1937, vol. 139, 227.

23 Vavilov to Muller, April 9, 1937, TsGANTD, f. 318, op. 1–1, d. 1436, ll. 102–3.

24 See ARAN, f. 201, op. 6, d. 4, ll. 1–3.

25 Darlington to Mohr, May 14, 1937, Mohr Papers.

26 Dunn to Jennings, December 19, 1936, Dunn Papers. Dunn here referred to the infamous 1925 trial of John T. Scopes, a school teacher who was put on trial for teaching evolution in a public school. For details, see, for instance, Jeffrey P. Moran, *The Scopes Trial: A Brief History with Documents*, New York: Palgrave, 2002.

27 For details of the next phase of the Vavilov–Lysenko debate in 1939 see Nikolai Krementsov, *Stalinist Science*, and particularly idem., "Printsip konkurentnogo iskliucheniia," in E. Kolchinskii (ed.) *Na perelome: Sovetskaia biologiia v 20-kh-30-kh godakh*, St Petersburg, 1998, pp. 107–64.

28 See, for instance, see Barbara A. Kimmelman, "The American Breeders Association: genetics and eugenics in an agricultural context," *Social Studies of Science*, 1983, vol. 13, 163–204; Paolo Palladino, "Between craft and science: plant breeding, Mendelian genetics, and British universities, 1900–1920," *Technology and Culture*, 1993, vol. 34, 300–23; and Robert Olby, "Mendelism: from hybrids and trade to a science," *Comptes Rendus de l'Académie des Sciences*, Ser. III, 2000, vol. 323, 1043–51.

29 See, for instance, R. D. Harvey, "Pioneers of genetics: a comparison of the attitudes of William Bateson and Erwin Baur to eugenics," *Notes and Records of the Royal Society of London*, 1995, vol. 49, 105–17.

30 William Bateson, "Common-sense in racial problems," *Eugenics Review*, 1921–22, vol. 13, 325–38, here—p. 325.

31 For details on Bauer's role in German genetics, see Johnatan Harwood, *Styles of Scientific Thought*, Chicago: University of Chicago Press, 1994, particularly, pp. 230–9.

32 See Erwin Baur, Eugen Fisher, and Fritz Lenz, *Grundriss der menschlichen Erblichkeitslehre und Rassenhygiene*, Munich: Lehmann, 1921.

33 For instance, R. Ruggles Gates used extensively the results of genetic studies on geographical races in deer mice to justify his idea that four major races of humankind—black, white, brown, and yellow, as he defined them—were in fact separate species. See R. R. Gates, "Genetics and race," *Man*, 1937 (February), vol. 37, 28–32.

34 Of course, the division of all reports into the three categories: "basic," "agricultural," and "eugenic" in a number of cases is somewhat arbitrary. In the following analysis, I classified as "agricultural" not only presentations that dealt explicitly with agricultural applications of genetics studies (new varieties of agriculturally important organisms, for example), but also those reports that dealt with "basic" problems, but were conducted on agriculturally important subjects, like corn or wheat. On the other hand, I qualified as "eugenic" certain researches conducted on laboratory organisms, like mice or doves, which had clear eugenics agendas, discussing issues of race or possible connotations of these researches to human genetics.

35 See *Trudy Pervogo Vsesoiuznogo S'ezda po Genetike i Selektsii*, Leningrad: 1930, vol. 1–6.

36 See *Biulleten' IV Sessii VASKhNIL*, December 20–30, 1936, no. 1–8.

37 See *Zeitschrift für induktive Abstammungs- und Vererbungslehre*, 1935, vol. 67, no. 2.

38 See "Papers read at the Pittsburg meeting of the Genetics Society of America," *American Naturalist*, 1935, vol. 69, 55–83.

39 See, for instance, Julian Huxley and Alfred Haddon, *We Europeans: A Survey of "Racial" Problem*, London: J. Cape, 1935.

40 In 1939, the American Anthropological Society issued a strong resolution condemning Nazi racial policy and "racial anthropology." For details, see Kuzhnik, *Beyond the Laboratory*, particularly Chapter 6. "Franz Boas Mobilizes the Scientists against Fascism," pp. 171–94.

41 See Krementsov, *Stalinist Science* and idem., "A 'second front' in Soviet genetics: the international dimension of the Lysenko controversy," *JHB*, 1996, vol. 29, 229–50.

42 "Scientific freedom," *Nature*, January 30, 1937, vol. 139, p. 185.

43 Demerec to Landauer, March 16, 1936, Demerec Papers.

44 See E. G. Conklin, "Science and ethics," *Science*, 1937 (December 31), vol. 86, 595–603, here—p. 601.

45 See Krementsov, *Stalinist Science* and idem., "Printsip konkurentnogo iksliucheniia."

46 See, for instance, Alexander Vucinich, *Science in Russian Culture, 1861–1917*, Stanford: Stanford University Press, 1970.

47 For a detailed analysis of the developing symbiosis between Russian scientists and their Bolshevik patrons see Kendall Bailes, *Technology and Society under Lenin and Stalin*, Princeton: Princeton University Press, 1978; Krementsov, *Stalinist Science*.

48 It was not only associated with the growing distrust of scientists as representatives of "bourgeois," "non-proletarian" strata manifested during the Great Break and the following campaigns for industrialization and collectivization. It also corresponded to the current personnel policies of the regime: the tremendous expansion of industry, education, public health, and science systems led to rapid promotion of a large cohort of "practical workers"—former peasants, workers, soldiers—with minimal education but "practical experience" to responsible administrative positions in all walks of Soviet life.

49 See RGASPI, f. 558, op. 11, d. 829, ll. 64–6.

50 Vavilov to Crew, October 1, 1938, Haldane Papers, Box 35.

51 A similar dissatisfaction of practical breeders with Mendelian genetics in Britain, which led to the institutional segregation of "academic" and "practical" research, has been discussed by Paolo Palladino, "Between craft and science: plant breeding, Mendelian genetics, and British universities, 1900–1920," *Technology and Culture*, 1993, vol. 34, 300–23; and idem., "Wizards and devotees: on the Mendelian theory of inheritance and the professionalization of agricultural science in Great Britain and the United States, 1880–1930," *History of Science*, 1994, 409–44.

52 TsGANTD, f. 318, op. 1–1, d. 1705. I would like to thank Tat'iana Lassan for calling my attention to this document.

53 See, for instance, Th. Dobzhansky, "Vavilov, martyr of genetics," *Journal of Heredity*, 1947, vol. 38, 227–32; James F. Crow, "N. I. Vavilov, martyr to genetic truth," *Genetics*, 1993, vol. 134, 1–4.

54 Dunn to Little, January 25, 1937, Dunn papers.

55 Dunn to Muller, January 7, 1937, Dunn Papers.

56 Haldane to Mohr, July 23, 1937, Mohr Papers.

57 Shull to Vavilov, September 23, 1937, TsGANTD, f. 318, op. 1–1, d. 1439, ll. 90–90 reverse.

58 Mohr to Dunn, September 9, 1937, Dunn Papers. Emphasis is Mohr's.

59 Muller to Huxley, March 9, 1937. Darlington Papers. C 24. D. 63. Emphasis is in the original.

60 This episode is described in details in my article "The 'second front' in Soviet genetics."

61 Dobzhansky to Dunn, July 4, 1945, Dunn Papers.

62 Lerner to Dunn, June 27, 1945. This letter is preserved among Michael I. Lerner's documents in APS. M. Lerner Papers, B: L 563.

63 Dobzhansky to Dunn, July 4, 1945, Dunn Papers. Emphasis is Dobzhansky's.

64 Aside from personal reasons, there may have been several equally important domestic reasons for such commitments by Western scientists in their discussions about Soviet genetics. One of the most important was the ongoing concern about possible future relations between science and the state in the West. In 1946–47, a number of articles about the Soviet science system were published in Western periodicals touching on the postwar organization of Western science. The most important subject of this discussion was the "freedom of science." Many disputants referred to the Lysenko controversy and the fate of executed Soviet geneticists as an example of the dangers presented by state control over science. See, for instance, Robert Simpson, "Science, totalitarian model," *Saturday Review of Literature*, 1946 (March 9), 28–32. In their critique of Lysenko's doctrine, however, most Western geneticists carefully omitted any political remarks.

65 Huxley to Demerec, December 31, 1945, Demerec Papers.

66 Ibid.

67 Demerec to Mohr, November 28, 1945, Demerec Papers.

68 Crew to Demerec, January 15, 1946, Demerec Papers.

69 Ibid.

70 Crew to the Soviet ambassador, February 11, 1946, in ARAN, f. 2, op. 1–1945, d. 401, 11. 18–20. A copy of this letter is also in the Demerec Papers.

71 See RGASPI, f. 17, op. 121, d.537, l. 26 reverse.

72 Demerec to Huxley, February 18, 1946, Demerec Papers.

73 Demerec to the IOC members, August 9, 1945, Demerec Papers.

74 On the honor courts see Nikolai Krementsov, *The Cure: A Story of Cancer and Politics from the Annals of the Cold War*, Chicago: University of Chicago Press, 2002; and V. D. Esakov and E. S. Levina, *Delo KR. Sudy Chesti v Ideologii i Praktike Poslevoennogo Stalinizma*, Moscow, 2001. For details on Zhebrak's trial, see Krementsov, *Stalinist Science*.

75 For details, see Krementsov, *Stalinist Science*.

76 See, for instance, Conway Zirkle, *Death of a Science in Russia*, Philadelphia: University of Pennsylvania Press, 1949; Michael I. Lerner, *Genetics in the USSR: An Obituary*, Vancouver, Canada: University of British Columbia, 1950.

Epilogue

1 On the fate of Soviet genetics during the 1950s and 1960s see Mark B. Adams, *Networks in Action: The Khrushchev Era, the Cold War and the Transformation of Soviet Science*, Trondheim: Trondheim Studies on East European Cultures and Societies, 2000.

2 Mohr to the IOC members, July 21, 1937. ARAN, f. 201, op. 5, d. 4, ll. 1–8.

3 See M. E. Vartanian (ed.) *Genetika i Blagosostoianie Chelovechestva: Trudy XIV Mezhdunarodnogo Geneticheskogo Kongressa, Moskva, 21–30 avgusta 1978*, Moscow: Nauka, 1981.

4 See Iu. N. Altukhov (ed.) *Voprosy Obshchei Genetiki: Trudy XIV Mezhdunarodnogo Geneticheskogo Kongressa, Moskva, 21–30 avgusta 1978*, Moscow: Nauka, 1981.

5 See, for instance, Leslie C. Dunn (ed.) *Genetics in the 20th century: Essays on the Progress of Genetics during the First 50 Years*, New York: Macmillan, 1951; Leslie C. Dunn, *A Short History of Genetics: The Development of some of the Main Lines of Thought, 1864–1939*, New York: McGraw-Hill, 1965; and A. H. Sturtevant, *A History of Genetics*, New York: Harper and Row, 1965.

6 See N. P. Bochkov (ed.) *Genetika i Meditsina: Itogi XIV Mezhdunarodnogo Geneticheskogo Kongressa*, Moscow: Meditsina, 1979.

7 See S. V. Shestakov (ed.) *Molekuliarnye Osnovy Geneticheskikh Processov: Trudy XIV Mezhdunarodnogo Geneticheskogo Kongressa, Moskva, 21–30 avgusta 1978 g.*, Moscow: Nauka, 1981.

8 See, Nikolay N. Vorontsov and Janny M. van Brink (eds) *Animal Genetics and Evolution: Selected Papers of the XIV International Congress of Genetics, August 21–30, 1978, Moscow*, Hague: W. Junk, 1980.

9 See, for instance, "Plodonosnoe drevo genetiki," *Pravda*, 21 August 1978, p. 6; "Uchastnikam XIV mezhdunarodnogo geneticheskogo kongressa," *Pravda*, August 22, 1978, p. 1; "Forum genetikov," *Pravda*, p. 2; R. Fedorov, "Zachem nuzhny khimery?" *Pravda*, August 27, 1978, p. 6; idem., "Genetika sozidaiushchaia," *Pravda*, August 30, 1978, p. 6; "K tainam nasledstvennosti," *Izvestiia*, August 22, 1978, p. 3; "Za geneticheskuiu bezopasnost' planety," *Izvestiia*, August 25, 1978, p. 2; "Takie vstrechi bestsenny dlia nauki," *Izvestiia*, August 26, 1978, p. 3; "Chto mozhet genetika," *Izvestiia*, September 2, 1978, p. 2.

10 "Chto mozhet genetika," *Izvestiia*, September 2, 1978, p. 2.

11 "Takie vstrechi bestsenny dlia nauki," *Izvestiia*, August 26, 1978, p. 3.

12 My account of Timofeef-Ressovsky's appearance at the congress is based on interviews with a member of the congress' organizing committee Evgenii Gus'kov, conducted in July 2003 in St Petersburg.

13 Almost exactly a year earlier, in 1936, Timofeeff-Ressovsky had also refused an invitation by Milislav Demerec to move to the United States. For details, see Mikhail Konashev, "Nesostoiavshiisia pereezd Timofeeva-Resovskogo v SShA," in E. Kolchinskii (ed.) *Na Perelome*, St Petersburg, 1997, pp. 94–106.

14 For details of Timofeeff-Ressovsky's biography see V. V. Babkov and E. S. Sakanian, *Nikolai Vladimirovich Timofeev-Resovskii, 1900–1981*, Moscow: Pamiatniki Istoricheskoi Mysli, 2002.

15 Robert K. Merton, "Science and the Social Order," *Philosophy of Science*, 1938, vol. 5, 321–37.

Index